A WRITER'S GUIDE TO ANCIENT ROME

MANCHESTER
1824

Manchester University Press

A WRITER'S GUIDE TO ANCIENT ROME

CAREY FLEINER

MANCHESTER UNIVERSITY PRESS

Published by Manchester University Press
Altrincham Street, Manchester M1 7JA
www.manchesteruniversitypress.co.uk

British Library Cataloguing-in-Publication Data
A catalogue record for this book is available from the British Library

ISBN 978 1 7849 9318 4 paperback

First published 2020

The publisher has no responsibility for the persistence or accuracy of URLs for any external or third-party internet websites referred to in this book, and does not guarantee that any content on such websites is, or will remain, accurate or appropriate.

Typeset by
Servis Filmsetting Ltd, Stockport, Cheshire
Printed in Great Britain by
Bell & Bain Ltd, Glasgow

As always, for Ellen Wynn Melody (1965–2016), Ursuline Academy (Wilmington, DE, Valedictorian 1983), University of Delaware (1987)

CONTENTS

VII

FIGURES

LIST OF FIGURES

Acknowledgements

There are many people and institutions to thank for their help, patience, and guidance with this volume. Many thanks to the History Department at the University of Winchester for their support and finding me teaching relief during the semester so that I could finish up this volume. Many thanks also to the editors at Manchester University Press, including Paul Clarke, Matthew Frost, Meredith Carroll, David Appleyard and Rachael Winterbottom who have helped to guide this project into being; thank you also to the anonymous readers who made excellent suggestions on the original proposal. Much of the content of this book would not have been possible without my students at the University of Delaware and the University of Winchester over the years, as many themes and ideas covered here were presented and discussed in class lecture and seminars in Classical history modules and student dissertation work. I owe much to my own Classical history and Latin teachers and lecturers over the years including Professor Nicholas Gross of the University of Delaware, and Professor Marvin Colker, and to Professor Elizabeth Meyer of the University of Virginia. Many thanks to my proofreaders, including Ms Kathryn Cephas at the University of Delaware, Morris Library. Particular gratitude goes to Professor Steven Sidebotham at the University of Delaware for over thirty years of mentoring, support, and as a model of good research practice, teaching, and presentation skills.

INTRODUCTION:
A WRITER'S GUIDE TO THE
ROMANS

Anyone who has picked up this book might fall into one of two general categories: someone who is interested in some way or form of recreating the Roman world, populating it with a set of characters, and putting them through their particular paces; *or* someone who is interested in how the process of reinterpreting the Roman world or re-creating it as historical fiction, film, or games might approach the subject. The fundamental goal here is not explicitly to direct the creative process; that would defeat its purpose of *guiding* an artist or a writer or a film-maker. This book isn't going to burden you with footnotes (although there are plenty of suggestions for further reading) or bury you alive under citations (although contemporary anecdotes are referenced). The novelist L.P. Hartley originated the expression 'the past is a foreign country: they do things differently there' (1953): as visitors who didn't grow up in a particular time or culture we will always look at that time and culture from the outside in. Historians love to categorise periods; they love to look for trends and developments that led to a particular outcome – we look backwards from a landmark event for all of the threads that led up to it both in our personal lives and in grander schemes. But just because you land on a particular spot, you cannot assume that, unlike all the roads in the Empire, these historical and cultural threads were deliberately leading down a particular path to a particular Rome.

Where do we find the real Romans? *Can* we find the real Romans? The answer is probably 'no'. Fiona Hobden (2009), in writing about how

Doctor Who portrays the Romans in the 2008 episode 'Fires of Pompeii', remarks that modern popular culture reinvents the Romans at about the pace of, if not somewhat behind, the scholarship – and even scholarship finds itself reinventing what we think and know about the Romans as new discoveries about them are made, or when sources are retranslated and re-evaluated. We are always looking for patterns that make strangers relatable to our own paradigms and understanding of the world. Because of the gulf of time and the fractionally surviving sources, the Romans are, to us, every bit as foreign as the Persians were to them. We inevitably put reflections of ourselves on to them – whether to make them more like 'real people' than alien objects studied through a careful reading of the texts, or to use them, much as the Romans did, to strike up parallels and commentary about ourselves. If the ancient Romans would be confused at how we portray them in our cinema, they might well be equally baffled at how we explain their customs and behaviour in our scholarship. Too many pieces are missing – not always because they have been lost to time, but because they weren't even recorded to begin with. For example, Hugh Bowden (2010) notes in his survey of ancient mystery cults that one of the reasons so little remains known about mystery cults is that the people who participated in them did not feel moved to write down the mundane aspects of their practices and beliefs.

Throughout this book, we look at the signposts that indicate what makes this person Roman, and that person not. We look at signs of status and wealth. We look for, as best can be recovered, attitudes and reactions in situations, and at those institutions that formed the framework of Roman life. At 350 pages, this book isn't going to provide aspiring writers with an encyclopaedic description of every facet of Rome's history, its people, economy, laws, games, and religion. No one author could possibly provide such a comprehensive study; fortunately, however, there exist excellent reference books, monographs, and specialist articles written by teams of experts in their particular fields.

Hence, we'll focus on sources and useful information about customs and practices around which you as author or artist might shape your characters and their physical and institutional environment. The scope here is limited to the general trends and themes from roughly between the late third century BCE and the early third century CE, with the occasional foray into the antecedents and legacy on either side of the period. Each chapter explicates its main themes with examples from the original sources. It provides additional sources to mine for the subject at hand and particular bits affected by scholarly debate, based on new discoveries or reinterpretation of written and material remains. This book is not *Mythbusters* or an exercise to point out all of the 'goofs' one might find in popular descriptions of Rome; it's left up to you whether or not you will produce a work of careful verisimilitude or anachronistic silliness (or any of the flavours in between). That's your call as creator.

A major theme throughout is the consideration of Roman identity: 'How do you *know* someone is Roman?' It's a tall order considering the diversity and mix of people and cultures in the Empire across the four centuries covered here. There is no one exclusive surviving paradigm that can provide us with exact fittings and fixtures about what your Roman might look like, talk like, act like. Fortunately for us, however, the Romans themselves wrestled with this very question, especially as the Empire grew and accumulated diverse territories, and they reflected on aspects of *us versus them*. The Romans were keen to categorise people – by occupation, by nationality, by status. They became concerned about what makes a Roman especially during those times when they encountered external foes and internal upstarts. This is an interesting prejudice considering that the Roman city-state itself was a bricolage of people and languages and cultures almost from the very beginning; the Etruscans, great traders that they were, incorporated many things into their own society from other cultures that were subsequently passed on to the Romans. In some respects, the Romans deliberately distanced themselves from the Etruscans when establishing the Republic in the late sixth and early fifth centuries BCE. For example, we associate Latin with the Romans – everything from Catholic Mass to lessons at school to *Monty Python's Life of Brian* and the 'Romans go home' scene – but the Romans *weren't* Latin originally; linguistically and culturally, they were Etruscan. The Romans began to identify with the Latin tribes only when they broke away from Etruscan rule – fighting with, conquering, and then allying with the Latin League in the fifth century BCE, a conglomeration of local tribes and city-states unified in protection originally *against* the Romans.

As the Romans encountered each new culture, especially the mainland Greeks in the third and second centuries BCE, some of the old conservatives at Rome were horrified that the young aristocrats such as Scipio Aemilianus (185–129 BCE) were becoming dandified with their love of Greek culture, entertainment, plays, and philosophy. Cato the Elder, a poster child for the old traditions, identified as a true Roman (see Plutarch's *Life of Cato*) as a result of his frugality, his simplicity, his love of the land. Order, respect for authority, and discipline were his watchwords; so it is interesting that it was a Greek, Polybius (c. 208 – c. 125 BCE), who wrote a straightforward account of Roman activity in the Mediterranean in the third and second centuries, and that he dedicated an entire chapter (6) to the tidy and disciplined order and respect for authority described by the Roman constitution and the Roman army – as a lesson for his fellow Greeks back home. Roman writers from moralists and rhetoricians to comedians and playwrights also took advantage of the new cultures and customs coming into the Roman world from the Greeks, from the Carthaginians, from the East, from Germany and Britain: but such treatises and comedies sometimes tell us more about the *Romans* than they might about the outsiders.

Thus Chapter 1 kicks off with a consideration of the Roman people and looks at indications of 'Romanness': traditional values, social status and standing, speaking like a Roman, and naming conventions. Considered here are family relations (public and private life), the role of the *paterfamilias* and *materfamilias*; marriage and children; the 'rules' of Roman behaviour – how you might be initiated into Roman culture and tradition, and some features of these. There's a discussion here of particular Roman characters and qualities, such as the *mos maiorum* (ancestor worship), consensus and deference, *nobilitas* and *auctoritas*. Unlike Greek heroes of epic who were demi-gods and individualists, far removed in achievement from ordinary men and women, Roman character and heroes were accessible – anyone from aristocrats to the poorest people could emulate Manlius Torquatus or Lucretia. The chapter wraps up with an indication of the social hierarchy and an introduction to the patron–client relationship and social mobility.

With your dossier on how to blend in with Roman society, next you need to feed and clothe your characters. Chapter 2 looks at food and drink, clothing and accessories. This chapter isn't going to provide explicit lists of what to eat and what to wear, but rather some broader themes to keep in mind as you provide your Romans with the basics. Taste and smell are amongst our strongest senses and conjure up memories and emotions; it is no surprise that the feast is a set-piece in any epic, myth, or history of a momentous event. Rome was a public society – entertaining and hospitality were a way to show off social status as well, and to gain praise for one's honour and generosity amongst friends and clients. Mealtime and offering of food was an important occasion in antiquity. Political deals were made, alliances cemented, establishment of one's social status and one's place in the pecking order were put on display at table.

The first part of this chapter considers food and meals – what to think about when planning a sumptuous feast or how to nourish your characters with the basic staples of the Roman diet. Topics in this section include a consideration of the banquet versus the humble repast; the Mediterranean triad and diet staples in general; dining etiquette, cookery books and recipes, with a particular focus on Apicius; and a beverage brief – not to mention which foods *shouldn't* appear on a Roman table. There's also a short section on New World nosh that has no business there. The second part of the chapter considers appearance and attire. Soldiers carried *diplomae* in brass cases which hung around their necks and contained their identity papers. Travellers on state business might have official documents giving them licence to travel and access to important places. Ordinary inhabitants of Rome, however, did not carry an ID card beyond their appearance. Clothing (and hairstyles) made the man and woman in our period. Considered here are basic wardrobe staples and the effects of social status on what one could and could not wear. Plenty of stories abound from the comic stage and the storytellers of mistaken identity due to loss or destruction of clothing, and how a long-lost aristocratic might be restored to his or her rightful inheritance on the discovery of a particular signet ring or other item of jewellery. Topics surveyed include the basic garments for men and women so that you can build a wardrobe; a primer on sumptuary law; colours and fabrics; the make-up box; and hair (facial and head).

Now that you've got people and they're fed and dressed, you might consider where and how to house them: in the country, the city, or the places in between. Fortunately, you have roughly 2.1 million square miles to play around with. Chapter 3 looks at some of the practicalities that go into creating the basics of civic space and on rural life in the Roman Empire. Status and identity feature here as with everything else: how basic or opulent your homes and accommodations will be will again depend on your characters' social standing and economic level. Décor reveals as much about the variety of goods on offer throughout the Empire and the cosmopolitan nature of the Empire as it does about your characters' wealth and good taste – or lack thereof. Whether or not your characters live in the city or in the countryside affects how they might view themselves or be viewed by others. Roman social snobbery related not only to someone's place on the economic scale but also to where someone lived, how many homes and villas they might possess, and the location of such dwellings. Here you can consider the ideal versus reality: the aristocratic dream was a home (or two or six) in the country or along the sea coast, or a place to escape the heat of summer or the dreariness of winter. Aristocratic poetry, satire, and letters abound in descriptions of lovely country estates, each run with the same order and efficiency of a military camp while remaining beautiful and cosmopolitan. Of course the reality was quite different: Cato (*De Agri Cultura*) and Columella (*Res Rustica*) might describe in their treatises on country living the best way to run such estates, but these are intellectual exercises for the aristocratic owner: the overseers were on a different plane altogether. As for the relationship between tenants and landlords, Juvenal's *Satires*, Martial's *Epigrams*, and Pliny the Younger's letters reveal that being a tenant and being a landlord in the first and second centuries of the imperial period led to similar sorts of headaches that tenants and landlords at present might suffer.

Topics in this chapter include the basic structure and parts of a city, essential especially if you're founding a colony, setting up a military outpost, or providing a clutch of provincials with a 'flat-pack' Roman city in emulation of them-down-there in Italy. There's a sample house layout and information on the types of buildings found in town and the various rooms one might find in a house, and different terms for various urban centres. Other topics include utilities (water and sewerage, heating and lighting), issues of safety and the dangers of city living (crime and fire mainly), and travel (conditions and directions). Finally, there is a consideration of the attitude towards city versus country living, the aristocratic ideal and the practical realities. Whilst you might include travel or the dynamic between someone from the far provinces encountering the life, noise, and speed of the centre in your storyline, you might also think about the city (or even the City) as a character itself – its appearance, contents, and 'personality' is as effective a catalyst for a plot as the individuals who inhabit it.

Now that your characters have character, have been fed and clothed, and are settling into their digs, they will need a bit of law and order. Chapter 4 surveys the basics of administration and legal business. Entire academic careers have been made over the past two and a half thousand years on the subject of Roman jurisprudence – not to mention the discussion, from academics and amateur enthusiasts, on Rome's principal means of peace-keeping: its army. Topics in this chapter include an overview of the administration of the Roman state, its magistracies and legal institutions, and its means of keeping order. You'll find a survey on how the Romans got things done (patronage and consensus), their love of hierarchy (organisation of the government), and the effects of status on their administrative, legislative, and military institutions. Two appendices act as handmaidens (or perhaps, since we're talking about administration and public order, *lictores* bearing *fasces*) to accompany this chapter. Appendix 1 is a chart of key conflicts, hotspots, opponents, and outcome or significance from c. 280 BCE through to 180 CE. Appendix 2 notes the main military and political movers and shakers of this period: a chart that matches up the big man or woman, what she or he is best known for, and a selection of the contemporary sources wherein you'll find his or her exploits. Long winter evenings will fly by as you sift through Justinian's formidable corpus of civil and criminal law accompanied with a side order of myriad contemporary texts on legal interpretation.

Chapter 5 looks at economic matters. Aelius Aristides famously called Rome 'the emporium of the world': 'All things converge here, trade, seafaring, agriculture, metallurgy, all the skills which exist and have existed, anything that is begotten and grows. Whatever cannot be seen here belongs completely to the category of non-existent things' (*Ad Romam*, 11–13). Aelius was part of the Second Sophistic, a group of Greek intellectuals who travelled about the Roman world, gave speeches for entertainment, and sometimes acted as ambassadors for the imperial government. His speech praises the great wealth of Rome, but there was in reality a tremendous gap between rich and poor in Roman society and far more 'not haves' than 'haves'. Between 200 BCE and 200 CE Rome prospered as its empire expanded. Major conquests in the East and Near East that brought in wealth and goods bolstered the economy, rising to heights during the *Pax Romana*, the first and second centuries CE. The provinces were great sources of revenue (and soldiers, who protected the peace and were supported by this revenue), which allowed for general political stability and peace in this era. The army built roads, and merchants followed; trade routes overland and across the Red Sea from the east brought in further goods, slaves, and wealth; urbanisation led to more marketplaces. As part of this survey on the economy, this chapter includes topics on the sources of Rome's wealth; land ownership and the labour force (with a focus on slavery); a coin spotter's guide and the value of money; shopping and foreign trade; taxation; and poverty and public relief. The Romans' characteristic preoccupation with status and social hierarchy is reflected in a discussion of their attitudes towards money-making and spending, and frugality and public benevolence.

All work and no play make Gaius a dull boy – and most modern audiences associate Rome with leisure, entertainment, and spectacle thanks to everything from Victorian art and novels through to cinema, television, and world-building games. Chapter 6 is a survey of a selection of Roman pastimes – there are far more, of course. It should come as no surprise that snobbery and social status affected the Roman outlook when it came to sport and entertainment – as far as our intellectual writers were concerned, popular entertainment was the stuff of the lower classes and a waste of a conservative Roman aristocrat's time – except when it wasn't. Tiberius, for example, loved dinner parties and held trivia competitions about Greek mythology (and God help you if he caught you with a crib sheet) (Suet., *Tib.* 56.1); Caligula used to host poetry competitions wherein the losers had to blot out their poor efforts with their tongues – unless they chose to be beaten with rods or thrown into a river (Suet., *Gai.* 20.1).

The most popular entertainment and escapism that cut across the entire social and economic strata were sports and spectacle, especially from the first century BCE onwards through to the end of the fourth century CE in the West, and a few centuries beyond that in the East. Sport and spectacle were big money-spinners, and, while we may not have much in the way of sources that precisely describe an actual gladiator match or the details of a particular chariot race, there are myriad references in contemporary sources and many material remains depicting them. The activities in the arena and the circus not only kept the Romans preoccupied but they also reinforced notions of social hierarchy and status (with seating arrangements and with the punishments meted out) and presented through their lavish splendour a symbol of the might, wealth, and authority of the Empire. Some sports became particularly politicised: during the era of the Republic, games could earn the sponsor the love if not the votes of the common people. During the imperial period, emperors used public entertainment as a means to demonstrate their power and might and to reinforce flagging popularity (see Mahoney, 2001: 71–90. for other contemporary examples): as Fronto remarked, the Roman mob was kept under control by two things: free grain and shows (Front., *Princ. Hist.* 17). The vicious riots at the arena in Pompeii (Tac., *Ann.* 14.17), commemorated in a fresco there, sadly have modern parallels in the violence that sometimes attends sporting events today. Many of these spectacles, at least superficially, continue to represent in modern eyes how Rome 'ought' to look. The key imagery for many modern stories set in Rome is the big scene at the arena, whether it's the showdown between the hero and his nemesis or the final moral victory for the Christian martyr against the pagan mob (or at least against the inevitable lions). This chapter scratches only the surface of the types of ways you can keep your characters entertained and amused. Here we'll limit ourselves to Roman attitudes towards spectacle, athletics, and public competition; chariot racing and gladiatorial games; baths and swimming; comedy theatre; dinner parties; music and dance; sexual entertainment and prostitution; gambling, dice, and betting (with a primer on a couple of board games).

The final topic that this guide considers in Chapter 7 is religion and religious practice. Religion of some form or another was inextricable from other aspects of Roman culture – public service to the state gods out of a sense of tradition, duty, civic responsibility; philosophy and intellectual study might take the place of impersonal ritual. The Empire encompassed a broad spectrum of beliefs, adapted and traded among the cultures in the Near East and into Western Europe. Religion and myth permeated all aspects of a Roman's life. It was impossible to tell where religion stopped and civic culture started; religion and myth were behind the inspiration for civic pride in the forms of art, athletics, build- ing projects. There was a constant vigilance in looking for signs and omens about the future. State cults and myths did not offer a set of moral and ethical codes – Romans learned behavioural codes of conduct from other sources, such as family or philosophy; mythological heroes and the history or biography of past statesmen and generals provided models for one's values and aspirations. The Romans maintained a contractual relationship between the gods and humans akin to the patron–client relationship: sacrifice and ritual included a material exchange (a sac- rifice) and visible reward – lack of either meant that people weren't performing their religious duties. Cults and sects from the Near East intersected throughout Roman life, across the Empire, in the form of Judaism, mystery cults, or, in the latter half of our period, Christianity. Eventually, after our period, state cults would be superseded by an official support of Christianity, but even then conversion to Christianity and Christian practices remained fairly superficial in terms of full conversion or universal dedication to beliefs in places even into the Middle Ages.

It would be, to coin a phrase, a Herculean task to include every aspect of religious practice in the Roman world, or a comprehensive list of sources, sourcebooks, and scholarship on the various flavours of religious practice in Rome and its impact on the state. Instead, see Chapter 8 for resources to get you started. We'll limit the discussion here to some of the major components of religion in the Roman world. These include discussion of foundation myths which provide the Romans with not only their heroes but also cultural values for emulation. Next is a look at the state cult (and a brief discussion of the pantheon and its origins) and the imperial cult (which became inextricably linked to the state cult). Also discussed is the *mos maiorum*, that is, the custom of venerating one's ancestors, as this practice plays a role in how Roman society and politics were folded together. State cults and the pagan gods were linked with civic duty, and the relationship between these gods and humans was impersonal. Other types of religious practice throughout the Empire fulfilled more emotional personal needs. Several instances of this type of religious practice in our period include the mystery cults, imported from the Near East, the Romans' relationship with the Jews, and the issue of the rise of Christianity. There is an entire industry of Roman fiction based around the relationship between the Christians and the Romans – with much of the basis of that literature and art going back to the earliest days of the Christians themselves. Fair play if you wish to revisit those experiences in your own fiction; here we focus more on how the Romans viewed the Christians – something one might not see as often in historical fiction and film.

Each chapter of this guide does make reading suggestions on the go. The last, Chapter 8, acts as a complementary standalone annotated bibliography and resource centre. Here you will find recommended resources, collections, and databases related to each chapter, as well as good places to start your research and reading of relevant scholarship. Particular trends and debate in the scholarship are highlighted. Keep in mind, of course, that limits of space prevent the chapter from being densely inclusive, and of course new publications are appearing in print and online all the time. The chapter includes suggestions on general textbooks for background reading, and then introduces you to online collections and databases of contemporary sources before addressing each chapter topically. The resources suggested throughout this book and this chapter are, for the most part, in English or English translations of scholarship; be aware that if you have other languages at your disposal you'll find a rich scholarship on the Classical world not only from Western European scholars, but from those studying the Roman world from the modern perspective of those cultures and civilisations who were once neighbours and long-distance trading contacts with the Roman world.

Finally, before we get stuck in, a final word about Classical reception. As we've noted, the Roman world in popular culture won't necessarily be a world that would be recognisable to a contemporary Roman: as a writer, historian, or designer, one may strive for historical accuracy in design, but how that design is adapted, used, and acted upon is a component of *Classical reception*, that is, how the ancient world is interpreted by the current audience who engages with it. This is especially true with depictions of Roman art and entertainment, because not only do current fiction, non-fiction, and scholarship engage with sources pertaining to art and entertainment as the Romans may have enjoyed it, but we also bring to the table our own cultural baggage.

Classical reception is an entire field unto itself – but if you are putting together your own fictional vision of the Roman world in a story, a novel, a motion picture, or a game, then it is well worth your time to invest in at least an introduction to this important scholarly field. Start with Lorna Hardwick and Christopher Stray (2008), Charles Martindale and Richard F. Thomas (2006), or Lorna Hardwick (2010). Don't overlook academic guidebooks such as David Schaps (2010). Dip into the seminal lectures of Arnaldo Momigliano (1992, for example) on the foundations of Classical historiography to understand how the study of the Classical world has been defined and redefined over the years by interpretation and re-evaluation of the sources – not only those by Roman writers, but how the views of Greek, Jewish, and other cultures influenced and continue to influence our interpretation of the Roman world.

Appreciation for film, television, and other popular media as part of Classical reception is fairly new in scholarship and complements what scholars of the Middle Ages refer to as *medievalism*. A key scholar for medievalism is Umberto Eco, who in his 1986 essay 'Dreaming of the Middle Ages' created a list of how the Middle Ages are used in fiction and filmed drama to particular effect; these categories may well be adapted as part of the Classical world on film and television. A good introduction to why the Rome we see on television or interact with through websites might not be recognisable to an actual Roman is Hobden (2009), who discusses how scholarship is constantly shaping and re-evaluating our own interpretation of Ancient Roman culture and society. McDonald (2008) provides a good summary of the debate in scholarship over the merits of film and popular depictions of the Classical world outside of modern entertainment. Fraser's 1988 monograph *The Hollywood History of the World* was initially dismissed by one of this author's post-grad tutors as 'dumbing down' the ancient world – that is, 'HollyRome' – but since the early 2000s the merits of HollyRome films have become a subject of scholarship in its own right: film, novels, and games aren't *meant* to be textbooks, but one must be aware that popular depictions of the ancient world are frequently based less on academic scholarship and more on popular culture itself: for example, the nineteenth-century novels *Quo Vadis* and *Ben-Hur* and works of art by Jean-Léon Gérôme, while rooted in Classical scholarship, were wildly popular works of entertainment that still have enormous influence on how Rome was and is still depicted in media across the board. It's important to develop an eye for critical reading not only of your contemporary sources but of influential popular histories of the era.

1 Woman with wax tablets and stylus, the so-called 'Sappho' portrait. Fresco, Pompeii, first century CE

This little guide is but a brief survey of a vast amount of resources, sources, and scholarship on the Classical world that is available for reflection, evaluation, interpretation, and creativity. It is intended to open doors for further reading and consideration as you construct your own Roman world – it's a welcome mat that invites you in to listen to the stories of the Romans and to contribute tales of your own. So *dextro pede* – best (right) foot forward, as the Roman would say – and enjoy.

Unless otherwise noted, all translations (and their flaws) are by the author.

1

ROMAN PEOPLE: OR, HOW DO YOU *KNOW* S/HE'S A ROMAN?

WHO ARE THE ROMANS, ANYWAY?

The basics for a Roman character sketch begin with the family. Traditional values so ingrained in Roman culture begin here: a love of authority, deference for one's elders, the importance of the group, and attention to status and hierarchy. Family, and especially one's *pater-familias*, were so important that Augustus remarked in his *Res Gestae* that the most precious title ever given to him was *pater patriae*, 'Father of the country' (Aug., *RG* 35; Suet., *Aug.* 58.1–2). He made his family *the* family in Rome – not only the one to emulate amongst Roman households but also the metonymy for the relationship between Rome and its provinces and allied states (Severy, 2003: 213–251). The *patron–client* relationship was the principal institution for how the Romans got things done (see Chapter 4). As a family might grow and extend into other households through marriage, so the state grew to include many other cultures, peoples, and practices. Assimilation might have been common practice, but social distinction remained strong across economic, political, geographic, and social lines – all going back to one's family, their status, and their reputation.

FAMILY RELATIONS

The *familia* included the extended family of relations by birth, marriage, or adoption (adoption of adults was more customary than of infants or

15

children), and the household slaves and servants (cf. Just., *Dig.* 50.16.195; Gai., *Instit.* 1.196). Family relations are a growing area of scholarship which takes into consideration a re-evaluation of literary sources, an examination of language and rhetoric, and material representations of the family to reconstruct a picture of household roles, family relationships, and use of domestic space. Key names to look for amongst the scholars of the Roman family and household are Rawson (1986, 2010), Dixon (1992), Treggiari (1996), and Bradley (1991); sourcebooks with excellent bibliography include those by Gardiner (1987), Wiedemann (1980), Parkin and Pomeroy (2007). Household hierarchy and relationships could be complex, and here you might find funerary inscriptions informative. Selected examples of these can be found in Parkin and Pomeroy (2007: 89–91); examples in L&R, 1: 523–525; and *ROL*, 4: 2–54. Excellent examples for the relationships amongst a *familia* over multiple generations from the affluent homeowners down through to their slaves are the funeral inscriptions of the Volusii (Treggiari, 1975). Here one finds not only intra-family relationships of free, freed, and servile members of a household but also the types of jobs that might be found within a large *familia*.

All stages of life were prescribed by Roman custom and tradition from birth to death. Members of the household were bound by domestic patron–client roles and (ideally) obligated by *pietas* ('devotion' or 'duty') towards their elders or the protection of weaker members of the household (Ulp., *Reg.* 11.1, 27; cf. Cic., *Off.* 1.53–58; Val. Max., 5.4.7). Parents were patrons to their children, and children, as their parents' legacy (and perhaps providers in their parents' old age), were their clients. The role models for such behaviour were the Roman heroes – such as Cincinnatus, a farmer on the one hand, but on the other a fiercely protective soldier when family or land was threatened (Liv.. 3.26–28) – or idealised wives and mothers who smoothly ran the household and produced sons for the good of the state (cf. Murdia, the perfect mother, *ILS*, 8394). Coriolanus's mother was a model (Val. Max., 2.1a–b; Liv., 2.40.1–13; Plut., *Cor.* 4.3–4, 34.1–2, 35.1–5, 36.1–5), and Cornelia of the Gracchi another (e.g. Plut., *TG* 1.1–5, 19.1–3; Val. Max., 7.1. Cf. Juv., 6.166–170). Unlike Greek heroes, whose desire and competition for individual glory saw them focused on attainment of mainly elite, aristocratic honours in the athletics, on the battleground, or political arena, Roman heroes (and heroines) embodied characteristics that could be attained by anyone at any social or economic level (see Neel, 2017). Even the private life of the family could be held up to public scrutiny. Augustus, for example, published a daily diary of the events in his household, and he scolded on more than one occasion the young women of his *familia* to keep this in mind (Suet., *Aug.* 64.2).

The head of the household was the *paterfamilias*; this was the oldest man in the family, and he could be a widower grandfather or a bachelor uncle (see Severy, 2003: 158–186; Val. Max., 5.8.1–3). His job was to protect and to provide for his family. In the days of the Republic, his word had legal sanction (Dion. Hal., *Ant. Rom.* 2.26.4; Ulp., *Reg.* 50.16.195.2a–b), and he had the power of life and death over his family (*Twelve Tables*, 4.1–4; cf. Manlius's punishment of his disobedient son, Val. Max., 5.8.3; Gai., *Instit.* 1.48–49, 52, 55; this authority was later limited in the era of Hadrian). The power of the *paterfamilias* was kept in check by the practice of the custom of the ancestors (*mos maiorum*). Other men in the family, when of age, acted as counsellors to his decisions, much as the Senate did in the days of Roman kingship. If he wanted his sons to defer to his wisdom and honour him after death, he would avoid being a tyrant and bully (see Liv., 7.4.4–7; cf. generational effects of a *paterfamilias* as tyrant, Pliny, *Epist.* 6.33). Despite this official position of the *paterfamilias*, however, a shrewish wife or a demanding child might direct the course of the *familia* (Plut., *Cat. Ma.* 8.2; cf. Plut., *Themist.* 18.5).

Other obligations of the *paterfamilias* included providing for the family's spiritual welfare: he made sacrifices to the household gods; he threw beans (*anima*) about the house to confuse the evil demons who would steal the family's spirits (*anima*) on the festival of Lemuria (Ov., *Fast.* 5.7.419–444). He protected his elders, as Aeneas did his father Anchises; he provided for his sons as they might continue the stability of the family and consequently Roman state, as Aeneas again did with his son Ascanius, also known as Iulus. A *pater* provided tutors for his sons' education; he saw to it that they secured work via his connections if not reputation, whether it was an apprenticeship, a military position, or a place in public life. If the *pater* couldn't help his sons establish their lives, they acquired a *patron* (see Chapter 4).

The *pater* also provided for and protected the women of the family. For example, if he were much older than his wife, which wasn't particularly uncommon, he might be obliged to continue her education in household management (*oeconomia*), as noted by Pliny the Younger (*Epist.* 1.16; 4.29, 19) and by the spouse of Turia (*CIL*, 4, n. 1527, in L&F, n. 191: 165–169). Some aristocratic fathers educated their daughters well enough to converse with them about their work in law or business (Hemelrijk, 1999: 30–40). Famous examples include Laelia, the daughter of C. Laelius (consul 440 BCE) who gave speeches as elegantly as her father (Quint., *Inst.* 1.1.6) and Hortensia, the daughter of the orator Q. Hortensius Hortalus (1.1.6; Val. Max., 8.3.3). On the complex relationship between elite Roman fathers and daughters, see Hallett (1984) and on women's education (including within the household), see Hemelrijk (1999). To murder a parent (or master) was the worst crime and was met with a ghastly, even highly symbolic form of execution called the *poena cullei*, 'the punishment of the sack' (see, for example, Cic., *Rosc. Am.* 26.7); for a description of the symbolism inherent in this punishment, see Marcian (*Dig.* 48.9.9), who describes it in his discussion of the *Lex Pompeii de parricides* (55 BCE).

The *materfamilias* lacked the legal powers of her husband, but she could have great influence over the family, especially her sons. Her duty as a good mother was to raise sons for the benefit of the state (as soldiers or statesmen); her behaviour and morals had to be beyond reproach, as she represented the domestic side of her husband's political life. Epitaphs are a good inspiration for the idealisation of the good wife and mother; see D&G (316–321) for a selection of contemporary references to Roman mothers. Sons were especially obligated to their mothers: Coriolanus was stopped from attacking Rome in revenge for political slights by his mother placing herself between his army and the city boundary (Liv., 2.40.1–13; Plut., *Cor.* 34.1–2, 35.1–5, 36.1–5). Another example is the mother of Agricola, Julia Procilla, lauded by Agricola's son-in-law Tacitus (*Agr.* 4.2–4). Overbearing mothers, at least according to an uncritical reading of the sources, included the empresses Livia (see Barrett, 2004) and Agrippina the Younger (see Barrett, 1996). The Julias of the Severan dynasty (Levick, 2007; Langford, 2013) are a study in how imperial women came completely and openly to pull the strings of administration for at least two child-emperors.

SOURCES AND SCHOLARSHIP ON ROMAN WOMEN

The study of Roman women is robust in terms of gender roles and the complexities of how the Romans defined what was masculine, what was feminine, and all of the shadings in between. The main caveat for studying Roman women is summed up in the introduction to Dixon's essential text *Reading Roman Women* (2001): written sources for Roman women were almost exclusively written by men; epigraphic and material representations were meant for public consumption and were thus formulaic or structured to embody physically the public face of Roman custom and tradition. As noted by Kampen in her study on women working in Roman Ostia (1981), there's no way to access private thoughts or feelings of women (or men, for that matter) on any point on the social hierarchy. The lives of women were bound by the many social institutions of Roman society. Variation and nuance can be extracted from the sources and used to create a variety of characters if you look especially at the women in the comedies of Plautus and Terence and the satires of Horace, Petronius, and Juvenal. Even Pliny the Younger's soppiest love letters and the devotion of Turia's husband, sweet or moving as they may be, were intended for public reading. Whilst the same can be said of piecing together the portrait of a male character, women tend to fall into particular rhetorical stereotypes – the innocent maid, the good wife, the wicked stepmother, the corrupt foreign queen, the *dux femina* (the dominating politician's wife), and the *mater impotens* (the pushy mother of a ruling son). All of these characters certainly have their purpose. A critical reading of such sources will clear a path to understanding how the exaggeration found in satire or the inversion found in rhetoric can inform a character study, as the extremes have to be believable in order to achieve the desired effect of humour on the one hand, or the outrage of an imperial critic on the other. L&R have a selection of literary portraits of model Republican and imperial women (2: nos 95–96: 347–352; no. 100: 358–361). For modern scholarship on how to sift through such public filters, see, for example, Segal (1987) and Konstan (1986) for comedy, Freundenburg, ed. (2005) for satire, and Ginsburg (2006) on parsing the rhetorical criticism of powerful women (of Tacitus in particular).

THE IDEAL ROMAN WOMAN: CORNELIA OF THE GRACCHI

Early imperial writers, reflecting on the ideals of the Republic as a way to criticise what they considered the disgraceful behaviour of the Julio-Claudian emperors, looked to the second-century BCE matron Cornelia, mother of the Gracchi, as the ideal woman. She embodied the traditional Roman values of *nobilitas* and *gravitas*; she was obedient; she was widowed and did not remarry, making her an *univira*, or 'one-man woman' (admirable, but impractical in a society where women might not have any financial or legal independence (Ulp., *Reg.* 1.27), especially if their sons were still under age, before their manhood ceremonies at the age of fifteen or sixteen). Cornelia raised her sons to be model politicians for the state – even if they broke with tradition and convention, insulted the Senate, and introduced violence into the political process that contributed to civil war and corruption that ultimately tore the Republic apart. Her calm and rational demeanour made her a model; she was identified as being a daughter of the heroic Scipio Africanus (and not identified as being the widow of her husband) (Plut., *TG* 1.1–7). Famously, when chatting with ladies who were showing off their bling, she waited until her sons had come home from lessons, called them over, clutched them to her bosom and announced, 'These are *my* jewels' (Val. Max., 4.7.1) She was elegant, chaste, modest – and somewhat insufferable: Juvenal mocked her in the second century CE for being a goody-two-shoes (6.166–170).

OPTIMA MATER: *WOMEN AND POWER*

Gender roles in the Classical world are complex and sometimes difficult to understand: the division of behaviour and attributes that fall under the 'masculine' and 'feminine' definitions suggested more about how aggressive and active (especially publicly and politically) a person was than about his or her sexual preference. Passive, or feminine, behaviour was seen as weak in a man but expected in a woman. Action and agency could be enacted through sexuality: passive partners took and received; active partners were assertive. Hence, when a man was mocked for being homosexual, it wasn't necessarily for being in a same-sex relationship, but rather because he as the passive partner was seen as weak and womanly (cf. Catull., 16, or Cic., *Phil.* 2.44–46 where Cicero shames Antony's youthful antics as a debauched boy who played the girl's part in sexual relations). Women were certainly expected to display feminine versions of masculine virtues and character. For example, they were to show dignity in the face of adversity or sorrow, as Plutarch counselled his wife on their death of their daughter (*Consolatio ad Uxorem*). But sometimes women might act in a manner that was 'too masculine', and they were held in disregard by aristocratic male authors; cf. Sallust's description of Sempronia, the wife of Decimus Junius Brutus (consul 77 BCE) and her sexuality (Cic., *Cat.* 24.3–25.5). Masculine traits in a woman included too much education, an interest in politics, and sexual aggression. A 'masculine' woman could be the one who dared to take on a public, political role, something officially forbidden but sometimes unofficially enacted, to the dismay of critics of the Julio-Claudian emperors Claudius and Nero. Inversion of gender roles was a popular rhetorical device that stressed the actions of such dominant women. They illustrated how weak their menfolk were and that the natural order of society was in chaos (see Aristophanes' Greek comedy *Lysistrata* – it's not 'girl power' that makes the play funny; it's that the world is in such chaos that women show more political sense than the men!)

MARRIAGE

The marriage ceremony was a ritual performed for family and friends – to make a public acknowledgement of the union (Gai., *Instit.*1.108–156, 136a–137a). The occasion called for loads of ritual and sacrifices to perform, traditional clothes and food, but there was no required officiator, and the marriage could be cemented by the simple 'Ubi Gaius, ego Gaia' ('Where he goes, I go'). It was the public recognition of the union that was important. The main impetus for marriage was to produce children – one's legal heirs and legacy, hence all of those Augustan laws on marriage (*ADA*, 166–198, abridged), rewards for having children (Cass. Dio, 54.16.1–2), and edicts against adultery and divorce (*ADA*, 112–128 and Suet., *Aug.* 34). Augustan legislation encouraged marriage and offered benefits and tax breaks for bachelors who got married – and stayed married, as divorce was rampant in the late Republic – and for women to have more than three children (Gai., *Instit.*1.45, 193). Part of it was Augustus's desire to promote the stability of the family, but part of it was to repopulate after the civil war and Senatorial purges. Upper-class families did not pair up their children in love matches, but looked for strategic alliances (cf. Pliny, *Epist.* 1.14) – one was considered fortunate if one fell in love with the marriage partner (see expressions of love from Turia's husband, L&F, no. 191, 27, 40; Pliny, *Epist.* 6.4, 6.7, and especially 7.5). It wasn't unusual for the lucky couple to meet for the first time on their wedding day, but this is an extreme, as the families – at least the fathers if nothing else – would have rummaged around in the various nurseries to find spouses to suit their own needs accordingly. For a collection of sources and laws on marriage and divorce, see Grubbs (2002: 81–218); there are also some examples including the *Lex Julia* and other Roman laws on marriage and adultery in L&F, nos 140–149: 128–134. Plutarch provides model advice for women on marriage in his *Moralia* 138a–146a.

In terms of sexual mores, keep in mind again how conservative upper-class Romans were meant to be. When it comes to love and sex, you'll find that one often has little to do with the other. There was a double standard when it came to youth and sex: young men were indulged (to a point) when they went out on the town in the evenings and sowed their wild oats, because the only women in the streets after dark would be prostitutes. Respectable young girls out after dark were foolish, and they were not sympathetic victims if they fell prey to these men. The 'rape plot' was a fixture of Roman comedy (cf. Plautus's *Casina* or Terence's *Hecyra*) and illustrates the social repercussions of sexual japes: it was jolly for the youth in the family to go out carousing and to ravish the women they encountered, but young women who were found to have lost their virginity (usually because they had fallen pregnant) were disgraced and brought dishonour on the family. Adultery, too, was a serious offence especially in the early Empire, as Augustus not only set a series of harsh penalties for committing adultery (*sturpro*) but also did not hold his own family above the law (with his daughter Julia being famously banished for her indiscretions) (cf. Val. Max., 6.1.12–13). Women were punished more severely than men – men could find relief from their wives with prostitutes (and Livia famously procured prostitutes for Augustus to keep him satisfied, Suet., *Aug.* 7.1), and it was not considered cheating. Women who were caught committing adultery were severely punished (e.g., *Cod. Just.* 9.9.22, 23 pr., 24, 26, 28L) and if allowed to live could lose their status, depending on the status of their lover (Paul., *Sent.* 2.21A.1–4L) (sex between aristocratic women and slaves was the most disdained; cf. *Cod. Just.*9.11.1 pr. L). *Sturpro* in the imperial family was tantamount to treason; Caligula banished his sisters on suspicion of adulterous plots to overthrow him (Cass. Dio, 59.22.6–9; Suet., *Gai.* 24.3,

29.1). They were lucky, as adulterous women could face capital punishment (cf. L&F, no. 130: 122).

Did husbands and wives love each other? Did parents love their children? It is a subject of debate amongst historians whether there was true love between husbands and wives, especially amongst the wealthier classes where marriage usually sealed a property deal or political alliance. You might consider a more dignified reflection on marriage and family, such as Plutarch's *Consolation to His Wife*, the *Laudatio Turiae* (a detailed, long funerary inscription dedicated to a devoted wife), Seneca's essay to his mother (*De Consolatione*), or the love letters Pliny wrote to and about his young third wife. Outside of marriage, you'll find plenty of love poetry about winning over girls you don't want to bring home to mother. For example, Ovid is famous for his saucy poems on winning a woman's love (*Ars Amatoria*; *Amores*); at the same time, his exilic poetry *Ex Ponto* and *Tristia* reveals that he has a devoted wife who misses him, wants to join him in exile, and at Rome remains an intercessor on his behalf when he's exiled (many instances in *Trist.* 1.2.37ff, 1.3.81–102, 1.6, 3.3, 4.3, 5.11, 5.14; and *Ex Ponto* 1.4, 3.1 in which he asks his wife directly to intercede with Livia on his behalf).

SEX AND ALL THAT

There are many contemporary sources about sex and scurrilous details (see also Chapter 6) to be found in the more scandalous biographies of Suetonius (whose *Lives of Famous Prostitutes* are sadly lost) and *Historia Augusta*. There is also love poetry and satire: look to Catullus, Ovid, Horace, and Juvenal for examples. Comedy is another good source of at least what's taboo or would get laughs in strait-laced, conservative society. In addition to Plautus and Terence, there are fragments of mimes and street plays; there is also the fourth-century CE *Philogelos*, which is a compendium that includes bawdy sex jokes. Studies of Pompeii have produced an entire industry devoted to the study of sex and prostitution. One might begin here with the work of McGinn, a legal scholar who has written extensively about Roman prostitution (1998, 2004). Medical textbooks by Galen and Soranus focused on 'women's issues' as a result of treating prostitutes – especially when it comes to illnesses and contraception. You can find selections of these and other commentaries on women's health in L&F (nos 423–481: 301–352) with useful sources on women's anatomy, pregnancy, midwifery, and physical health as found in the writings of contemporary philosophers, doctors, laymen, female physicians, and epitaphs. The plight of prostitutes also shows the dichotomy of the female image. The highest-paid courtesans were witty, well educated, and politically influential, such as Praetia, who influenced one of Sulla's generals (Plut., *Luc.* 6.2–5). The lowest of the low, the *pornai* (from the Greek 'to sell'), were women who sold themselves in desperation to hold their households together, especially if they were widowed.

CHILDREN

Ideally marriage produced children, and the study of Roman children, youth, and the bonds between parents and children (in all of their variations), wet-nurses and wards, and masters and slaves are all growing fields of scholarship. The relationship between Roman parents and children may seem stiff, distant, and formal to modern eyes; much of this is again down to Roman reserve and the idea that not every child would survive – or even be accepted into the family. Pregnancy and birth were dangerous conditions; childbirth was a leading cause of death due to lack of understanding about infection and post-natal care. There are depictions of midwives and birthing chairs that survive; medical literature describes the conditions of birth and its complications. Roman writers debated over the use of wet-nurses (Tac., *Dial.* 29; L&F nos 297–301: 237–239, including a Roman version of *The Grapes of Wrath* adult breast-feeding at no. 303: 240) versus breastfeeding (Aul. Gell., *NA* 12.1). They also debated when and how much affection ought to be shown to a child (Tac., *Dial.* 29). The idea of loving devotion towards children appeared as a result of the increasing numbers of foreign slaves brought into Roman society from the second century BCE onwards; Roman women were encouraged, from the early imperial era to become more (publicly) demonstrative towards their offspring (Quint., *Instit.* 1.4–7; Plut., *De Lib.* 6–7) so as not to be outdone by the affections slaves showed their own children or to be replaced by the wet-nurses caring for the free offspring of their owners (Plut., *De Lib.* 5). Nero's mother and aunt publicly fought over establishing their affections for him (Suet., *Ner.* 7), but at the (literal) end of the day, it was his wet-nurse to whom he had the strongest loving bond as she and the emperor's mistress were the only ones who dared to care for his body and burial after his suicide (Suet., *Ner.* 50). Likewise, Domitian's wet-nurse Phyllis stole and buried his body after he was assassinated (Suet., *Dom.* 17.3; Cass. Dio, 68.18.2).

One of the Republican *paterfamilias*'s legal rights was to decide if infants born to the household would live or die. The newborn child was laid at the father's feet, and if he rejected it it might be taken off to the dung heap to die of exposure or to be picked up by slave traders. The *paterfamilias* could order unwanted children to be exposed. The extent of the *paterfamilas*'s authority in the matter of children was discussed when Pliny the Younger and Trajan discussed the fates of foundlings (Pliny, *Epist.* 10.65–66). An example of such decisions amongst ordinary families is found in a letter from Egypt around 1 BCE in which Hilario advises his wife Alis to keep their child if it is a boy, but to expose it if it is a girl (*Oxy. Pap.* no. 744 = Select papyri no. 105 in L&F, no. 295: 236). If the *paterfamilias* accepted the new baby, he raised it aloft and named it.

DEATH AND MOURNING

As for the end of life, death was more public and more familiar than in the modern era: infant and child mortality high, warfare endemic (especially in the late Republic with both foreign and civil wars), and increasingly lavish public spectacles in which death was a component of the entertainment, especially from the first century BCE. Augustus raised mourning for his own heirs – he outlived several of them – and family members to a high art; see Lott (2012) for a recent exploration of how Augustus helped to create sensational public ritual of mourning for imperial family members. A look through various funerary inscriptions and laudations found in D&G, L&F, L&R, *ROL*, and so forth will indicate the public side of death and mourning in general, a sentiment not dissimilar to the ritualised public mourning of Victorian tombstones and the sentimentalising of death and funerals.

2 Tombstone of a family in Aquincum, first to second century CE

ROMAN NAMES

In an era without ID cards, names were hugely important as indicators of family, reputation, and status. Indeed, this idea persists in modern stories of Rome, too: it's a dramatic moment in *Gladiator* (2000) when the vengeful Gladiator reveals his true identity to his nemesis the Emperor Commodus: Maximus Decimus Meridius. I'd like to think the emperor's stricken response was less concern that his old man's factotum Maximus had escaped assassination and was now before him seeking vengence, and more distaste about the strange construction of the Gladiator's nomenclature.

Roman aristocrats had three names: the praenomen, the *gens* (or family/clan), and the cognomen. The praenomen comes first: *prae* means 'first' or 'before'. There are only twenty or so of these, which is why they're frequently abbreviated. The family name is the *gens* – Julius, Claudius, Cornelius. The clue is in the ending – the 'ius' stem. Remove the '*i*' and you have the founding member of the clan: Julus (son of Aeneas, so the Julian clan were old and venerable), Claudus, Cornelus. The *gens* is always in second position. Flexibility comes with the third name, the cognomen (*cognos* – 'known by'): this is colourful, creative, and often has particular meaning, one of the most famous being Cicero, which means 'chick pea'. Cicero was called after an uncle who picked up this nickname because of a physical deformity; the younger Cicero was advised to use his other names (Marcus or Tullius) in his public career, but he refused out of deference to his ancestor (Plut., *Cic.* 1.3–4).

Additional names called *agnomines* could be added, especially for men who had distinguished themselves in battle or in their public career. Some add-on names distinguish like-named family members similarly to modern English 'Junior' – Maior and Minor, for example. *Agnomines* could be a sign of respect and honour: G. Cornelius Scipio had *Africanus* added to his name after he led the Roman army to victory against Carthage in 202 BCE to defeat Hannibal and end the Second Punic War (Liv., 30.6–7). They could also reflect ignominy. General Gn. Cornelius Scipio gained his nickname 'Asina' after his disastrous command at Lipara (Polyb., 1.21.11, Liv., 22.23); yes, it does mean 'jackass,' and yes, as far as his battle plans went, he was one. Fabius Maximus was called *Cunctator* ('delayer') because he refused to engage Hannibal no matter how many times the Punic general attempted to tease him into battle

(Plut., *Fab.* 5.2–4). It is an improvement on *Verrucosus* (Warty) due to his complexion and *Ovans* (Sheepy) as he was called as a shy schoolboy (Plut., *Fab.* 1.3). *Magnus* – 'The Great' – was a sarcastic moniker hung on Pompey which he decided to keep (Plut., *Pomp.* 13.4–5), maybe because his other nickname, *Adulescens carnifex* or 'the teenaged butcher' was too long to fit on the loyalty card application. Which of a person's names would become the one by which he or she was familiarly known follows no particular pattern.

FREEDMEN AND NAMING CONVENTIONS

Their freed names were a prized possession of freed men and women and indicated their new status. They frequently adapted their erstwhile owner's name into their own, indicated by the insertion of a G or C (for Gaius or Caius), = in the middle of their name – this is again found in many inscriptions. Example: the former slave Glyco, owned by Gaius Julius Caesar, might want to show both his freed status and to whom he owed his freedom (his patron). So Glyco might become G. Julius Caesar G. lib. Glyco. Glyco's son would be G. Julius Glyco, a free man.

NAMING GIRLS AND WOMEN

Up through the first century CE, aristocratic girls did not have particularly original names: their names were variations of their father's gens. Hence Cornelia was the daughter of Publius Cornelius Scipio; Octavian, son of Gaius Octavian, had two sisters called Octavia – distinguished by the addition of Maiora and Minora. Other girls ended up as Prima, Secunda, Tertia – First, Second, Third. More creativity can be found amongst the lower classes, and a greater variety of aristocratic women's names appear from the mid-first century. Inscriptions, letters, and epitaphs are a fruitful source of female names.

SOURCES FOR NAMES

For aristocratic names, mine the obvious literature: historians and biographers (Livy, Plutarch, Suetonius, Tacitus, Josephus, Sallust, Caesar, the *Historia Augusta*). Sift Cicero's and Pliny's letters or the poetry of Catullus, Horace, Ovid, and Vergil. Other wellsprings include the dinner-table anecdotes and conversations found in the miscellany volumes by authors such as Aulus Gellius, Cornelius Nepos, or Valerius Maximus. The names of ordinary people will also be found in inscriptions and graffiti – from buildings, from the letters at Vindolanda (a fort on Hadrian's Wall in Britain), from funerary epitaphs. Sources for inscriptions in translation include the *CIL* as found on www.attalus.org, which includes over five hundred translated inscriptions from the *CIL*, many papyrus sources, and other inscriptions from Greece and the Near East. Fraser and Matthews have published a lexicon of Greek personal names (1987–2005); Swanson (1968) put together a collection of names found in Roman verse. Finally, if all else fails, there's the *Roman Name Generator*. Don't forget the family pooch – see *Names for Roman Dogs* (see bibliography).

EVERY TOM, DICK, AND HARRY: LIST OF PRAENOMINES

Appius, Aulus, Decimus, Gaius, Gnaeus, Lucius, Marcus, Manius, Numerius, Publius, Quintus, Servius, Sextus, Spurius, Titus, Tiberius, Vibius. Change the -us to -a for the feminine version. Praenomines were usually abbreviated. There is no hard and fast rule whether a man will be known by his praenomen, gens, or cognomen: e.g. the Emperors Tiberius and Gaius (Caligula), Emperor Claudius, Emperor Vespasian and Nerva.

LONGEST NAME

The grand prize winner here is the Senator Quintus Pompeius Senecio Roscius Murena Coelius Sextus Iulius Frontinus Silius Decianus Gaius Iulius Eurycles Herculaneus Lucius Vibullius Pius Augustanus Alpinus Bellicus Sollers Iulius Aper Ducenius Proculus Rutilianus Rufinus Silius Valens Valerius Niger Claudius Fuscus Saxa Amyntianus Sosius Priscus (*ILS* 1104, in Salway (1994: n. 51)). Note that his *agnomines* are, in fact, in sets of three full names, as he's glomped family names on to his own, an extravagant version of the double-barrelled surname in the modern English-speaking world.

ROMAN VALUES: DOES S/HE *BEHAVE* LIKE A ROMAN?

The family unit defines so much about your Roman characters: reputation, status, eventual place in the world (and how they might rise above or fall below that place). It's also where people were initiated into Roman custom and tradition, whether they grew up within Roman culture, adopted it wholesale, or had it thrust upon them. In the days of the early Republic, the Romans didn't think about things such as what made a Roman a Roman. In the fifth century BCE, in their desire to break free from Etruscan rule, the Romans narrowed their sights at their closest neighbours, the Latin tribes who had formed a defensive League against Etruria. This League did not want the Romans to join up with them, Rome being an Etruscan city-state. The Romans had other ideas, however; they went to war with the Latin League, defeated it at the Battle of Lake Regellus (496 BCE), and became its *de facto* leaders. Together with their new allies, the Romans eventually overcame Etruscan rule. How the Romans treated their new allies and how these allies interacted with the Romans set a template that continued in the West, arguably, clear into the eighth century CE.

Like the Etruscans, the Romans were magpies when it came to other cultures, and mongrels when it came to their own identity. After chucking out the last king, Tarquin, because his son had raped a Roman matron (Liv., 1.57–60), the Romans claimed cultural affinity with their Latin neighbours. They also began to absorb neighbouring tribes into their own (for instance, famously the 'Rape of the Sabines' to acquire wives: Liv., 1.9.1–16, Plut., *Rom.* 14.1–2). The Romans could be absolutely brutal when it came to conquering adjacent territories. Afterwards, though, they were unlike the Greeks who rarely mingled with the locals, were stingy about granting citizenship, and formed federations and allegiances only under extreme duress (only to revert to scrapping like cats the moment external threats passed). The Romans, conversely, devised interstate relationships with their victims and vanquished to establish a system of mutual benefits politically, economically, and culturally. They created formal alliances with these peoples by making them various flavours of provinces, federated states, or clients. A fair degree of autonomy was allowed locally (language, religious custom, law), although ultimate allegiance was owed to Rome, as were taxes and military obligation. For examples of the Roman presence on and its intervention in local affairs, you might sift through the Gospel of John to look at Jesus's trial as his case was punted back and forth between local Jewish authorities and Roman governor. You'll also find Roman presence in the provinces in the Acts of the Apostles and various letters of Paul in the New Testament, Josephus's *Jewish War* (*De Bello Judaicum*) and *Antiquitates Judaicae*, the letters of Pliny the Younger and Apuleius's *Metamorphoses*. A number of emperors took an interest in the civic proceedings of the provinces, including Claudius, Trajan, and Hadrian; Caracalla extended citizenship across the Empire in 212 CE (Giesson Papyrus no. 40 col. 1 = Abbott-Johnson, no. 191 = *FIRA* vol. a, no. 88, in L&R, 2: no. 106: 380), not out of patriotic benevolence but to squeeze taxes out of the wealthy Greek half of the empire (see Chapter 5) – up until this time, most grants of citizenship had been provided more freely in the West. Thus, look through accounts of their reigns for imperial interaction in the provinces as described by Suetonius, Tacitus (*Annals* and *History*), and the *Historia Augusta*. The Romans, too, created different levels of citizenship amongst their allies; benefits of being a Roman citizen included the privilege of appealing directly to the centre, rather than local, authorities. For example, when arrested by provincial authorities, Paul of Tarsus (d. 66 CE) got an audience with the Emperor Nero, proclaiming *Romanus sum* (Acts 22:28). The Egyptian administrator Philo, a Hellenistic Jewish philosopher, took his case from Alexandria to Rome in 40 CE hoping to get from the Emperor Caligula firm adjudication on the conflict between the Jewish and Greek communities (cf. Joseph., *AJ* 18.8.1) – he got more than he bargained for when he saw the scandalous behaviour in the imperial court; see his account *Legatio ad Gaium*.

Romanitas extended beyond simply aping Roman custom or creating villas and public buildings in the hinterlands (cf. Fishbourne Palace in West Sussex) to impress the centre. It included the opportunity to participate in Roman life. This comprised both the privileges (rising to the heights of politics locally) as well as the obligations of doing so (paying taxes or supplying human resources to the army): effectively the list of benefits grudgingly compiled by the People's Front of Judaea in the famous 'What have the Romans ever done for us?' scene in the film *Monty Python's Life of Brian*. Romanisation wasn't always welcome, and there was resistance in places (usually met violently) but ambitious local leaders soon saw advantages – and, since most people just wanted to get on with their lives, they adapted. Roman culture was spread by conquest and settlement: those who resisted or did not keep up with their obligations might find their city-states levelled as an object lesson (e.g., Corinth in 146 BCE: Cass. Dio, 21.2; Zon., 9.31, and Athens in 87–86 BCE: Plut., *Sull.* 13–14), their territory absorbed into the Roman state without discussion (Macedonia in 146 BCE), and their autonomy crushed for almost two millennia (Judaea after 136 CE; see Goodman, 1993, 2007, amongst others).

Note that while the Romans had their hands full on the frontiers with attacks and raids from Germanic, Celtic, and Gallic barbarians (Boudicca in Britain, Teutoberg Forest, assorted tribes pouring over the Danube during Marcus Aurelius's reign), the cultures who most resisted Romanisation were the oldest ones in the East (especially Greece); western provincials tended to embrace *Romanitas* more readily and wholeheartedly. This is most evident in Spain, Gaul, and North

Africa, provinces where military camps and veterans' colonies were often established. Especially in the West, locals came to trade with if not live in this society, and they realised there would be benefits if they learnt Latin, adopted Roman ways, and so forth. Those locals who 'became Romanised' stood to gain the most. Subsequently, there was competition among the provincial administrators and local strongmen to get noticed, sometimes to the economic detriment of their constituency; for example, Hadrian had to pass a law banning excessive spending on public works and entertainments in the provinces (*HA, Hadr.* 22.7–8). Britain was one of the exceptions in the West as the locals there were not as easily subdued: on the one hand, the Romans built three series of fortified lines across their northern British boundaries (not so much to keep the northern tribes out as to establish tighter control over checkpoints, much like the *limes* along the Rhine frontier), the Gask Ridge (70–80 CE), Hadrian's Wall (from 122 CE), and the Antonine Wall (142 CE). On the other, despite some impressive examples of Romanisation whilst the Romans were there (Fishbourne Palace, the tomb of Classianicus now in the British Museum, London), once they were gone, the German tribes overran the province and established fairly quickly their own laws and customs. Simon Young's *Farewell Britannia: A Family Saga of Roman Britain* (2008) is a recommended read here, a fictionalised account of the impact of the Romans on a single household over the course of four centuries.

EMPIRE AND IDENTITY

Whether Rome set out to conquer an empire or stumbled into ruling one has been a topic of debate not only amongst modern historians but also amongst contemporary Romans, especially from the third century BCE. Busy for centuries with subduing their Italian neighbours and settling their own domestic political and economic struggles between the plebeian and patrician classes (see Chapter 4), the Romans found themselves engaged with the big players on the international scene first with a cousin of Alexander the Great, Pyrrhus of

Epirus, then the Carthaginians in two wars, and a series of wars with and the alliances amongst Greek and East Aegean city-states against the Macedonians. One effect of these wars was a need, especially among Roman conservatives, to define what made a Roman *Roman*. The wars in the East brought into the Roman world an influx of Greek culture in the form of art, literature, philosophy, and history writing, amongst other cultural effects. Younger Roman aristocrats embraced all things Greek (especially philosophy); the older, conservative generation feared for the loss of old-fashioned Roman traditions and customs. That is, simply put, a preoccupation with family (*mos maiorum*, deference, consensus), farming (land was the basis of the Roman economy), and fighting. *Virtus* was an especially important quality that defined a man – *vir/*'man' being the root of the word – and virtue as a result of the *gloria* that fighting to protect home and family that military service could bring.

This period of Hellenisation, too, not coincidentally, was when the earliest Roman historians appear. One of the earliest prose histories of Rome was written by the second-century BCE historian Polybius, a former Greek hostage who became close to a group of young aristocrats who are referred to as the 'Sciponic Circle' as it included Scipio Aemilianus, hero of the Macedonian wars and the (adopted) grandson of Scipio Africanus. Polybius very much admired the discipline and respect for order the Romans had in their government as well as their daily lives: read Book 6 of his history of Rome, which not only lays out how the Roman government and the *cursus honorum* works but also has bang in the middle of it a discussion of how the Roman army was organised. Polybius's account of the Romans was intended for a Greek audience, and he admired the discipline and authoritative respect of the Romans that coloured both military and civilian life.

By the middle of the second century BCE, the Romans had become intensely involved in Greek affairs, which led to absorbing from Greek (Athenian, really) culture: art, literature, and drama, rhetoric and oratory, and other 'effeminate' arts such as medicine and teaching. One effect of Hellenisation was that conservatives felt that the younger

generation was becoming too 'Greekified' and losing site of the traditional, simple Roman character (cf. Plutarch's *Life of Cato the Elder*).
The Romans had always been very conservative in their way of thinking
and public expectations of their behaviour. This is one of the reasons
that Plautus flourished in the mid- to late third century BCE – he co-
opted and adapted for Roman audiences plays by Greek New Comedy
playwrights. None of his characters is ostensibly Roman (they're mostly
Greek), but they subvert Roman behaviour and customs. It was all right
to laugh at their scrapes and mishaps and terrible manners, and audiences found the theatre a cathartic release from the pressure of conform-
ing to social norms. Comedy revels in subverting these conventions, and
many of Plautus's targets remain familiar: social climbers and toadies
(consider Basil Fawlty, and how he treats the cross-section of society
who stay at Fawlty Towers) or the clever slave (the cunning Blackadder)
who connives at the expense of his foolish aristocratic masters. Women
in these comedies were beautiful McGuffins, formidable battleaxe wives
and mothers-in-law who actually ran the household, or prostitutes with
hearts of gold.

SOCIAL HIERARCHY: IN WITH THE IN CROWD

The family unit was a microcosm of Roman society. Where your fictional
family fits into the greater scheme of things depends on both a vertical
and a horizontal hierarchy that are at once strictly defined and fairly
fluid. One's place in society was reflected in one's appearance, work,
economy, law, travel, entertainment, and religion. The Roman social pyramid was complex and nuanced – and keep in mind that advancement
was not always admired, and demotion not always pitied. Hierarchy was
important to the Romans as it affected the roles of patrons and clients,
that social contract which effectively kept Roman society moving. As
business was conducted and life was lived primarily out of doors – in the
assembly, in the forum, in the public baths and latrines, in the arenas –
the visible signs of stability and status and of visible order and power are
important considerations.

The Romans defined their social classes by a number of criteria; one of the most obvious was wealth. The social pyramid would show that there were very few 'haves' at the top and everyone else as 'have-nots' on the bottom. Sometimes change was dramatic: one's fortunes could sour overnight, and members of the patrician elite could find themselves in a dire situation due to war or sudden poverty. Similarly, one might rise quickly to a comfortable state of living through manumission from slavery, thence to business success as a freedman; one's children could rise into the equestrian class and onwards into public life. Military service could also bring changes in status. There was no middle class in the Classical era as defined by later industrial and capitalist economies. There was, however, a thriving merchant class, and there were plenty of social climbers and social achievers. There existed, too, horizontal social status, in that each layer of the Roman social pyramid was further divided in terms of family, wealth, and origins. Elite families amongst the Senatorial patricians competed with each other for status and distinction, for example, and there were multiple smaller hierarchies amongst slaves – slaves could own slaves, as seen in the inscriptions of the multi-generation tombs of the Volusii family (see Treggiari, 1973, 1975). Examples of elite attitudes, snobbishness towards freedmen, and conditions of slavery can be sampled in L&R (2, nos 43–48: 155–173 and no. 50: 176–182).

One would think that with the opportunities available to move up into a higher status through trade (as the equestrians and freedmen did) and because Romans assimilated so many cultures into their own, that Rome was an open society when it came to people changing their status. Instead, the Romans could be social snobs when it came to wealth, family connections, or provincial origins. The Romans loved to point out the inversion and subversion of social norms – it's a rhetorical as well as comedic device. Examples of snobbery abound in the sources of our period; it's found between aristocrats, against provincials, against the *nouveau riche*, against the poor, against foreigners or barbarians. No matter what a person's social status, he or she could find someone else upon whom to look down. Examples abound throughout our period. The plebeian politicians Tiberius and Gaius Gracchus snubbed the Senate and paid the highest price for it (Plut., *TG*). Sulla, a patrician and part of the old guard (the *Optimates*, a conservative faction of politicians during the late Republic), was mocked for hanging out with singers, dancers, and actors in the pub rather than associating with his social equals (Plut., *Sull.* 2.2–4). Tacitus slammed the elite politicians and leaders of Rome through his lionisation of the savage but noble Germans in *Germania*. Ovid complains about living amongst the yokels in Tomis, Bythnia, his place of exile in *Tristia* and *Ex Ponto* (cf. Ov., *Trist.* 5.10.35–40). Juvenal mocks the effete and precious rich kids of the city of Rome throughout his *Satires* on their choice of food, pastimes, and holidays. Intellectuals looked down on the general mob: Cicero regarded the games and chariot races as a waste of intellect (e.g. *Fam.* 7.1; cf. Sen., *Epist.* 7.1–5); Terence was infuriated that the production of his new play *Hecyra* was disrupted (Ter., *Hecy.* 1–42) not once, but twice, by his audience racing out of the theatre on hearing that a tight-rope walker (1–5) and gladiators (39–42) had come to town.

The Roman elite also mocked social climbers whether they were Roman natives, provincial wannabes, or ambitious freedmen. Old wealth and prestige earned respect – but only inherited or married-into wealth (next best was wealth earned in retirement, as by veterans of the army). Wealth accrued through trade or labour was considered vulgar; business ventures, investments, and mercantile pursuits were not only looked down upon, they were legally *verboten* to the top patrician class. This affected how the Senatorial patricians viewed the equestrian class (also known as *equites*) of plebeians or 'new men' who sought to hold political office, and who, especially, rose to prominence in the later Republic, ignoring completely the proper routes to power up the *cursus honorum* (see Plutarch's lives of Marius and Pompey, for example). Plebeians had been allowed to hold office since 367 BCE (*Lex Licinia-Sexta*), but this did not deter their patrician peers from snubbing them, catty oratory being their weapon of choice. Cicero looked down on his political rivals, especially amongst the new men, his very peers; his second *Philippic* against Mark Antony is a tour de force of abuse hurled at one plebeian new man against another. No surprises really as the most conservative Romans tended to be plebeian – *equites* and freedmen. Do a Google image search on Cato the Elder and you'll see what I mean, for example: a fierce visage similar to the severe expressions found on many tomb effigies of freedmen and women. These two groups in turn were mocked by the aristocratic classes for aping the appearance of fine society without completely understanding the proper behaviour meant to go along with unearned wealth. Petronius's *Dinner with Trimalchio*, a set-piece in the *Satyricon*, is a scathing portrayal of a freedman and his freed wife as vulgar *nouveaux riches*. Read about Trimlachio's dinner party side-by-side with inscriptions left behind by well-to-do freedmen and women who acted as civic patrons and were very respectable and conservative in their new status (examples are found in *ROL*, 4, of civic inscriptions and of such public munificence). Compare the difference between the images found in comedy and in real life; consider the audience for each.

Senatorial patricians, *equites*, and freedmen were in turn united in their disdain for provincials who, too, desired to advance up the social ladder, to become big fish in their provincial ponds, and perhaps come to Rome to serve in imperial business. Provincials from older, established areas mocked the upstart barbarians who copied Roman custom: examples come from the letters of Gallo-Roman Sidonius Apollonarius. He lived a couple of centuries after our period, but his colourful letters are imbued with lofty humour about the Goths and Germans he encountered on a day-to-day basis – many of them the local administrators if not leaders. He mocks how they attempt to ape Roman custom and mangle the Latin language, and he gives advice on how to tell a barbarian from a civilised man (Sid. Apoll., *Epist.* 8.3). For example, he tuts with amusement to his friends about how funny some of the barbarians – including Arbogast, a worthy barbarian who otherwise was praised by Sidonius for his eloquence and *Romanitas* (4.17) – were in their attempts at civilised dining – as well as appearance (2.1.3, 3.2.2). Compare his praise of Theodoric the Goth (1.2.6), Veltius as a model Roman (4.9), and the Frank Sigismer who dresses like a Frank but manages to remain elegant and refined in manner (4.20). Likewise he writes to his friend Syagrius about how funny the barbarians could be when they attempted to be cultured and eloquent (5.5); Sidonius tells his friend, who is Roman but bilingual, to take care that he doesn't lose his Latin lest he be mocked. He is urged to maintain his Frankish speech, so that he can join his fellow Romans in laughing at the locals.

Social distinction and competition all played out publicly, and all aspects of Roman society reflected the social league table. The social hierarchy was reinforced publicly and visibly through many aspects of Roamn life – taxes, laws, punishments, and even apparel and where to sit at the games and dinner parties, all reflected one's social status. The point of such stratification, even after gaining wealth, was that it was a means for the aristos to protect their own prestige and exclusiveness. As much as the elites may have mocked them in comedy and even rhetorical writing, the freedman class may not have felt the sting, as they lacked the cultural baggage with which the elites were burdened. As ex-slaves, they could be seen as truly liberated. They had no family honour or reputation to uphold, no inherited code of conduct, no national or caste customs to restrain them at all from every means to the end of making money. They, like the equestrians who likewise lacked the trappings of aristocratic heritage, became important players in the imperial bureaucracy as they were appointed by, and thus could become clients of, the emperors and other administrators. They were considered less likely to become corrupt in their desire to compete. To see how the elites felt about *that*, consider Suetonius's *Life of Claudius* or Seneca's *Apocolocytonis* (a satire that mocks Claudius's deification) and complaints found therein over the emperor's overdependence on his freedmen (6–8; Suet., *Claud.* 24, 28–29).

SOME ROMAN VALUES AND CUSTOMS

Roman values and traditions were initially defined by the likes of Cato the Elder and early Roman historians and poets such as Ennius, Naevius, and Fabius Pictor during the period of Hellenisation in the third and second centuries BCE. These traditions were codified and reinforced again following Augustus's settlement of the Empire from 27 BCE as he sought to bring stability to it. It is the historians, biographers, and rhetoricians of this latter period who define for us most strongly the key customs and cultural institutions of what makes the Romans Roman.

mos maiorum
Honouring the customs of the one's ancestors; showing respect to one's elders and betters.

dignitas
Similar to the idea of the British stiff upper lip and keeping calm and carrying on, *dignitas* is how you receive others' admiration and appreciation of your self-worth. When this is insulted, then you act: as Coriolanus (see Plutarch's *Life*) or the First Triumvirate of Pompey, Crassus, and Julius Caesar, or, later, Alaric the Goth (described by Orosius, Claudian, Zosimus, and Jordanes cribbing from Cassiodorus's account) did when they thought the Senate had insulted them in spite of the great deeds they had performed on behalf of the Roman state.

nobilitas
The ability to carry on soberly and without displays of emotion even in the worst of times. Cornelia was the model of *nobilitas* in the face of the deaths of her sons (Tiberius and Gaius Gracchus).

auctoritas
The main corollary to *dignitas*, loosely translated as 'charisma'. You did not earn it; it was not given to you. By virtue of your character, station, and acknowledged superiority, you would be listened to by the people. Augustus and Hadrian were its embodiment.

pietas
Duty and devotion towards one's family, one's ancestors or the state gods – even under the most adverse of situations. Aeneas is called

pius Aeneas throughout the *Aeneid* for his devotion not only to his father but also towards his destiny and duty to get his son out of Troy and into Italy so that the Roman state could be founded. Marcus Aurelius, a scholar by nature and a reluctant soldier, was a real-life embodiment of pietas who nevertheless carried out his duty to the state throughout his troubled reign (160–180 CE).

libertas

The freedom not to challenge or change established order, but rather to do what the *mos maiorum* and the laws allowed. The Romans were not democrats; they did not challenge authority. Even when the emperors behaved badly, it was the man who was replaced, not the office. Society functioned because it was content to accept at least a minimum of personal rights despite unequal privileges and responsibilities.

consensus and deference

Along with the patron–client system (see Chapter 4), these ingrained traditions were how the Romans got things done. Everything in Roman politics was geared towards collegiality and group think: multiple magistrates on every level, the Senate, the Assemblies, for example. Manlius Torquatus executed his own son, a renowned general, for jeopardising the Roman army in the pursuit of his own singular glory (Liv., 8.9–22). Polybius describes decimation or *fustuarium* (6.37–38): every tenth soldier chosen at random and then beaten to death by their fellows, whether they were guilty of the crime or not. Such is the emphasis on consideration for one's fellow soldiers or fellow Romans (see also Chapter 4). Consensus was found throughout Roman government and administration: a single ruler (king or queen) was regarded with suspicion of being a power-mad, corrupt individual. Of course there were individuals in Roman society, but anyone outside the system would be regarded with suspicion if not contempt by those within. Good examples of how outsiders and strangers were treated until their identity is established are found in Apuleius's *Apologia* and *Golden Ass* (*Metamorphoses*) – for example, in Book 3 of the latter, when Lucius is put on trial for murder – as a joke by the locals – or in Book 4 when a young noblewoman is captured by robbers to sell as a slave, but the tattered remains of her fine clothing give her away as an aristocrat (4.23–28). Deference and following the correct procedure are linked inextricably with *pietas* and the *mos maiorum*. Even at their angriest or rudest in the Senate, the senators would maintain public deference to their colleagues ('I agree with my esteemed colleague') – check out Cicero's legal speeches and addresses in his court cases for just how elegant and lofty such expressions of deference could be.

impudia and *infamia*

Shame and infamy. Roman life was public, and it didn't matter if you were on the lowest rung on the urban mob ladder or the highest senator: your behaviour was held up to public scrutiny. The Romans wrote and indulged in biographies not only to learn about the lives of particular men (there are no biographies devoted exclusively to women) but also to see their good deeds remembered for eternity and their bad deeds held up to public scorn. On *damnatio memoriae*, see Varner (2004) for a study of imperial portraiture and Flower (2011) on memory and commemoration.

THE SOCIAL ORDER AND STATUS: A GENERAL GUIDE

Keep in mind there are overlaps and grey areas of distinction among certain of these designations. See *VRoma* on social classes at www.vroma.org/~bmcmanus/socialclass.html for a complementary chart of the social order.

PATRICIANS AND PLEBEIANS

This was a fundamental division of society, but avoid assuming that all wealthy aristocrats were patricians and that all poor people were plebeians. According to the myth of Romulus (found in some detail in Plutarch's *Life*), certain families were designated as the true rulers of Rome, that is, those who came to make up the Senate as an advisory body originally to the king. These patricians (root word *pater/* father) are the old families who, until the resolution of the Conflict of the Orders (mostly through compromise from the fifth through to the third centuries BCE; see Chapter 4 on administration), held exclusive political power in Rome. During our period, patricians and plebeians could intermarry (originally forbidden by the *Twelve Tables*, 449 BCE, 1.45.18–19; the *Lex Canuleia* repealed this law in 445 BCE; cf. Liv., 4.1.1–3, 6.1–11 on plebeians holding office and marrying patricians in the early days of the Republic), and plebeians could hold any and all of the magisterial offices (the Licinio-Sextian laws described by Livy, 6.35.1–5). Women could be patricians or plebeians and fall into any of the social categories below as wives of the Senators and equestrians, as wives of and workers in trade, as freedwomen and slaves, but they could not hold any political office or vote.

SENATORS

Augustus reordered the economic levels of society: to qualify for the Senatorial class, one had to be worth 1 million *sesterces*. Originally they were synonymous with the patrician class, but, once the magisterial offices were open to plebeians, the character and make-up of the Senate became a mix of patrician and plebeian. Senators were appointed to their positions by the consuls and later by the censors. Senators were also former magistrates who had seen out their terms in office. From the time of the late Republic, provincials could also join the esteemed ranks. There were occasional purges of the Senate and restructuring to make the body friendlier to the incumbent faction or ruler. Its administrative power slowly diminished from the time of the Gracchi, and the Senate was pretty much a court society by the end of the first and into the second century CE.

EQUESTRIANS

The equestrians (*equites*) came from the next wealthiest class of Roman society, originally those men provided with a horse for battle (an expensive piece of equipment to maintain). Members of this class were frequently *new men*, or the first in their families to hold public office. They had wealth of at least 400,000 *sesterces*, and they sometimes tended to be far more conservative than the old landed aristocracy. Equestrians came from the plebeian class. Equestrians could rise economically to the Senatorial class but were scorned by their old-moneyed, patrician peers. Unlike members of the Senatorial class, equestrians could earn money through business interests. Vespasian was the first equestrian emperor, fifty-four years after Augustus's death.

FREEDMEN AND FREEDWOMEN

Former slaves who either bought or were granted their freedom. Some could do quite well for themselves, as they, like equestrians, did not have the stigma hanging over them that earning money or working in trade and industry was vulgar. Freedmen and freedwomen and their new riches might be mocked in the works of Petronius, but freedmen became an invaluable part of administration and bureaucracy from the time of Augustus. While their freed status was visible in their names, the names of their children gave no indication of any humble origins. A number of tombs and inscriptions reflect the wealth, conservative nature, and civic contributions of urban-dwelling freedmen and freedwomen all over the Empire. No freedman ever became emperor, but Pertinax was the son of a freedman (*HA, Pert.* 1.1).

SLAVES

Not quite the bottom of the social pyramid, although life for agricultural slaves and miners was grim, to say the least. Treatises describe how slaves ought to be treated; laws were enacted during the early second century CE to try to protect them from vicious masters. Slaves had a distinct hierarchy within their servile status. Roman citizens were not to be enslaved, and the sources of slaves were captives and prisoners of war, as well as slaves born into their position in households and estates. See Wiedemann (1980) for a selection of documents on slavery.

URBAN AND FREE POOR PEOPLE

At the bottom of the Roman status pyramid. Moved into the city in time of economic crisis, especially from the second century BCE when many small farmers lost their lands and the owners of the great *latifundia* replaced them with the new slaves brought in as a result of the Eastern wars. They were despised by the higher classes as poverty was considered vile and the result of bad luck. The poor hated back with equal viciousness, but they had little power to assert their resentment. They tended not to revolt as a result of the long tradition of knowing one's place. The mob played an important part in political corruption (voting and gang control over urban districts) during the Republican civil wars. Emperors kept them happy with spectacles and dole programmes such as the *alimenta* as long as there was money in the treasury (otherwise diverted to the army).

LATINS AND OTHER ALLIES; PROVINCIALS

The Latins and other allies were *not* below slaves, of course; these close allies had many if not all of the rights as citizens of the City of Rome itself. The further one travelled from Rome, the more of a stigma being a provincial could be. Many provincials, especially in the West, could appear to be more Roman than the Romans, since they had to scramble to put into place quickly all of those attributes that would identify them as Roman. Tacitus tells us that the great secret revealed in the civil war of 69 CE was that 'emperors could be made in the provinces' (Tac., *Hist.* 1.4) as this was the source of the powerbase for the four men who fought to be emperor that year. The first truly provincial emperor, however, was Hadrian, born in Spain. Claudius had been mocked for granting citizenship to so many from Gaul (where he had been born as his father was on military assignment; Suet., *Claud.* 2.1); only a century later, emperors such as Trajan and Hadrian strove to emphasise the cosmopolitan nature of the diverse provinces of the Empire.

BARBARIANS AND OUTSIDERS

'Barbarians' were not necessarily primitive brutes, but anyone with customs and practices alien to Roman traditions – and no interest, at least initially, in assimilating. Barbarians could manifest as wild rural tribes (Gauls, Germans, Celts) – the root of *civilisation* is *civis* or *city*. Other signs of barbarism included practising human sacrifice (Carthage, Druids), kingship (Parthia, Egypt, Celts), believing in magic and *superstitio* (Christians) or having an interest in democracy (Greeks).

2

THE BASIC NECESSITIES: FOOD AND CLOTHING

Whilst you can sift through literary sources or material images for inspiration about what food to put on your Roman table or how to dress your Romans and their neighbours, keep in mind again that this is a public culture. A Roman's identity, social status, economic level, and culture background are accessible through his or her dining customs and attire. Excess and splendour get noticed because they are out of the ordinary and frequently reported in the sources as scandal and satire for people to tut over. Such titillation is timeless: the red-tops and the monologues of late-night television satires find plenty of cannon fodder in the current exploits and the youthful indiscretions of politicians, athletes, and celebrities in pretty much the same way that Suetonius's breathless discussion of Tiberius's (e.g. Suet., *Tib.* 43, 44, 61–62) and Gaius Caligula's excesses (*Gai.* 20, 24, 26–27, 37) would have been received by contemporary audiences. More mundanely, not only did food-sharing indicate status, but meals were also important social and political gatherings. A banquet was a time to impress allies if not enemies; meals provided opportunities to exchange hospitality and patronage between hosts and guests.

The finer details of the dinner table and the wardrobe are, as ever, up to you. Included here are representational case studies and suggestions of contemporary sources. First up is a general look at food. Topics here include the swanky meal versus the humble repast; the staples of diet in the Mediterranean; common beverages; dining clichés and some foods to avoid – not because they might be disagreeable but because, despite what Hollywood set-dressing might imply, the Romans didn't shop for goods in the New World or Australia. The second part of the chapter provides you with a sketch of fashion and clothing in the Roman Empire across the different social classes, covering basic wardrobe choices, fabrics, colours, and accessories (including hair, cosmetics, and jewellery). As always, the discussion here isn't meant to restrict or dictate your choices for your characters, but rather to provide general themes to consider when creating your fictional Rome.

ALL ORGIES, ALL THE TIME: BANQUETS AND BLING OR A HUMBLE REPAST?

You know you're in Rome when the banqueting scene hits the screen (or page): it's one of the key signposts of the Classical world in popular culture, along with the chariot race or the gladiatorial match (or indeed throwing Christians to the lions). They're always vibrant scenes: Dancing girls! Scurrying servants! Flowing wine, or, if you're on a 1960s TV budget, Ribena, which shows up well as red wine on black-and-white videotape (BBC 1965)! Plates of extravagant, gilded food set down before diners who are festooned with flowered garlands and draped over couches – when they're not making a dash for the *vomitorium* to make room for the next course.

Of course not everyone ate like an emperor (or freedmen and freedwomen showing off their wealth). The extravagant banquet or symposium (the Greek version of a dinner party, adapted by Romans) is the one that gets the press – and not necessarily for wowing the audience, but often as a means to criticise the host. When the extravagant stuff is mentioned in sources, it's because it is unusual or because it's satire on the part of the author. Most people went about their daily meals in a humble fashion, sat upright at table, and ate simple food. Whilst the rich lived in isolated, walled houses in town, the urban poor generally lived in flats over shops or in several-storeyed *insulae* (apartment houses) which had an effect on how they ate. For example, they wouldn't necessarily have access to running water or an oven in their house (due to size and expense as well as fear of fire), so they would go to local wells and fountains for water. Bread and other goods were baked up the street at the local communal bakery (see Pliny, *NH* 18.25–27 on bread-making and baking). If the average person had meat at table, it would be most likely pork (as oxen were kept to be used as farm tractors, and sheep and goats a source of milk, cheese, and fleece). Festivals and street vendors could supply more exotic fare and 'junk food' on special occasions, but at home simple meals would generally include grains (mainly in the form of bread), olives, and food more readily available – and deemed more suitable – to those of humbler economic status. These staples for all included the so-called 'Mediterranean triad'.

STAPLES: MEDITERRANEAN TRIAD AND GENERAL FOODSTUFFS

The Roman economy was a subsistence agrarian economy (see Chapter 5), and Roman politicians were always concerned about feeding the army if not the civilian population. References to food production and prices can be found throughout the works of the historians and biographers as invariably the great men passed laws about grain prices and control of grain trade and production. Most foodstuffs would have been produced locally, if possible; taxation records for trade from the provinces are useful to find out which provinces produced what type of foodstuffs, and how likely it was for such items to appear on the table (see L&R, for example, for a whip-round of provincial products, 2, no. 23: 76–85; see also *CAH*, 11: 405–678, for a look at the provinces during the high Empire in the second century CE).

The 'Mediterranean triad' consists of grapes, grain, and olives – the basis for everything from the most humble of meals through to the most elaborate. These foods grow well in the environment and climate found in Greece and in southern Italy especially; this is why, during the eighth and then later in the sixth century BCE, the Greeks founded colonies to North Africa, Spain, and southern Italy, as these crops thrive there. During the third and second centuries BCE, the Romans consolidated smaller farms into large estates called *latifundia* (cf. Cic., *Off.* 24.84–85; App., *BC* 1.1.7; Pliny, *NH* 18.4), and these estates frequently focused on a single, major crop. Spain, for example, was turned over to large-scale olive growing – like the Greeks, the Romans used olive oil for almost everything – cooking, heating and lighting, even washing. These estates became the backbone of political struggles from the time of the Gracchi (from the last third of the second century BCE).

PERSONAL HYGIENE

While the Romans sometimes used a plant beaten in water to produce lather for washing, olive oil remained the main way of cleaning the body: oil up, then scrape off with a small device called a *strigil*. Soap as we think of it, cakes made from rendering fat, ash, and lye, is a product of the Middle Ages.

SOURCES FOR YOUR MENUS

As for essential and traded foodstuffs, the Vindolanda Letters from the north of Britain provide an excellent example of military outposts and food – there are surviving receipts and requests not only for everyday food fare but also for food and drink required for religious festivals (Bowman, 2011; *Vindolanda Tablets Online*). Everyday repasts might also be found literally on the floors of Roman houses; they decorated their mosaics with foodstuffs both common and exotic. Collections of these images as well as discussion about the kinds of food that were sold by vendors in street markets and restaurants can be found in works on Pompeii and Herculaneum. Other sources of inspiration include farming texts that will give you overviews of gardens and food production. Gentlemen naturally aspired to become farmers, or so says Pliny the Elder (*NH* 18.3.22). Cato the Elder, Columella, and Varro describe kitchen and herb gardens (in addition to their discussions of large estate management, see Chapter 3). Whilst these works may be more intellectual exercises than practical handbooks, you'll find in them sections on how to lay out an estate, raise meat animals including sheep, goats, pigs, and cattle, and information about poultry, fish, beekeeping and dormice. On kitchen gardens, Pliny the Elder (*NH*, 12–20) discusses plants including medicinal herbs, exotic plants and spices from the East, fruit trees and planting and caring for them, farm management, and garden plants for food, fabric (flax, for example), and dyestuffs. Both Pliny the Younger (second century CE) and Sidonius Apollonarius (fifth century CE) describe in their letters other estates and produce at great length (e.g. Sid. Apoll., *Epist.* 2.2).

KEEPING ROME FED

Key provinces for keeping Rome fed: Egypt, North Africa, Gaul, Spain, the Black Sea regions of Bithynia.

KEEPING ROME FED

The availability of particular foodstuffs depended on season and weather: one bad growing season could lead to subsequent famine years. Cities lived off their surrounding countryside; Rome was the greatest urban parasite of all. This was not only to feed its enormous population; Roman food laws and taxes, especially on grain (*annona*), mostly related to the need for keeping the army fed. Urban centres were home to those rural poor and former farming families whose farms were swallowed up by landlords, *latifundia*, or other economic issues. To keep the urban mob (and especially their children) fed, imperial and urban *alimenta* ('eating') programmes were initiated during the peaks of the Republican and imperial period. Trajan codified and had the most generous of these programmes (e.g. *CIL*, 11.1147, in L&R, 2: no. 70: 255–259). But you'll find sifting through Plutarch's lives of Republican leaders – especially the Gracchi brothers, and Suetonius and Tacitus on Caesar, the Julio-Claudians (notably Claudius, Suet., *Claud.* 18.2, 19, 20.3), and the Flavian emperors – that regulating corn prices, taxes on foodstuffs, and food distribution were issues during their administrations. Keeping the mob fed was key to keeping people happy – modern American sporting events might have 'T-shirt cannons' to fire prizes into the audience between innings of a baseball game; those who paid for the *munera* or games in the arena had food and other prizes flung into the stands of spectators (e.g. Suet., *Ner.* 11; Cass. Dio, 66.25.5). Paul Erdkamp (2009) is a key scholar for background and discussion on the importance of food and grain especially, and his study will take you through the complexities of the effects of grain and grain trade on the economic, political, and social affairs during the imperial period. See the indexes for L&R, 1 and 2, under 'grain distribution' (or *annona*) for examples of laws, issues, and distribution of food.

DINING ETIQUETTE

Sadly, no single work of a Roman 'Miss Manners' survives on proper etiquette or ritual at a Roman dinner party. There are, however, surviving works that provide titbits about custom and etiquette for the dinner party. Aulus Gellius, for example, quotes Varro on the ideal number of guests to have at table (*NA* 13.11): one should begin with the Graces and end with the Muses, that is, there should be no fewer than three guests and no more than nine. Although his text dates from the fifth and sixth century CE, Macrobius provides anecdotes about the Julio-Claudians and (alleged) traditions from this whole period in his *Saturnalia*. Another later writer is Sidonius Apollonarius, a fifth-century poet and letter writer who was also a civil servant; he spent much of his adult life on diplomatic embassies between Roman politicians and Germanic or Goth commanders. Reading through his letters will give you examples from a well-read aristocrat who enjoyed dining and leisure with his friends (for example, *Epist.* 1.11.10–11).

Other rules of behaviour at meals – at least what *not* to do – can be found in satire and comedy. For example, Petronius's derision of Trimalchio's dinner party in the *Satyricon* and its participants – both men and women – is a good indication of how the aristocracy looked down upon newly wealthy freedmen. Because satire depends on the rhetorical practice of inversion for their humour, the description of the party indicates *good* behaviour by showing bad behaviour. Thus you can pick up titbits on etiquette, such as how guests must cross the threshold of the host's house correctly and not bring bad luck: be sure to step with the right foot first (*dextro pedes*) as some guests are scolded when they're about to cross into the house literally wrong-footed (Petron., *Sat.* 30–31). Trimalchio demonstrates vulgarity with every course of the meal, from serving ostentatious food (33, 35, 36, 40, 47, 49, 60 – a cake shaped like the god Priapus – 65, 68, 70) and from announcing the price of the wine (34) and other costings. He also throws valuable presents of food and trinkets at his guests and discusses the value of his wife's jewellery (67). At one point, he sweeps the table clear so that he can lie down on it and pretend he's on his funeral bier – forcing the guests to give his eulogy (71–72). It's over the top and makes the *Beverley Hillbillies* look like *Remains of the Day*, but the excesses and inversion of expected norms are precisely what's needed for laughs and can be reverse-engineered to work out expected social niceties. Other comedy sources include the plays of Plautus – his plots are filled with stock characters (many adapted from Greek comedy), and amongst them is the cook. Cooks were popular characters in comedy; for example, one of them is the hero who helps to bring down the braggart soldier in *Miles Gloriosus*. *Captivi* has a character who is obsessed with obtaining a free meal, and the subplot of his kitchen-raiding is interwoven throughout the main plot of captured prisoners, mistaken identity, and reversal of fortunes. Farcical dinner party scenes in *Menaechimi* would probably remind one of similar scenes in *Fawlty Towers*. For scenes of shopping and foodstuffs in the marketplace, there is the evil pimp Ballio in *Pseudolous* who orders his slaves in his brothel to 'negotiate' for the various foodstuffs needed for his birthday party (Plaut., *Pseud.* 225–229).

BANQUETS

The Emperor Elagabulus threw colour-themed banquets in the summer (blue one day, green another, rainbow-hued on yet a third (*HA, Helio.* 19.2)). In addition to using exclusively silver dinnerware, most of which was decorated with obscene images, as 'in imitation of

Apicius' he 'often ate camel heels, cockscombs taken from the heads of living birds, the tongues of peacocks and nightingales (because it was said the eater of such would be immune from plague)' (20.5–6). He also served up mullet-guts, the brains of flamingos and thrushes, partridge eggs, the heads of parrots and pheasants, and the beards of mullets (20.6–7). His dinner parties gave the fictional Trimalchio a run for his money in terms of excess, inedible over-the-top gilded and gem-encrusted dishes, and floor shows (21–22) – even his dogs got goose paté (21.1).

CONVERSATION

Table talk was another indicator of good character. If meals were a place for the host to demonstrate his hospitality, travellers and guests might be expected literally to sing for their supper and to pay for their meal with storytelling or tales of far-off places (e.g. Petron., *Sat.*, 61). No need for your characters to be at a loss for words in this case: there are plenty of contemporary handbooks that provide the anxious (upper-class) dinner-goer with ice-breakers and conversational topics. Sources include Aulus Gellius's *Attic Nights*, the *Miscellany* of Cornelius Nepos, and the same of Arrian. Conversation ought not be too vexing or heavy-handed, we learn: guests should avoid being too talkative or too reticent, or to speak of anxious or perplexing affairs. The conversation should instead focus on common life experience and be diverting and cheerful so that the interest and pleasure conveyed refine one's character (Aul. Gell., *NA* 12.1.1). Other sources that that can be mined for conversational topics include popular contemporary travelogues, such as that of Pausanias or Strabo: tales of other places – tall and true – and bizarre lands. At the most refined aristocratic table, it might be wise to brush up on one's knowledge of Greek myth or hone one's skill at verse. Tiberius was known for his perverted extravagance at his Villa Jovis (Suet., *Tib.* 42–45), but he and Gaius Caligula (and other well-educated Roman aristos such as the latter's father Germanicus) had a familiarity with Greek literature, tragedy, and myths, and they *loved* showing this off. Tiberius was known to quiz his guests on obscure trivia at table and severely punish people caught cribbing (*Tib.*, 56, 70, and especially 71). Gaius Caligula would have poetry contests (which allegedly might end with the loser having to lick clean his poetry off the page) (Suet., *Gai.* 20).

THE *TRICLINIUM*

For special occasions, the wealthy had a separate room for dining called the *triclinium* after the three long couches (which might each accommodate up to three people) arranged around the table. The *triclinium* might be its own indicative room of the house, or it could be out of doors to take advantage of mild weather and the garden. More extravagantly, the emperor Tiberius's infamous *triclinium* was a water-based folly built into the grotto at Sper Longa (Tac., *Ann.* 59.1; Suet., *Tib.* 39), where the guests reclined on floating couches while servants swam about to serve them, surrounded by illustrations of Odysseus painted on the cave walls. Diners reclined on their couches; where they sat in relation to the host was also a critical indication of their status and social position. Sources indicate that at the most important person (after the host) needed to be in a key position, but remain vague as to which was the plum spot, including the location of the host himself or herself. The main thing is that the host's seat was the best, and the status of his guests was determined from there. For example, 'Very tasty and inviting appetisers were brought in, as by now all the couches were occupied except for Trimalchio himself, for whom, after the new fashion, the foremost place was reserved' (Petron., *Sat.* 31). Horace pokes fun at the dining social order in *Satire* 2.8. Roller (2006) covers the bases from men and women to children and includes a catalogue of illustrations to inform your scene taken from funerary monuments and wall paintings.

THAT ROMAN COOKERY BOOK GUY ... APICIUS

For actual recipes, one can turn to Apicius, the author generally associated with a collection of Roman recipes that your teacher might have used when your Latin class did the Roman Banquet module. The oldest copy of the recipe book that survives is from the fourth or fifth century CE, but Apicius is referenced by earlier authors from the late Republic and early Empire including Athenaeus (Ath., 1.7), Seneca (*Epist.* 95.42, *Brev. Vit.* 11.4, *Cons. Hel.* 10.8–9), Cassius Dio (57.19.5), and Pliny the Elder (*NH* 10.133). As with other Classical miscellanies, the cookery book contains recipes attributed to Apicius from other sources; in her edition, Alcock (2001) notes, for example, that some of the more medicinal recipes probably originate with the Asia Minor physician Marcellus. Excluding the common types of manuscripts copied in the early and into the Carolingian Middle Ages (that is, grammars and particular texts of Vergil and Cicero as models of Latin grammar, not to mention Scripture), Apicius's recipe book was one of the most widely copied manuscripts in medieval scriptoria. We are missing whole swathes of Livy and Tacitus, but we've got plenty of copies of recipes from simple through to extravagant meals – the *Penelope* online project has an English translation of Apicius (adapted from Hill's 1936 translation) for ready reference (though as of this writing in June 2019 only about half of the transcribed translation has been checked).

Whichever edition you dip into, you'll find a collection of recipes which range from the humblest milky toast to meals that are the culinary equivalent of modern Las Vegas floorshows. The *Penelope* (and more recent Loeb) edition, for example, is arranged by type of food item across ten books containing nearly five hundred recipes. This information could help you shape your story as you consider who would have access to some of the finer herbs and spices and who might be involved with sourcing the ingredients along the trade routes between Rome and India, for example. Taken at face value, and with the continuous popularity of the text, it's easy for modern readers to assume that the Romans were all extravagant gourmands. Apicius, however, was associated with the worst excesses of gluttony, excess, and debauchery – this is the fellow who, according to tradition, killed himself out of despair of not being able to find and feed himself with the ultimate extremes of fine dining (Sen., *Cons. Hel.* 10.8–9; Cass. Dio, 57.19.5; Isid., *Etym.* 20.1.1). So he, his lifestyle, and his recipes were associated with wasting food and crazy meals, which, in a conservative, subsistence economy, was symbolic of extreme wealth and decadent folly amongst the upper class and social climbers. Pliny the Elder remarked that Apicius's recipes were aimed at the gourmand and the extravagant: 'Apicius, the greatest glutton amongst the spendthrift gourmands, taught that the flamingo's tongue has an especially fine flavour' (Pliny, *NH* 10.133). According to one story, the future commander of the imperial guard, that is the Praetorian Praefect Sejanus, prostituted himself for Apicius's pleasure and patronage (Tac., *Ann.* 4.1). The unknown author of the *Life of Elagabulus* claims that the teenaged emperor 'himself declared that his models Apicius among commoners, and, among emperors, Otho and Vitellius' (*HA, Heliog.* 18.4). The association between Apicius and gluttony persisted into the Georgian age, as Thomas Courture, writing in 1847, compared George IV to these same emperors in his gourmand excesses.

IT'S NOT ALL PEACOCK'S TONGUES AND GOLD-PLATED FISH

Recipe 181: Milk toast (adapted from Thomas H. Corcoran's translation for the Loeb edition, 1971)

Pultes tractogalatae

- Put a pint of milk and some water on the fire in a new clean pot.
- Break round bread into it dry.
- Stir well to prevent burning.
- Add water as necessary.

Tractum is a thin sheet of pastry; one could use a stale bit of bread or a roll.

BUT IF YOU MUST INDULGE ...

Recipe 231: Flamingo and parrot (adapted from Corcoran's Loeb edition, 1971)
In phoenicoptero

- Scald the flamingo, wash and dress it.
- Prepare the flamingo for parboiling by placing it in a pot.
- Add water, salt, dill, and a little vinegar.
- Finish cooking with a bunch of leeks and coriander, and add some reduced must to give it colour.
- In a mortar crush pepper, cumin, coriander, laser root, mint, rue; moisten with vinegar, add dates, and the broth of the braised bird.
- Thicken, strain, cover the bird with the sauce and serve.

Parrot is prepared in the same manner – just make sure Polly comes from the Old, and not the New, World.

CAVEAT ANACHRONISMS!

The Romans ate fruit and vegetables as they were available in season and locally – just make sure 'local' refers to 'indigenous to regions actually known to and occupied by Romans' and not 'Tesco Direct'. Do your homework, and keep the New World off the table.

NO: Avocados, tomatoes, pineapples, potatoes, peanuts, pumpkins, maize, blueberries or cranberries, cashews, or Brazil nuts. No chocolate! No turkey.

Do not embellish your scene with exotic birds. Fauna indigenous to Australia and South America frequently pop up in banquet scenes in television and films – the Romans got around, but not quite that far. No macaws, New World parrots, or white cockatoos.

A BEVERAGE BRIEF

The famous wines for the Romans were Opimian and Falernian, and guests neck them in *The Satyricon* with abandon: 'While we were perusing thoroughly the [wine] labels, Trimalchio clapped his hands and said, "Alas! How much longer does wine live on than a little man. So let's drink 'em up! There's life in wine. This is genuine Opimian, I guarantee it. I offered nothing as good yesterday, though my dinner guests were far more respectable"' (Petron., *Sat.* 34).

- Wine: keep it flowing and keep it watered. *Calda* is a warm mulled wine popular in winter; *posca* is vinegar diluted with water fit for soldiers, the poor, and other ruffians. Beer is the beverage of barbarians.
- Milk drinking is unusual except as fresh as possible from handy goats or sheep as there's no way to preserve or pasteurise it. Milk is consequently consumed instead as cheese.
- Water flowed into cities via aqueducts and filled fountains and baths; rarely used as a beverage.
- Apicius includes many recipes for beverages, sauces, and gravies, including *garum*, everyone's favourite rotten fish sauce.

WHEN THE MEAL IS THE FLOORSHOW: EXCESS AT TRIMALCHIO'S DINNER PARTY

'After we applauded this declamation, a course followed but not the size we expected – it was so unusual, though, that it drew every eye to it. There was a circular tray around which were shown the twelve signs of the zodiac, and on each the caterer had placed the food most relevant to the sign: so over Aries, there were ram's-head peas, on Taurus a piece of beef, on Gemini a pair of kidneys, on Cancer a crown, on Leo an African fig, on Virgo the womb of a barren sow, on Libra there was a pair of scales with a bun on one plate and a cake on the other, on Scorpio a small marine fish, on Sagittarius a bull's-eye, on Capricorn a lobster, on Aquarius a goose, and on Pisces two mullets. In the middle there was a piece of cut sod on which lay a honeycomb with grass around it. An Egyptian slave-boy passed bread around from a silver serving dish. In the most loathsome voice Trimalchio himself croaked out a tune from the mime "Asafoetida". Seeing that we seemed sad at the prospect of tucking into such vile fare, he said, "Let's tuck in, I beg of you – this is only the appetiser for the main course!'" (Petron., *Sat.* 35–36).

VOMITORIUM, OR NOT?

While eating themselves silly, Trimalchio and his guests go in and out of the main dining room to vomit and make room for the next course. It remains part of our image of Roman dining: stuffing their faces, then throwing up the first course to make room for the second. This is allegedly how the assassins got Claudius when the poisoned mushrooms he was served didn't work (Tac., *Ann.* 67.1). Because the mushrooms made Claudius feel ill, he called for assistance vomiting, so allegedly a poisoned feather was stuck down his throat in between courses to finish him off (Tac., *Ann.* 67.1) – by his doctor Xenophon no less (Suet., *Claud.* 33.1). Seneca remarked that the Romans ate to vomit, to vomit what they ate, and that they didn't even deign to 'digest the feast for which they ransack the world' (Sen., *Cons. Hel.* 10.2).

Vomitoria was the term for the gangways and exits of the theatres and especially stadia, a colourful image of the building disgorging its patrons. So which came first? There's plenty of references to vomiting, emetics, and fine dining amongst Roman sources; one is spoiled for choice amongst the poets (Verg., *Geor.* 3.516; Ov., *Met.* 2.119), the satirists (Mart., 7.67.10 and 11.90.6; Juv., 6.432; Petron.,

3 Mosaic of an amphora for holding garum, from the house of
Aulus Umbricius Scaurus, found in Pompeii, first century CE

Sat. 56.6), and amongst the lives the usual suspects (Suet., *Gai.* 57.4;
Ner. 20.1). Pliny the Elder provides discussion of vomiting in his
Natural History: (8.106, 23.5, 25.57, 20.107, 21.128, 26.67 and elsewhere) and the ins and outs, as it were, of purging (colour, shape,
frequency, etc.), and at the dinner-table itself, there is Cicero (*Phil.*
2.104) and our pal Aulus Gellius (*NA* 17.15.4) for examples of those
who couldn't make it to the designated area. If you do include the
vomitorium, don't forget to have slaves on hand to wipe up the spit-
tle and others tasked with collecting the vomit of the drunks (Sen.,
Epist. 47.5).

SPICING THINGS UP

Freshness was a tricky issue – one advantage of local produce was getting the freshest goods, but originally, markets were held every ninth day in Rome (*nundiae*), and the quality of the goods with limited shelf life depended on how quickly the farmer or merchant could get into town and set up his wares. Without refrigeration, the Romans did not have many options when it came to food preservation. Instead, they used salt and brine (i.e. pickling). Spices not only added flavour but also disguised the smell and taste of food that had gone off: Plautus, for example, mocks fishmongers flogging rotten fish (Plaut., *Capt.* 813–819) – how would a nation of people who devoured garum by the boatload would even notice …? Apicius again describes some means of short-term food preservation: Book 1 of his cookery advises variously on food preservation, including honey, pickling, spices, and sawdust. Recipe 27 suggests that one can keep truffles (*tubera ut diu serventur*) by drying them out, packing them in dry sawdust, then sealing them in a vessel with plaster to be stored in a cool place. NB: do *not* try this at home.

SALT

Salt was *very* expensive, as there was no means to collect it without intense physical labour: *salus* is the root of *salary*, as every schoolchild knows, and small bags of salt were much prized as soldiers' wages. To be sentenced to the salt mines was a death sentence. The average prisoner of war who was sent to the mines, as those unfortunates captured on the failed Sicilian expedition of 415–413 BCE learned, had a life expectancy of three miserable months (Thuc., 7; Plut., *Nic.* 12–30 and *Alc.* 17–21).

PRESERVING

Apicius suggests preserving fruit, such as peaches (Recipe 28), by soaking them in brine, then sprinkling them in salt, immersing them in vinegar, and sealing the container. There is a caveat to this type of preservation: Apicius warns that a number of methods that preserve foods also act as laxatives – a source for some mundane realism in fiction.

CLOTHING MAKES THE MAN (AND WOMAN): CLOTHING, COSMETICS, COIFFURES

Appearance was an instant indicator of status, position, and wealth in the Roman world. Clothing signified how one had moved up in the world and broadcast this news publicly, as seen on the tombs of freedmen and freedwomen, wearing attire their reflected their wealth, surrounded by illustrations of objects that indicated the means of their material well-being. A famous example is Regina and Barates, the latter a Palmyran living in Britain in the second century CE, who wanted to show the world that his bride, a former British slave, had become a proper freed Roman matron. On her tombstone, Regina is dressed in the sober gown of a Roman matron with her jewellery and valuables on display, and Barates' loving inscription commemorates her as a lady.

Discussion of appearance in contemporary literature is usually connected to morality and social status. Male, aristocratic authors writing on the subject go to the extremes of either expounding on the great virtue exhibited by those with modest, conservative appearances (such as the simplicity of Cornelia, mother of the Gracchi, see Chapter 1) or mocking the vain excesses of those who slathered on the paint and draped themselves in jewellery (such as found in the satires of Martial, Juvenal, Petronius, or Ovid in Book 3 of his *Ars Amatoria*). A rare exception is Ovid's *Medicamina Faciei Femineae* – an unusually positive discussion of a lady's toilette and use of cosmetics in Roman literature. Another somewhat objective source on the subject is Pliny the Elder's discussion of exotic unguents and perfume (*NH* 13.4–5). Livy's discussion of women's public protest against sumptuary laws demonstrates that sacrificing for the state only goes so far: once austerity measures were out of the way, women wanted back their finery (34.4; on the Oppian Laws, 34.4.1–8).

How you dress your characters might be folded into how strangers and 'outsiders' were identified and consequently treated by the locals – it can make quite a difference to the storyline if a stranger shows up in the big city or in a back-country village on his or her travels (or misadventures). In Plautus's play *Rudens*, for example, frightened girls pray outside of a temple to Venus so loudly that the priestess, Ptolemocratia, comes outside; she speaks scornfully to them, assuming from their rags that they are paupers rather than bedraggled survivors of a shipwreck (Plaut., *Rud.* 265–266, 270–278). Other instances of merit and status associated with appearance are found in Apuelius's writing. According to his *Apologia*, while stopping at a small town, he was accused of witchcraft and a local murder because he was the stranger on the scene (Apul., *Apol.* 1.2.8–12). Mistaken identity (and changed identities) also occur throughout his work *Metamorphoses* (*The Golden Ass*); this pastoral novel follows a young man as he wanders the provinces, searching for his own identity. He is accused of a crime because he's the new guy in town, and, terrified, he's put on trial for murder. To his relief, he discovers that the people he 'killed' in his drunken state were wine-sacks (Apul., *Met.* 3.5–12) – and the whole thing is a prank played on him by the locals. Subsequently, he meets other people who fake or have lost their identity. This is a common plot point in comedy and satire: once a man (or woman) has lost their original clothing, the only way to distinguish a *princeps* or a pauper is usually some significant scrap or piece of jewellery left in his or her possession. For example, a girl imprisoned in the mistaken belief that she was a slave is found to be wearing ragged silk clothes (*Met.* 4.23–28), a mark of distinction that she's actually an aristocrat. Lucius is recognised as a youth of good standing because of his clothing, but Milo, a wealthy man, is ridiculed as a miser, because he wears clothing that is old and shabby and does not reflect his status – he does so to avoid being asked for handouts (1.20–21). Elsewhere, in Terence's *Hecyra* a lost ring restores the status of a young woman's virtue, and a ring is an indicator of status in Plautus's *Milos Gloriosus*. Apuleius's Lucius suffers the extremes of changes to his external appearance, as he spends much of *Metamorphoses* stuck in the guise of an ass and treated quite badly as a consequence.

BASIC GARMENTS: COLOUR, SHAPE, AND FABRIC

As with lavish meals and parties, expensive, extravagant clothing is described because it is unusual. Excess is mocked as an affectation of the *nouveau riche*:

> Then we went into the bath, and there we stayed until we were drenched in sweat; then we at once plunged into the cold water. Now Trimlachio was anointed all over and rubbed down, not with towels, but with blankets made from the softest wool. Meanwhile, three masseurs drank Falerian wine right in front of him, and when they argued and spilt some of it, Trimalchio said that they were toasting his health. Then he was rolled up in a scarlet cloak made from wool and placed on a litter. (Petron., *Sat.* 28)

The basic ground rule is to start simply as most clothing in the ancient world was based around the squares and rectangles that came off the weaver's loom. How you add to the basic design will indicate the status and identity of your characters. Just remember, no buttons and certainly no zips (which abound in older Hollywood blockbusters). Unless there's a seam, pins and brooches (*fibulae*) of all shapes and sizes should be used to fasten clothing at the shoulder.

Some clothing did come in other shapes: the toga, for example, which is a large semi-circle of woollen cloth. Other shapes, mainly for accessories, might be felted: wool boots, mitts, or caps. Hat were also sewn and woven into circular shapes out of straw and other plant fibres. There was even a type of knitting from this period now called *nålbinding* – 'knitted' cotton socks dating from the third century CE onwards survive from Dura Europa and Coptic Egypt, vibrant cultures just to the east of Rome's territories. (There is no word equivalent of knitting in either Greek or Latin, however.)

CLASSICAL-ERA FABRICS

These include wool, cotton, and linen (from the flax plant). Cotton production in antiquity was labour-intensive, making it an expensive fabric. Silk was not produced in the Roman world until far after our period, with the legend of Justinian sending henchmen into India in 552 CE to steal silkworms to bring back to the Byzantine Empire (Proc., *Goth.* 8.17.1–8). Silk *was* available in our period, but only as a very expensive import from India.

COLOURS

Colours depend on natural dyes made from plants (including lichen), minerals, and other materials such as ground shells. They are set into the fabric with metallic salt solutions called *mordants* (from the Latin *mordare* or 'to bite'). Without them, dyes are not fast and will eventually rinse out or fade in the sun. Colours can range across the spectrum, but natural dyes tend to be more muted than the vivid chemical dyes that appeared in the nineteenth century. Most dyes produce variations of yellow and come from the stems, leaves, and plants, such as onion skins and marigolds. Blue (in the West) is derived from woad. True green is next to impossible from natural dyes, but overdyeing yellow-dyed material with woad produces blue-greens. Madder roots produce red, and lichen in northern climes also produces red and purple (deep, rich red comes from cochineal, a New World insect). Purple comes from *murex* shells – and it is the dyestuff of the aristocracy and emperors, as this is the costly Tyrenian purple.

SPINNING AND WEAVING

Spinning was ubiquitous in the ancient and Classical world. Everyone except aristocratic men spun – women of all classes, even certain men, particularly sailors and prisoners. There are many depictions of spinners in artwork across the Empire, and it was an important symbol of women's work in the Classical era: Harlow and Nosch (2015) and Nosch (2014), for example, have written extensively on textile production in terms of practicality and its economic, social, and cultural implications. Scheid (2001) has studied themes and symbolism of weaving and cloth production in Classical Greece and Rome. This drudging, labour-intensive but endlessly necessary household task had an element of sociability to it and carried an image of the well-run household. Augustus, for example, bragged that all of his and his family's clothing was made by his sister Octavia, his wife Livia, his daughter Julia, and his granddaughters (Suet., *Aug.* 64.2, 73). Many funerary inscriptions for women sum up their entire character by saying, simply, 'She spun'. Even in the lengthy panegyric *Laudatio Turiae* (*CIL*, 6.1527, in L&F, n. 191: 165–169) one of Turia's main accomplishments is that she spun for the household. This image of Roman domesticity is strangely inverted in Petronius's satire: Trimalchio the freedman brags about how everything at his extravagant dinner party being produced right there on his estate, including clothing and household goods, but he is mocked for being so cheap that he has everything that he can made on the premises (Petron., *Sat.* 38).

AIDS TO THE APPEARANCE: SLAP AND BLING

Ovid saw women in their natural state akin to a blank canvas – and he refers here not only to their physical form but also to the state of their minds. He is the only male Roman writer to offer up positive commentary on the dos and don'ts of choosing clothing, styling hair, and applying make-up. He emphasises basic hygiene as well as judicious application of cosmetics; *Ars Amatoria*, Book 3, and his short didactic poem *Medicamina Faciei Femineae* (*Cosmetics for the Faces of Women*) are treasure-troves of advice to women on enhancing their charms. Other sources for the make-up box include Horace, who warned that women ought never to spoil the illusion of their beauty by allowing their menfolk to see the tools of the make-up trade, which might include vermilion, rose petals, chalk – or crocodile dung (Hor. *Epod.* 12.10–11). Pliny the Elder provides practical discussion of the substances, both benign and foul, that go into the lady (or man's) toilette (for example *NH* 20.6, 21.73, 22.82, 27.88; cf. Ov., *Ars* 3.270).

CULTUS

When the Romans talk about one's beauty regimen, they use the word *cultus*, which refers not only to cosmetics, perfume, and accessories but also to the cultivation of one's manners or customs in order to present one's best character, whether demonstrating one's *nobilitas*, brushing up on one's language skills or literary knowledge, or taking good care with one's appearance.

Many literary sources mock excess and extravagant attention paid to the details of grooming by men and women. Juvenal likens a women's daily regimen of choosing her clothing and arranging her jewellery and cosmetic box to a soldier or gladiator preparing for battle (Juv., 6). Note, too, the word *medicamen* used in reference to cosmetics. There is a blurry line of distinction made between medical potions and cosmetic supplies in, for example, the work of Pliny the Elder or of physicians such as Galen (his treatises *On the Constitution of the Art of Medicine* and *The Art of Medicine*, both available through Loeb translations, are well worth a look). Martial and Juvenal (6.47–9) make fun of the cheaply painted slut, and they describe the worst of the cheapest cosmetics and potions: smelly if not caustic horrors made from animal fat, lead, or other cheap materials that went rancid on the skin (when they weren't sloughing it off). Compounding the stench was an application of cheap perfume to covering up (cf. Sen., *Con.* 2.21) or failing to mask body odour (Mart., 6.93). The problem was, then as now, that the 'good stuff', such as the traces of the 'Londinium cream' (a foundation made from animal fat, starch, and tin) found in contemporary compacts, was expensive. Common, cheaper beauty nostrums were made out of inferior materials that went bad quickly. Even the finest stuff required constant application as it was sweated off throughout the day – chalk may have whitened the face (Hor., *Epod.* 12.10) (and hidden the effects of poisoning, such with Claudius's son Britannicus), but a sudden cloudburst could lead to disaster (as with Britannicus's funeral) (Suet., *Ner.* 33; Cass. Dio, 61.4); Martial warned women to stay out of the rain lest their creamy pale complexion (i.e. chalk dust) washed off (2.41).

ATTITUDES TOWARDS THE BEAUTY REGIMEN

The Romans associated the use of cosmetics and their effect on appearance with the quality of character, gender roles, and social standing. Male writers argued that good, modest ladies needed only their natural beauty to impress, and that vulgar women (that is, the poor, the social climbers, sex workers, and street performers) painted themselves up with inferior products. Use of depilatories indicated loose morals, as women were expected to shave prior to having sex (cf. Mart., 12.32, 21–2). Perfumes were useless trifles: the best scent of a woman was her natural state, according to Cicero, although Pliny the Elder describes deodorant made from alum which might be a preferable alternative (*NH* 21.142, 35.185, 21.121). Vain women showed their weak character by spending too much time in front of the mirror. Jewellery was an expression of vanity and folly: Trimalchio's wife Fortunata wears all of her gold at once at the dinner party, while Trimalchio reels off the cost of each item (Petron., *Sat.* 67). The man himself wears so many rings at once he can barely move his fingers (32.71); gold and ivory bangles ladder up his arms (32–33). According to the noble lady Cornelia, mother to the Gracchi, the only jewels a woman needed were her sons (Val. Max., 4.4 pr.). Jewellery *was* an important part of one's property. Even the smallest items would be carefully inventoried for tax and will purposes, and handed down in families as part of the family estate. In times of need jewels and plate could be used for survival; consider a woman who was found in an inn at Pompeii clutching a handbag of her precious jewellery, grabbed as she tried to escape from the falling ash.

AS FOR MALE DEDICATED FOLLOWERS OF FASHION ...

Ovid says, 'avoid the man that makes a ritual [*cultus*] of his fashion and his good looks, and frets lest his hair should get ruffled ... What they say to you, they've said to a thousand girls: their love wanders and never stays in one place. Woman, what can you do with a man more high-maintenance than you and who probably has a greater number of lovers?' (*Ars.* 3.433–438). Emperors who used make-up (such as Otho) were seen as feminine, and those who perfumed and shaved their body hair (such as Elagabulus) were seen as not only unmasculine (Juv., 2.99–101) but also immoral (Cass. Dio, 80.14.4).

THE EYES HAVE IT ...

Eyes were an important feature – kohl around the eyes is an effective sun blocker, and an effective highlight, as the Romans found large and distinctive eyes exquisite. Eyebrows were darkened and brought almost together over the brow with soot or antimony; lids might sparkle with green or blue shadow made from crushed minerals. Pliny the Elder advises fluffing up the eyelashes as they fall out during sex – bare eyes indicate sexual depravity (*NH* 11.1.54). The effect here is seen in the Egyptian sarcophagoi paintings of both men and women; large, exaggerated eyes also became an artistic style on sculpture from the middle of the third century CE as first Stoicism then Christianity affected the association of eyes with intellectualism and mystic beliefs.

MEN'S HAIRSTYLES

There are myriad descriptions of hairstyles as well as material depictions, so there is no excuse for some of the daft anachronisms one sees especially in mid-twentieth-century HollyRome films. There's variety in Roman hair that can be as traditional or as mad as one wants, so don't jar your readers or viewers out of the moment with 1950s Brylcreemed Tony Curtis style or the painfully 1990s mop on the child Lucius Verus in *Gladiator.*

Men's hairstyles in our period run from the 'classic' short, fringed haircut of the mid-Republic through to the curlier (and shaggier) Hellenistic styles adapted by the Graecophile emperors in the second century CE. The short style and clean-shaven faces on Roman men again relate to identity and status: in the Republic this style became popular not coincidentally around the time when the Romans were emphasising their separation from their longer-haired Etruscan forebears (and erstwhile kings) as well as men from the East and hirsute Gallic tribesmen. Graecophiliac locks and beards indicated intellectualism and cosmopolitan outlooks from the time of Hadrian. Consequently, short hair and shaved faces alternated with longer styles and beards from the second century CE onwards depending on the emperor's interest in Neo-Platonism, his provincial background, or a desire to distinguish those men with (claims of) Roman pedigree from the increasing number of Germanic and Gothic officials in the Roman army and administration.

There is room for vanity in your characters, especially amongst upper-class men: Pompey, for example, was famous in his youth for his good looks and his lush blond hair (Plut., *Pom.* 2.1). His rival, Caesar, on the other hand, was embarrassed by his thinning hair and wore laurel crowns to hide his baldness (Suet., *Iul.* 45.2). Gaius Caligula, who inherited the baldness gene, was thinning on top, but bodily hirsute; jealous of men with full heads of hair, he made it illegal for anyone to see him from above or to mention goats in his presence (Suet., *Gai.* 50.1; cf. 35.2 where he forced mean to shave their heads). Vespasian, however, was completely bald, and, if he didn't give a toss about people mocking the constipated look of his resting facial expression (Suet., *Vesp.* 20.1), he probably wasn't fussed about his hairline. Nero and his generation, which included the slightly younger, future emperor Otho, experimented with trendy styles; statues of Nero in his later reign show him with longer hair that curled on the nape of his neck, for example – which made him mutton dressed as lamb, as only younger men wore their hair at that length (Suet., *Ner.* 51.1). Later busts of Nero and those of Otho and other young, aristocratic men in the late 60s CE show them with their hair combed forward; it lies flat on the crown and puffs out around the lower part of the head – not quite a Marcel wave, but not unlike the modern dreaded 'hat hair'. Perhaps the style was deliberately cultivated to resemble the look that was then common amongst the lowly but madly popular charioteers who sported a similar style. One of the most vain of all was Lucius Verus, appointed co-emperor by Marcus Aurelius in the *Historia Augusta*, who was told once too often how beautiful his blond curls were. To make sure everyone noticed, he sprinkled gold dust in his hair to make it glitter even in the dimmest of lights (and, apparently, to shine to rival the sun during the day) (*HA, Ver.* 10.7.8). Sadly, he died in 161 CE, and so never made it to Studio 54.

CLEAN-SHAVEN OR SCRUFFY?

Egyptians shaved off or used depilatories on all of their body hair out of hygienic practice. The Romans didn't go to those extremes, but Roman men with their clean-shaven faces and cropped hair were distinctive from Jews and Germans. If you need any indication of Roman determination and dedication to hard work and pain in life, keep in mind that razors (*novaculae*) were made from easily dulled bronze. A close shave was not easy to acquire or to maintain; one alternative solution was simply to pull the hairs. Professional barbers (*tonsores*) were part of the influx of all things Greek that began to show up in Italy and the West from the third century BCE, and wealthier men might have a barber amongst their household slaves. There were barbers' shops; amongst the tools of the trade uncovered by archaeologists were dice and rudimentary dental tools. Beards were not fashionable amongst aristocratic, conservative Roman men during the mid- to late Republic and early imperial period; Nero is depicted with a beard because he loved Greek culture, not because he actually wore one. Beards are found throughout the East during our period; in the West they indicated Greeks, Jews, Celts, Gauls, or Germans until the second century CE when Graeocophile emperors, beginning with Hadrian, begin to sport them, neatly trimmed, setting a trend. Did Hadrian wear a beard because he was keen on Greek culture (Cass. Dio, 68.15.6) or because he was hiding a facial disfigurement (*HA, Hadr.* 26.1)? Believe what you want – the sources support either supposition.

WOMEN'S HAIRSTYLES

Women's hairstyles (and their jewellery) were the ways in which women could distinguish themselves. In the Republican era, hair might be drawn back modestly and caught up in a bun at the nape of the neck (certainly the common style for young girls to signify their youth and innocence). Matrons covered their hair; Vestal Virgins (and brides) are depicted with complex plaited styles under their headdresses. You'll find more physical depictions of women after the imperial period, but the modest hairstyles of early Julio-Claudian women are indicative of simple Republican styles. One example is Agrippina the Elder, who is typically depicted with her hair parted in the middle and drawn back and clasped at the nape of her neck. Similarly, her daughter Agrippina the Younger is sometimes depicted with this style. Simple buns and knots of hair also appear on the busts and coins depicting early imperial women as well. As with the emperor's, hairstyles of imperial women would be widely copied not only by aristocratic women but also by women of the lower classes and represented the traditional modesty and conservatism of the Republic that Augustus promoted.

Amongst the tools on the woman's dressing table were curling tongs (*calamistrum*), combs, and ornaments; any museum collection worth its salt will have an abundance of hair pins – so ubiquitous that you can find them cheaply for sale on eBay. Women wound their hair with ribbons (called *vittae* or *fasciae* – cf. the *fasces* or tied bundle of rods representing Roman power and unity) which can be seen in paintings from Egyptian sarcophagoi and frescos and paintings from Pompeii. Curls were popular amongst both men and women, although curling one's hair could be fraught with peril as the tongs were simply metal rods laid on a heat source; hair could be scorched or even melted off. Women might also wear pieces much like tiaras and Alice bands; these would be decorated with precious jewels, pearls, or bits of gold, glass, and paste gems. Mirrors were made from polished bronze – this does work; don't let endless illustrations of corroded green mirrors jade you, as it were. The British Museum has on display, amongst its Etruscan mirrors, a polished bronze mirror. It's as effective as a modern mirror; reflections in water might be somewhat clearer, but highly polished bronze works well enough for purpose. Women (and men) did dye their hair – and colour their grey. There was also a lively trade in wigs – blond hair taken from German slaves and captives was popular; later red wigs became fashionable after forays into the Celtic world. Wrote Ovid:

> Ah, you women! Oh, how nature indulges your beauty! How many ways to repair the damage! Sadly we men are exposed, and our hair is snatched away by age, just as the leaves fall, then the Northern Wind strips them away. A woman will dye her grey hair with German herbs; and seeks a better colour by their art. A woman steps forward densely coiffured with store-bought curls instead of her own; she pays for another's. No blushes at all – we see her come quite openly. A woman will appear wearing a mass of hair that she has just purchased. For a little money she can buy another's tresses. She'll do the deal without a blush, quite openly, before the eyes of Hercules and the virgin in front of the Muses' choir. (Ov., *Ars* 3.159–168)

Search *crines* on the Loeb database for descriptions of and satire about *crines* or hairstyles worn by both men and women.

FORENSIC HAIRSTYLING

The Baltimore hairstylist Janet Stephens has re-created the styles of the Vestals, the styles of Faustina the Younger and Empress Plotina, and Cleopatra. Her results (2008) have challenged scholarship about how women's hairdos were constructed. As of this writing (January 2019), Stephens maintains walk-through styling videos on YouTube which might prove inspirational, or you might check out her website for further modern reconstructions (with suggested modern substitutions in place of Roman implements as well as providing video). See Eveleth and Pesta in bibliography, and many other hits on Google.

NOTED WOMEN'S HAIRSTYLES

- The simple *nodus* (which means 'knot') of the matron which demonstrates her modesty. This is a style from the time of the Republic adopted by Augustus's women as a physical reminder of how Augustus had restored the stability of the Republic. This style is seen on images of Augustus's sister Octavia, his niece Antonia, his wife Livia, and his daughter Julia, and Claudius's daughter Octavia, all late first century BCE and early first century CE. It's achieved by combing a long section of hair forward, then lifting the section back over the head; the section is held in place at the back so that the front of the hair creates a little puffed bump over the forehead. Other women such as Agrippina the Elder simply parted their hair in the middle and gathered it in a bun.

- *seni crines* – This is comprised of the tall wrap of plaits worn by the Vestals, which is also significantly the style worn by Roman brides. Janet Stephens has videos on YouTube in which she demonstrates how to re-create this style.

- Flavian styles of the 70s–90s, especially the construction of towers of curls over the front and sides of the head: hair drawn into a bun at the back, and masses of curls in a high arch over the head. Some women used hair pieces and in some cases actual wigs to get the effect, and some managed it more elegantly than others if surviving images are any indication. This trendy style is mocked by Juvenal as tall from the front, but short from the back (6.501–503). Domitian's wife wore this style.

- The Julias (early third century CE): Septimius Severus's Syrian wife and in-laws had distinctive, Eastern hairstyles. His wife Julia had a long hairstyle that was set off by a centre part and then the hair drawn up to the back of the head in a loose twist (while framing the face) – her clothes and hair were very trendy and widely imitated in the early third century. You'll see a variety of changing women's styles amongst the empresses from the early second century onwards.

SUMPTUARY LAWS

Ostentatious spending was considered vulgar by the Romans; spending curbs were important means of public good especially during the Republic. Indeed, Livy notes that frugality was a positive trait during the wars of the third century BCE, when even women and children gave up any gold or silver that they had to the state, following the model of the Senators. To live simply demonstrated 'modesty and purity' and virtuous living – especially amongst Roman women (Liv., 34.6). Sallust (or, more likely, Pseudo-Sallust) warned Caesar that the best thing he could do was to give up chasing wealth and riches (or at least reduce his wealth as much as he could to live frugally). Greed and the pursuit of wealth overcome intelligence, education, experience, and natural good will, Caesar is warned, and those who value riches over honour, merit, and good deeds are not worth ruling. Virtue and honour, the respect of the people:

4 Unknown Roman Matrona, found at Aphrodisias, second century CE

these are won through good deeds rather than through largesse or osten-
tation. (Sall., *Epist. ad Caes.* 7.1–9).

The censor, a magistrate elected outside of the *cursus honorum* (see
Chapter 5), put checks and balances on extravagance, and, in this public-
facing society, apparel and lavish parties were places where spending and

conspicuous consumption were visible. Laws that curbed extravagance, notably passed in the third century BCE, were clustered together under the title of *sumptuariae leges*; the *Twelve Tables* also allude to these types of law (Aul. Gell., *NA* 2.24, 20.1). In modern usage, 'sumptuary' refers specifically to clothing, but for the Romans this legislation covered clothing, jewellery, banquets, entertainment, and expenditure on food.

Particularly notable sumptuary laws from the era of the Republic include the *lex Oppia* (c. 213 BCE) which was passed during at the height of the second Punic War (218–202 BCE) after Rome's disastrous defeat by Hannibal at Cannae (216 BCE). This law determined the amount of gold that women could wear. It also legislated the colours of women's clothing: they could not wear dresses 'of different colours' as certain dyestuffs, especially reds and purples, were expensive. There may have been political implications to this law as well, as purple dye came from Phoenicia, specifically Tyre, a city-state with ties to Carthage. The *lex Oppia* was repealed twenty years later when the crisis passed, and the women of Rome took to the streets in 195 BCE demanding that the law be struck from the books (Liv., 24.1; Val. Max., 9.1.3). Livy notes that the women complained that, because they were expressly forbidden to partake of magistracies, priesthoods, triumphs, badges of office, gifts, or spoils of war, they took as their badges of pride the elegance and finery of beautiful clothes (Liv., 34.5).

The Julio-Claudian emperors also attempted to pass sumptuary laws affecting expenditure on banquets and festivities, but these were difficult to uphold (Tac., *Ann.* 2.33; 3.52,3). Nero, for example, tried to pass laws checking extravagant clothing and accessories, but this is the man who built an entire palace of gold so that he could, as he allegedly said, 'At last [I can] live like a human being!' (Suet., *Ner.* 31.2). For a brief checklist of these and other sumptuary laws on the books, their repeals, and attempts to enact them between about 215 BCE and into the middle of the first century CE, see the Tufts University *Perseus* database online, which has transcribed *Sumptuariae leges*, keeping in mind that this is a work in the public domain published originally by Smith (1898); the link is in the bibliography.

THE BASICS: MEN'S AND UNISEX GENERAL WEAR

Tunic

The basic garment wore by men and women, free and slave: a simple rectangle held together with sewn seams down the sides and shoulders. Gender determined the length. The under-tunic was called the *subacula*.

The toga

The garment of the Senatorial class. To wear one not only showed high status and dignity; putting and keeping one on required high status (a dresser to help) and dignity (to keep from tripping over its folds and falling on one's face). *Togae* can be wrapped around the wearer in different ways so that the folds lie in different patterns to create pockets (*sinus*). Men of the Senatorial class also pulled their *togae* over their heads when at prayer or making sacrifices.

Toga candida

Candida means bright or shining – this toga was bleached to make it as white as possible. Keeping such garments clean was also difficult and expensive. A candidate for office wore the *candida* – its brightness symbolised the purity of the wearer's character.

Toga praetexta

This is the one with the broad purple stripe worn by the Senators and magistrates (i.e. consuls, praetors, etc.). Rank determined the width of the purple stripe, with the emperor having the widest stripe, and perhaps an outfit made entirely from purple cloth. The dye comes from the *murex* shell, and it was extremely expensive.

Toga pulla

A dark-coloured toga for mourning.

Outer garments: cloaks
The outer cloak was versatile because it was wool; it kept the wearer not only warm but also dry. Men and women wore outer cloaks held together by brooches, *fibulae.*

Outer garments: hats
Just about everyone in the Roman world, especially in the Mediterranean, suffered from pink eye; straw hats were common headgear to block the sun to try to alleviate it.

Socks and underwear (*udones*); trousers
The Romans (and Greeks) dismissed trousers and undergarments as barbaric – because, in their experience, outsiders wore them: the Persians in the Greek world and the Germans in the Roman world. Concessions were made, however, especially in colder climates: check out the letters from Vindolanda for requests for clothing on the northern frontier, amongst which are a letter asking about more socks and underwear (Vindolanda Tablet 346, leaf 1, *Vindolanda Tablets Online*).

Shoes and footwear
Explore the myriad Google returns with discretion – descriptions of shoes and footwear are mixed in with discussion of clothing. Websites aimed at schoolchildren provide simple, sometimes useful information. Top hits when Googling 'Roman shoes' are usually *caligae* – but these aren't shoes: they're military boots or sandals.

THE BASICS: WOMEN'S WEAR (ADAPTED FROM *LIVIUS.ORG*)

Intusium (tunic)
An under-tunic similar to the man's *subacula*, except longer. Women tended to layer tunics, for modesty and warmth.

The *stola*

The most common long tunic, this was a wool garment layered over another tunic or the *chiton* to distinguish married women and matrons from girls and unmarried young women. It had side seams and could be belted; the shoulders were held together by *fibulae*. It was allotted (although not required) by law during the Republic to married women, and it was an important sign of their married status. Livia wore the *stola* publicly, emphasising the importance of women's role in the domestic sphere. The *stola* was usually plain-coloured, but it might feature a multi-coloured or decorated border (*instita*).

The *palla*

A long cloak worn by respectable women; made of wool, it was rectangular and draped and thrown over the body. As with the toga on men, the 'cowl' of the *palla* could be pulled up over the head to protect the hair or as an expression of deference.

Undergarments

Women sometimes wore a short bodice under their clothing called a *strophium*, similar to a cropped camisole. No one can say for sure exactly what women wore under their frocks, although plenty of websites offer conjecture for role players. Most of these garments are based on the famous ball-playing girls fresco at the Villa Romana del Casale near the Piazza Armerina, Sicily.

The peplos *and the* chiton

Borrowed Greek fashion, the *peplos* was a long dress fastened at the shoulders with *fibulae*. Its basic shape is a square. The *chiton* was similar to a long tunic, sewn up the sides to the arm; several pins went across the shoulders to hold the garment closed. The chiton was more common; both dresses could be colourfully dyed. They were made from more lightweight fabrics such as linen, or, if very luxurious, silk.

The toga

Another example of the Roman love of inversion and gender roles is that prostitutes wore *togae*. They were also simultaneously admired and scorned for their finery, elegantly coiffed hair (or wigs), and unabashed use of make-up. Despite their exaggerated female sexuality, they were regarded as masculine – because they were independent, like men, and because they sold their bodies for sex (making them the assertive partner). Prostitutes were the only women permitted by law to wear *togae*. This was to indicate that they were the 'opposite' of other women, that is, they were sexually assertive rather than passive.

3

LOCATION, LOCATION, LOCATION: DOMESTIC AND PUBLIC PLACES AND SPACES

THE CITY AS A CHARACTER

How do you know you're in a Roman city – or in *the* City, that is, Rome itself? Cinematic shortcuts usually involve a sweeping panoramic shot of iconic buildings such as columned temples, aqueducts, and an amphitheatre. Real-life Roman cities and towns might arise from the crudest beginnings, for example, military outposts such as Caerleon in Wales or Aquicum in Budapest. Even along the farthest frontiers familiar buildings would spring up: temples, baths, an amphitheatre, and a theatre. Initially meant for the soldiers or the inhabitants of a colony, these new urban centres grew to include marketplaces and shops along with housing. There's no one set paradigm for a Roman city, however, although the ones established as colonies especially in the West may have more of a 'flat-pack' sense of establishment than those older, sprawling cities found in the Eastern provinces.

In addition to bespoke colonial cities whose foundations were similar to the square-and-crossroads foundation of a military camp, the Romans might adapt indigenous infrastructure to accommodate their own buildings. The baths in Bath, for example, have clearly Celtic influences in their décor and temple. Likewise, many older cities in the Eastern provinces gained a Roman stamp amidst their own architecture in the form of aqueducts and circuses. Athens, for example, contains a number of Roman buildings established by Hadrian, including its music theatre; the remains of Corinth are Roman, not Greek, courtesy of Lucius Mummius levelling the place in 146 BCE (Cass. Dio, 21 (Zon. 9.31); Vell. Pat., 1.13.2). In fact, the Roman presence in terms of rebranding and rebuilding is so endemic in the Greek East that one has to come back to the West, that is, the islands off the coast of Italy, to find Classical Greek temples; elsewhere very few mainland Greek structures such as theatres remain 'unRomanised' (Epidaurus is one of the rare ones). Western cities demonstrate Rome's heterogeneity as well. Locals in the Western provinces would construct buildings, houses, roads, and monuments in emulation of their Roman masters. Such urban centres reflected provincial loyalty to the state, and, with luck, drew attention to a local strongman hoping to gain administrative privilege from the centre. So as you create your settings, consider how local culture might reshape Roman foundations and demonstrate the architectural crossroads of *Romanitas* and *barbaritas*. How do your provincials ape the metropolis? What monuments will the local movers and shakers create in imitation of the Caesars at the centre?

URBAN PLANNING AND THE FICTIONAL TOWN

Rome provides a template for emulation of an organic urban plan: it has been, of course, built upon, remodelled, and changed over the centuries. Pompeii and Herculaneum are freeze-framed, well-preserved and well-documented towns; De la Bedoyere's succinct *Cities of Roman Italy* (2010) is a good starting place for a survey of Pompeii, Herculaneum, and Ostia. Pompeii even features on Google Street View if you can't walk around an ancient site in person. Similarly, one could look at the remains of the Roman city in the modern town of Caerwent, Wales: amongst the houses and streets of the modern village are a partially uncovered forum, shops, houses, and a temple. Aquincum in Budapest is another substantial site largely excavated, and it provides a good layout of an outpost that developed in a thriving commercial town on the European frontier.

BLUEPRINTS AND CITY PLANNING

If you're looking for a template on construction and buildings to place in your city or town, you might start with David Macaulay's *City* (1974). Written by an architect with a background in ancient and medieval architecture, *City* begins with the basic cross-roads of a Roman settlement and fills up with the typical buildings that sign-post a Roman urban space. Macaulay grows his city over a period of two to three hundred years to reflect the evolving character of Roman identity as well as the Romans' ready absorption of outside cultures. Gorski and Packer's work (2015) on the Roman Forum complements Macaulay. They reconstruct the Roman Forum with scaled, digital plans, providing historical, architectural, and archae-ological context from the time of the Republic through to the end of the reign of Septimius Severus. For Pompeii, do have a look at the Pompeii Bibliography and Mapping Project. This site allows you to access the city on a phenomenal scale and is an ongoing project. *Curiasum Urbis et notitia de regionibus*, online at *Lacus Curtius* (http://penelope.uchicago.edu/Thayer/E/Gazetteer/Places/Europe/Italy/Lazio/Roma/Rome/_Texts/home.html) is a gazetteer of Rome that you can use to explore the different districts and neighbour-hoods of the city. A recent, comprehensive work is Carandini (2017), who has put together an atlas of the ancient city of Rome; you'll find here not only maps, photos, and 3D reconstructions but informa-tion on the latest scholarship on the topography of the city.

A useful contemporary source for city planning is Vitruvius's work on city planning and construction; recent editions of the text are lavishly illustrated. He will tell you everything you need to know about building a city, from construction materials (Book 2 on bricks, sand, lime, concrete), the machinery involved in civil engineering (Book 10), sourcing water and building aqueducts (Book 8), public spaces including the forum, entertainment buildings, and harbours (Book 5), private houses (Book 6), and gendering space in those houses (Book 7) amongst other topics.

FOUND A CITY OF CLAY, LEFT IT IN MARBLE ...

The blinding, pure white city that gets depicted in the blockbuster films would have baffled a contemporary visitor or inhabitant, as both Greek and the Roman architecture was garishly coloured. Buildings were painted, and often hung with tapestries and decorations of flowers and garlands for celebratory occasions. Many Roman statues, carvings, inscriptions, and structures still have bits of paint clinging to them to indicate colour. What we think of as empty-eyed statues wouldn't have been in antiquity, as hair, eye colour, and skin tones were painted on. The Ashmolean Museum in Oxford has a reproduction of the famous statue of Augustus Prima Porta as it might have appeared to a contemporary viewer. See the Smithsonian's article about Vinzenz Brinkmann (Gurewitsch, 2008), an archaeologist who has made eye-popping, colourful reproductions of Classical Greek statues. Similarly, Beard (2007) has a brief column on the subject, 'Were Ancient Statues Painted?'

CONSTRUCTION (AND DESTRUCTION)

Cities and towns were not static, and ongoing construction can and should be noted in a fictionalised Roman town or city. There's been plenty written on individual buildings and their fates over time as buildings suffered neglect, disuse, and rejuvenation at various points during our period. Hadrian rebuilt the Pantheon of Marcus Agrippa, for example (*HA, Hadr.* 19.10); Julius Caesar restored the forum and started a basilica (Suet., *Iul.* 10.1; Plut., *Caes.* 29.3) that Augustus finished (Aug., *RG* 20.3); Suetonius and Augustus himself talk about Augustus's building projects and restoration schemes (Suet., *Aug.* 29–30; Aug., *RG* 19.1–21). The 'life' of a particular structure or monument over time would lend itself to a dedicated story in the same way that Young's *Farewell Britannia* (2008) follows the fortunes of a family over four centuries in Roman Britain: for inspiration, check out Beard's short works on the Parthenon (2010) or the Colosseum (with Hopkins, 2011), for example.

Depending on the size and prosperity of your city, construction would be going on all the time. For example, a triumph or the *adventus* of a visiting dignitary might warrant new monuments. These might include a giant arch to celebrate a military victory, for example to Caesar and Fortune (Mart., 65.5), for the recovery of lost Eagles (Tac., *Ann.* 41.1), for a heroic general such as Scipio Africanus (Liv., 37.3.7), or for imperial triumph (Suet., *Claud.* 1.4). There might be victory columns, such as the ones dedicated to Trajan or Marcus Aurelius; columns also mark imperial divinity (*HA, Heliog.* 25.7). Maybe the city's fortunes are running low, and the only thing affordable might be a modest fountain such as the *nymphaeum* of Severus Alexander (*CIL*, VI.31892d.5; Amm. Mar., 15.3; Jord., 1.1.478). Monuments were intended to impress the visitor, amaze the tourists, and fill the locals with civic pride. City patrons, both men and women, also contributed new buildings and structures to their cities. For example, Livia paid for temples in Rome including to Concordia and the Porticus Livia (Ov., *Fast.* 6.637–648 and *Ars*1.71–72; Pliny, *NH* 1.5.9 – although Augustus provided the land: Suet., *Aug.* 29.4). Elsewhere, wealthy freedmen and freedwomen paid for the erection of monuments and public buildings to enshrine their memory; for example, Modia Quintia paid for a portico (L&F, no. 227: 192–193) and Eumachia dedicated a building to the local fullers' guild (L&F, no. 222: 191). *ROL* (vol. 4) has many inscriptions related to this type of civic euergetism (that is, related to civic munificence); Cornell and Lomas (2002) discuss civic patron in general, and Hemelrijk (2015) women patrons and donors in particular. Don't forget the more mundane decorations that proliferate in the city landscape: graffiti and advertising. There are plenty of examples throughout the Empire, especially Pompeii, military camps, and tourist attractions such as the singing statues of Memnon in Egypt. On the latter, see Callistratus's description *On the Statue of Memnon* (9.25ff), and on touristy emperors Septimius Severus (*HA, Sev.* 27.17.4).

The flipside of public remembrance was the *damnatio memoriae*, that is, visible and deliberate removal of one's existence from the public record. Examples include Torquatus, an enemy of Nero (Tac., *Ann.* 15.35) and Opimius (Cic., *Rep.* 1.3.6; cf. Cic., *Cael.* 30.71); other famous *damnationes* include that of Sejanus, Messalina, Domitian, and Geta (the brother of Caracalla). In such cases names were chiselled out of inscriptions, faces rubbed off from coins or paintings, and heads defaced or replaced on statues. Entire buildings might be razed as part of this process: the Colosseum was constructed on the gardens (Suet., *Vesp.* 9.1) that once formed Nero's *Domus Aurea* (Tac., *Ann.* 15.42; Suet., *Ner.* 31); Titus's baths (Suet., *Tit.* 7; Mart., *Spect.* 2), and later Trajan's baths (Paus., 5.12.6), were planted square on top of the house itself.

DOMESTIC SPACE

The Roman home, from the biggest and grandest to the smallest and humblest, is the *domus*, a term synonymous with the members of *familia*, or household, itself. The *domus* ranges from the smallest unit of physical space in Roma as well as the largest: the imperial *domus* became not only a model for the most humble of households but also represented Rome as a whole. Symbolically, a well-run and well-organised *domus* represented the order and hierarchy that the Romans valued. Everyone within the household knew his or her job and place; the home was governed by the authority of the *paterfamilias* and familial patron–client relationships. Space in a house could be public or private; its spaces were engendered. The contents and decoration of that space illustrated its use as well as reflecting the owner's status, responsibilities, and ambitions.

Working from the designs found in, for example, Vituvius (see Chapter 8), planning a large fictional villa or estate is fun; the floor plan for villas such as the larger houses in Pompeii, the Palace of Fishbourne in Sussex or the Roman Painted House in Dover, provide ideas for describing the stately home of a wealthy family in the city or out in the provinces. Most houses had small and dark rooms; even the mightiest of residences had fairly pokey rooms, lavishly painted for illusion of light and space. Going bang up the scale would be Nero's Golden Palace: built at public expense after the fire in Rome, the palace was not only meant to be the pinnacle of Roman might and wealth (it was to be open to the public) but also came to represent the excesses of Nero's demands for

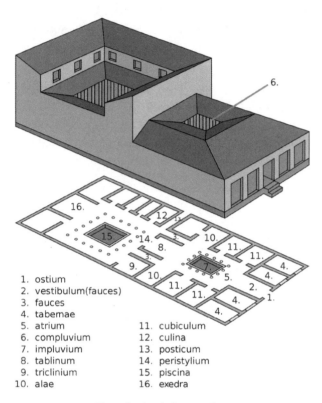

1. ostium
2. vestibulum(fauces)
3. fauces
4. tabernae
5. atrium
6. compluvium
7. impluvium
8. tablinum
9. triclinium
10. alae

11. cubiculum
12. culina
13. posticum
14. peristylium
15. piscina
16. exedra

5 Plan of a simple Roman *domus*

creature comforts. Once his private rooms were finished, he allegedly took one look at them and exclaimed, 'At last [I can] live like a human being!' (Suet., *Ner.* 31.2). Both Suetonius (*Ner.* 31) and Tacitus discuss the opulence, waste, and extravagance of the palace (Tac., *Ann.* 15.4.2), which has been recently excavated. It's in a terrible state, sadly, as other stuff was built on top of it directly after Nero's reign – deliberately, as the Flavians wished to bury Nero literally and figuratively.

HUMBLER HOMES

The majority of the population lived in cramped *insulae*, some of which are still standing in Pompeii. They can stand as high as five storeys and have shops and services on the ground floors. These flats would have been dark inside, partly because windows might be small and covered with grilles (see Lighting, below) and partly because the buildings were so close together. Martial, for example, quips about being able to reach through the window and touch his neighbour's house (Mart., 1.86). There wouldn't be much in the way of amenities – no indoor plumbing, no source of heat, no kitchens. Rarely did *insulae* have any access to land onsite or even what we'd think of as an allotment for kitchen gardens. The average city-dweller, especially in the larger cities such as Rome, would be completely dependent on markets for food, services, and material goods No wonder Juvenal's and Martial's satires and epigrams are filled with laments about exchanging city life for a small place in the country, no matter how mean (e.g. Mart., 3.52) – *if* you could afford to get out of town.

DECORATION

The décor and public rooms of a house spoke volumes about how the Romans viewed their place and identity in the hierarchy of Roman society. What they put on display sent messages about their wealth, status, and accomplishments to visitors who might include family, friends, or clients. The frescos and paintings at Pompeii, for example, tell us about the interests, education, and accomplishments of not only the men in the family but also the women. In *The Satyricon*, Trimalchio brags about his possessions and holds them up for his guests to see and marvel at (e.g. Petron., *Sat.* 33.34); Tiberius decorated his walls of his sea-cave triclinium with stories of the *Odyssey* (Tac., *Ann.* 59.1); Hadrian's villa at Tibur is a mishmash of styles created from his travels around his Empire, and viewing his home – *the Domus* – gave the guest a representation of the Empire as a whole (*HA, Hadr.* 26.5). Walls and floors were the platform for most of the décor – frescos and paintings on the walls, and mosaics mainly on the floor. This artwork can be simply decorative or grandly applied to create an illusion of space in the smaller rooms of houses. To make rooms look bigger, the Romans used *trompe l'oeil* images: you'll find inspiration from sources on Pompeii and Herculaneum. Underneath the modern streets of Dover there's also the Painted Roman House, which houses some of the best surviving wall paintings outside of Italy – an example of what's going on in terms of copying Roman style and keeping up with the centre even way up on the northern frontiers. Many floor mosaics survive from across the Empire and run the gamut from patterns and geometric designs to complex artwork featuring stories from myth, sporting events, animals, food. Fishbourne is famous for its mosaic floors, where the craftsmanship ranges from exquisite to amateur (sometimes in the same room on the same design). See Cunliffe (1998) for a short introduction to the villa and its floor mosaics. The Villa Romana del Casale (and work on the Piazza Armerina, in Sicily), a bit later than our period (fourth century), is famous for its mosaics and frescos of sport, hunts, and athletics (including the so-called 'Bikini Girls'); Wilson's study of the villa (1983) will provide you with an English text and illustrations of its layout.

If you seek a 'Roman IKEA' then have a sift on museum websites for furniture and furnishings in their collections – frequently only the best material is on public display, but research collections will include images of items in storage. Archaeological remains and museum collections of both artefacts and artworks which depict household goods are also go-to sources for household furnishings. Pompeii and Herculaneum frequently pop up for the organic goods that survive from this era. The Museum at Naples has most of the material excavated from the houses that wasn't stolen by gap-year aristocrats and antiquities collectors between the seventeenth and the twentieth century. Sources on Roman Egypt as well as Roman Britain will also have other perishable goods from opposite ends of the Empire that survive from our period. The Museum of London has an exhibition on what typical rooms in a modest Roman house would have looked like furnished.

Enjoy decorating your houses: you can match the contents to your characters' economic status as well as the period. It is true that valuable household items were passed down through the generations, but avoid accidental time travelling ... the dramatic moment in *Gladiator* when Russell Crowensius chooses a helmet to hide his face prior to performing in front of the emperor is a bit jarring when one sees that amongst the choices is the Sutton Hoo helmet – a magnificent piece of Anglo-Saxon art from about three hundred or so years after the events in the film.

PERILS OF URBAN LIVING

Augustus reported that he found Rome a city of clay and left it a city of marble (Suet., *Aug.* 28.3) – a majestic transformation, but also a practical one, as marble doesn't burn as readily as clay. Fire was a common problem in the more crowded quarters of the city due to the close proximity of the *insulae* (Cass. Dio, 66.24; Juv., 3.194–202; Tac., *Ann.* 15–64), the use of braziers for light, heat, and cooking, and a lack of a professional fire-fighting department in the modern sense. Fire-fighting was one of the civic management duties of the *aediles*, but privateers could profit easily from the disaster (Juv., 14. 306–308). Crassus, for example, exploited his position to extort fire insurance money out of people. He'd show up with his 'fire brigade' at a burning house, offering to buy the property in exchange for saving the owner's possessions. Consequently he ended up owning a substantial amount of prime real estate in downtown Rome (Plut., *Crass.* 2.3–5). A couple of generations later, Nero was accused of starting the fire of 64 CE as a means of clearing out a section of town in which to construct his Golden Palace (Suet., *Ner.* 37.1–3). Profiting off disaster was commonplace enough for Juvenal to remark witheringly, 'Then we weep on behalf of the City, then we hate fire; as it burns, comes one rushing up who offers marble and collects donations' (Juv. 3.214–16). He remarks that the wealthiest seem mysteriously to gain even better things as a result of the disaster; the poet muses on such men as potential arsonists for profit (220–223). The Great Fire of 64 (Tac., *Ann.* 15.38) and the fire of 80 (Suet., *Tit.* 8.4) are indicative of how quickly fire could spread through the *insulae* that jammed the streets; fire jumped quickly from building to building across narrow ways, and those who wanted to help were hampered by the cramped streets. Tacitus and Suetonius note that, despite his reputation for strumming a lyre while Rome burned (Suet., *Ner.* 37.2–3; Tac., *Ann.* 15.39) (and hints that he might have been instrumental in its ignition, Cass. Dio, 62.16.1–3, 37.2; Tac., *Ann.* 15.44), they remark that Nero passed legislation to create preventive measures against future fires (*Ann.* 15.43; Suet., *Ner.* 26.11). For example, he cleared out the *insulae* and slums to try to widen the streets to make fire-fighting easier and drew up codes about building materials to make the *insulae* more fire-proof. The Emperor Titus was praised for paying out of his own purse sums to help rehouse those left homeless by the conflagration during his reign (Suet., *Tit.* 9.3–4; Cass. Dio, 66.24.3–4).

Another urban problem was street crime, exacerbated by the highest authorities themselves as they allowed their own children to indulge in antisocial behaviour. (There was no 'police force'; for discussion of crime and protection, and the *vigiles*, see Chapter 4.) One aspect of male (especially aristocratic) youth culture was being allowed to harass people in the streets with no consequences except a shrug and a 'just being lads' attitude in the face of complaints. Hence a key plot point in Terence's comedy *Hecyra* is a young man sowing his wild oats by raping any foolish girl caught out after dark, yet abandoning his fiancée when she herself is attacked and becomes pregnant (there's a happy ending because, huzzah, it turns out that he's the young man who actually raped her). The Emperor Nero also enjoyed running about with thugs:

> As soon as twilight was past, he'd put on a cap or a wig and go to the taverns or wander around the streets playing pranks which were not, however, without danger: he used to beat up men who were returning home from supper; he'd stab anyone who put up resistance and throw them into the sewers. He even broke into the shops and robbed them, setting up a 'commissary' [*quintana*] in the imperial palace – where he'd divvy up the lot he'd grabbed, sell it at auction, and squander the profits. (Suet., *Ner.* 26.1)

The thrill came from the risk; Nero gave up the mugger's lifestyle when the senator-husband of one of his victims beat him up. After that he travelled only with protectors who hung back at a discreet distance and would step in if he seemed threatened (*Ner.*, 26.1).

Violence was part and parcel of Roman street life: 'Even during the day [Nero] would be carried privately to the theatre in a sedan, and from the top part of the proscenium he'd watch the brawls of the pantomimic actors and encourage them. When they came to blows and beat each other up with stones and broken benches, the emperor himself threw many missiles at the people and even cracked a praetor's skull' (Suet., *Ner.* 26.2). Juvenal also complained about endemic street crime: 'If you go out to dinner without making a will, they'll think of you as merely careless, oblivious of those tragic events that occur: there are as many ways to die as there are open windows watching you when you go by at night' (3.272–275), 'for after the houses are locked up, when the shop shutters are chained and sealed, when everywhere is silent, there will still be someone around to rob you' (3.302–304). Juvenal likens Rome to a hunting ground for thieves similar to a big game preserve (3.308).

Other complaints about city life include excessive noise day and night, the time when deliveries were made and the streets filled with carts and workers: 'Many a sick man has died from insomnia here ... for which lodgings allow you a good night's sleep? You have to be mighty rich to sleep in the City. Indeed – that's the source of our illness, the constant traffic in the narrow, twisting streets, and the swearing of the driver at his halted cattle would snatch sleep away from Drusus [Emperor Claudius]' (Juv., 3.232–238). Living in the city was costly, whether expenses came in the shape of extortionate rents or high prices in exchange for shoddy services: 'All of Rome comes with a price!' lamented Juvenal (3.183). He complains, 'It's hard to climb the [political] ladder when limited personal funds block your talents, but in Rome the effort is even harder. It's expensive, wretched lodgings; it's expensive, the bellies of slaves; it's expensive, a meagre supper' (3.165–168). Another source of grumbling was immigrants, says Juvenal – 'I can't stand a Rome full of Greeks!' – and then goes on to complain that no one in Rome seems actually to *be* from Rome (3.61–81). And finally, there was even danger from above; remember, most houses had no indoor plumbing 'So make a wish and a wretched prayer on your way that they will be content to empty their full chamber-pots over you' (3.276–277). According to the aristocratic poets, these and other issues are why the sensible person made an escape to the country, and why, as devotees of the cult of the land, (aristocratic) Romans lauded and praised country living.

BASIC UTILITIES: LIGHTING

It was rare to have glass windows in a Roman building – glassmaking was an expensive process. Smaller windows might be covered in opaque shale or mica to let dull light in, but were often open and covered with iron grilles. Natural light came in via the gardens and *atria* (if you were wealthy enough to have a house that large), but most of the interior rooms of houses, whether grand or mean, were lit by lamps, one of the most common artefacts found throughout the Roman world. Lamps were usually oil-fuelled and ranged from tiny nightlights to multi-flamed 'chandeliers'. They might be plain, mass-produced and utilitarian, or highly decorated. Outside the house, there was no street lighting but what you carried with you. Anyone who went out at night was taking his or her chances unless he or she had bodyguards and slaves to light the way with torches: says Juvenal in his third satire: 'Me, the thief hates, as I go home by the light of the moon, as usual, or in the short-lived light of a candle, whose wick I take care of and regulate' (3.286–287).

On lights and lamps, you might start with simply a catalogue of lamps for inspiration: suggested works include Sussman (2012), Frecer (2015), and Bailey (1972). Lamps abound in museum collections, so have a look on their websites under research information and image catalogues.

BASIC UTILITIES: HEATING

In Italy and Greece the weather varied from hot in summer to mild and rainy in winter. When needed, interior heating came from braziers and stoves (hence the great danger – and common occurrence – of fire in *insulae*, as heat and light sources got knocked over). Posh dwellings and baths had hypocausts in certain rooms – raised floors underneath which either fires burned or hot water was channelled as part of the heating system. Hypocausts didn't cover the entire house as they had to be (laboriously) maintained by hand by slaves and servants. Other *villae*, especially in the northern climes, benefited from naturally occurring hot springs – the later Roman poet and letter-writer Sidonius complained to friends if he were sent as envoy to a villa that had no springs or hot baths. Hypocausts were costly to install and maintain in private dwellings; the state maintained the ones found in the public baths. You can recognise their remains on Roman sites because of the stacks of flat bricks that supported the floor above, lifting the room's floor up and away from the hot air or water channels. Ready sources for heating and how hypocausts work include Macaulay's *City* as well as Book 10 (especially sections 1, 2, and 4) of Vitruvius on engineering and architecture.

SANITATION AND WATER SUPPLY

Spending time in the public baths and latrines was all part of one's daily social activities whether one was rich or poor. Much action can take place at these locations: political intrigue, murder plots, diplomatic missions. Frontinus's work (*De Aquae Ductu Urbis Romae* or 'On Aqueducts') is an engineer's dream, discussing pipe diameters, wells, and adjutages. He describes in minute detail repairs and costs affecting the running of the aqueducts and sewers in Rome based on hours that he spent combing through imperial records, receipts, and laws pertaining to water regulation. You also learn about how people steal from the pipes and aqueducts by diverting the water channels (Front., *Aq.* 2.97) and the exciting tasks borne by the water commissioners. Don't rely on him for accurate numbers about how much water the channels and pipes actually delivered, however; until the invention of fluid mechanics, no one could provide accurate statistics. If you really need to know how Frontinus fudged his numbers (and *loads* of academic writing wrestles with his numbers and where he went wrong), see Rushkin (link in the bibliography). Appreciate Frontinus for his record of the detailed levels of bureaucracy and complexities involved in keeping the city watered. A modern survey on civic plumbing is Hodge (2002), who looks at everything on bringing water supplies into the city – water sources, aqueducts, designing and supplying the water channels, distributing water through the urban centre, wells, and finally where it all drains away in the sewers.

Speaking of sewers, and the fascination everyone seems to have with sponges on sticks, very little has actually been written on toilets and waste until fairly recently. Pompeii to the rescue again, partly because so much of the city is intact, but also because the study of sanitation is an archaeological task. On the subject of human waste and sanitation, check out Hobson's (2009) survey on facilities mainly in Pompeii and Britain (where most examples survive) – public toilets for civilians, military latrines, and private toilets in homes. Hobson includes loads of illustrations and a discussion of the kinds of bits and pieces found down in the sewers. A more recent survey by Koloski-Ostrow (2015) complements Hobson. She provides a general introduction to sanitation in Italy using the best-known cities as case studies (Rome, Pompeii, Herculaneum, Ostia), and looks at the nuts and bolts of the physical aspects of latrines, sewers and sanitation from the archaeological record and literary sources on Roman hygiene practices, status, and sanitation. The final chapter is a bonanza of contemporary references to toilets and human waste (production of, uses of, jokes about, and so forth) in written and material sources.

WEATHER AND CLIMATE

Weather and climate affect travel conditions and also show provincial Romans' defiance of the elements in their pursuit of emulating the centre: a good case study is the modern mock-up of the gardens, outdoor *triclinium*, and fishpond at Fishbourne Palace in West Sussex – a striking contrast can be found in January between beautiful and typically Roman architecture and grey, chilly British winter skies. As you consider your forecast, you're including a diverse area from Britain to Spain, to North Africa to the Middle East, plus the Mediterranean basin which was mild and wet in winter, and hot and dry in summer, and subject to the occasional chance of volcanic eruption. It's tempting to do a study of current weather and forecasts in the area in which you have your characters living, but keep in mind that there have been various climate changes and indeed topographical changes over the past two thousand years.

The modern idea of weather forecasting is a product of the British, the barometer, and the telegraph in the nineteenth century. In antiquity, 'weather' forecasts included prodigies and natural phenomena. Contemporary sources include Greek writers (scientists and philosophers): Aristotle's *Meteorologica*, and Theophrastus of Eresus, and selections in Irby-Massie and Keyser (2001). Hellenistic Greece overlaps the beginning of our period, and from 200 BCE Greek science and teaching were becoming more and more popular in Rome as part of the Hellenisation of Rome. Other meteorological sources include Pliny the Elder's *Natural History* and Seneca's *Natural Questions*. Sources on prodigies and general natural weirdness include the miscellanies of Cornelius Nepos and Arian; Pausanias and Strabo's works on travel and geography include bizarre travellers' tales and marvellous sights from the ends of the world that would be useful in your auspices-dependent society.

RELATIONSHIP BETWEEN TOWN AND COUNTRY

The Romans loved their cities, but they elegised the countryside. Roman literature on rural life is frequently idealised by contemporary authors who viewed the life of a 'gentleman farmer' as a virtuous ideal. *Rusticus*, associated with country living and the origin of the modern word 'rustic', derives from a word that means 'outside the city'. Escape from the noise, crowds, and stink of the city to a bucolic villa or hideaway in the country was a common theme with Juvenal (Satire 3) and Martial (e.g.1.86, 4.64, 4.66). Aristocrats regarded living in the countryside as an idyllic exercise, but they viewed the native inhabitants – either the actual poor who scratched out a living from the soil or simply local folk who lived in towns and provinces away from Rome – as ignorant wretches no matter how upscale or successful they eventually became. It was a double standard: a heroic farmer such as the legendary Cincinnatus was seen as a simple man (albeit an aristocrat and an ex-consul) willing to take up the sword to protect his land (Liv., 3.12, 26–29), but provincials were frequently the target of mockery. One sees examples of this in such tales as the rustic encounters of aristocratic Lucius in Apuleius's *Metamorphoses* or of Apuleius himself during his witchcraft trial in *Apologia* as he plays up to the yokels on his jury. Even emperors weren't exempt: Hadrian had a hard time at winning over the Senate because he was born in Spain, and Claudius was mocked for his affinity towards the Gauls (he had been born in a military camp in Lugdonum).

Aristocratic men, forbidden by law to work as businessmen or in trade, defined their wealth and status by how much land they had, and land ownership was described as an idyllic pursuit for the gentleman. As Cicero noted, all a man needed was his library and his garden: '*Si hortum in bibliotheca habes, de erit nihil*' (*Fam.* 12.25). By aristocratic standards, of course, 'gardens' either occupied space in one's villa or might encompass an enormous estate called a *latifundium*. Between the third century BCE and the second century CE entire books were written on the joys of land ownership: for example, Vergil's *Georgics* are pastoral poems celebrating the beauty of the land and the idyllic pastime of being a gentleman farmer. When the younger set of aristocrats became 'Hellenised' during the third and second centuries BCE, conservatives such as Cato the Elder felt that they had lost sight of the old Roman virtue of conservative simplicity. These attitudes are found in a long work he produced on the ideal estate (*De Agricultura*). He, as well as two other writers, Columella (*De Re Rustica*) and Varro (*De Re Rustica*), wrote treatises about managing an estate and what, ideally, would be found on a large Roman farm. These tracts contain much information about how land ought to be set out, what crops to grow, animals to husband, equipment to keep on hand, and how to acquire, maintain, and treat one's slaves. Detailed as they are, these works might be considered as much as intellectual exercises that reflect the Roman love of order and organisation as much as they describe how to run a large estate. These authors emphasise the *Romanness* inherent in land management, even as they emulate Greek writers who wrote about the countryside from a moralistic point of view. The rustic life, they believed, was in in tune with nature and sufficed people to better themselves. This sort of life lay closer to the ultimate source of all bounty and peace, filled with all the good foods and sources of health to lead (the rich) to a long life.

How these estates were *actually* run is a completely different matter: unfortunately, little survives to describe day-to-day running of the *latifundia*. One useful source for the hassles of being a landlord and aristocratic property owner is the collection of letters by Pliny the Younger. The governor of Bithynia during the reign of Trajan in the early second century CE, Pliny owned and managed properties both close by and at a distance from his own patch. His letters refer to buying and selling property, the bureaucratic tasks interrupted so that he could travel and inspect his properties, and the problems he had with tenants (especially when rent was overdue) (see, for example, *Epist.* 1.24, 2.4, 3.19, 7.11, and 10.54). Also surviving are a pair of land registers. They describe different areas at two different points in time of our period, but they are indicative of large estate management at the hands of the freedmen overseers and the slaves on the property. One is the Table of Veleia, also called the *lex Rubia* (dating from around the mid-first century BCE) and the other *Ligures Baebiani* (from a settlement of Ligurians in Samnium, Italy, in the second century BCE). Both documents concern *alimenta* schemes (that is, government programmes of food distribution) and indicate loans, property values, and owners in these two areas. The Latin text is found in the *Corpus Inscriptiones Latinae* (Baebiani, *CIL*, IX 1455; and Veleia, *CIL*, XI 1.147). To complement these registers, you might find useful a set of surviving peasants' contracts from North Africa. These are inscriptions from Ain-el-Jemala and Ain Wassel (c. 117–138 CE), and Suk-el-Khmis (c. 180 CE) which illustrate the need for regulation to prevent abuse from the overseers as well as the owners of these estates (L&R, 2: 97–99). Flach (1978) is still considered to have the best (German) translations (and notes) on these three inscriptions (see also *CAH*, 11: 531–534; the Latin text can be found in Smallwood, 2011).

THE IDYLLIC LIFE OF A COUNTRY GENTLEMAN

'Our friend Faustinus's Baian farm, Bassus, does not occupy an ungrateful expanse of broad land, laid out with useless myrtle groves, sterile plane-trees, and clipped box-rows, but rejoices in a real unsophisticated country scene. Here close-pressed heaps of corn are crammed into every corner, and many a cask is redolent with wine of old vintages. Here, after November, when winter is at hand, the rough vine-dresser brings in the ripened grapes; the savage bulls bellow in the deep valley, and the steer, with forehead still unarmed, yearns for the fight. The whole muster of the farmyard roams at large, the screaming goose, the spangled peacock, the bird which derives its name from its red wings, the spotted partridge, the speckled fowls of Numidia, and the pheasants of the impious Colchians; the proud cocks caress their Rhodian mates, and the turrets resound with the murmur of pigeons. On this side mourns the ringdove, on that the wax-coloured turtle-dove; the greedy swine follow the apron of the bailiff's wife, and the tender lamb bleats after its well-filled mother. Young house-bred slaves, sleek as milk, surround the cheerful fire, and piles of wood blaze near the joyous Lares. The steward does not, through inactivity, grow pale with enervating ease, nor waste oil in anointing himself for wrestling, but sets crafty nets for greedy thrushes, or draws up fish captured with the tremulous line, or brings home deer caught in the hunter's toils' (Mart., 3.58.1–28, D.R. Shackleton Bailey, *Martial: Epigrams*, Cambridge, MA: Harvard University Press, 1993, pp. 227–229).

AND THE REALITIES OF BEING A LANDLORD ...

'I am detained here because I find it absolutely necessary to let my farms on longer leases than usual, and have to make arrangements accordingly, which will require me to form new plans. For during the last five years the arrears have increased in spite of the great abatements I have made, and for that reason, many of my tenants are now not taking the slightest trouble to reduce their debts, inasmuch as they despair of being able to meet the whole of them. They even seize and consume the produce of their farms, as though they had quite made up their minds not to stint themselves in any respect. I must therefore grapple with this evil, which is growing worse daily, and find some remedy for it. One way of so doing would be to let the farms not for rent but for a proportion of the produce, and in that case, I should have to appoint some of my household as overseers to see the work was done and to take care of my share of the produce. I think there can be no better form of rent than the produce of the soil, the climate, and the seasons. This would require great honesty, sharp eyes, and many pairs of hands, but the experiment has to be made, and now that the disease has taken a firm hold, some change in the treatment must be tried' (Pliny the Younger to Paulinus, explaining why he must miss Paulinus's first day as provincial consul, 107 CE, *Epist.* 9.37, trans. J.B. Firth, from www.attalus.org/info/pliny.html, accessed 23 July 2018).

TRAVEL

Although wealthy aristocrats had estates out in the country, they were often politicians who didn't dare to leave the urban centre during the summer (when elections were held), or they were lawyers (who didn't want to miss important cases), except perhaps in the early spring when

the Senatorial calendar was lighter. When they did escape to the country, it was to flee from the heat (as found in comments from Cicero's
letters, Juvenal's and Martial's satires, and later letters of Sidonius) or
to act in their capacity as landlords, usually in September (during the
Ludi Romani, a religious festival with games, held 12–14 September) and
October (during the vintage harvest). Augustus made autumn travel
easier by reorganising the administrative rules regarding how many
Senators were needed for quora (Suet., *Aug.* 35.3; cf. Cass. Dio, 55.3.1–4
where Augustus fixes the dates when the Senate meets), but still most
were stuck in Rome during the hottest months. When a bigwig did get
away to his holiday home, he might stroll in peaceful gardens as Hadrian
did at Tivoli (*HA, Hadr.* 26.5), or as Cicero did at Arpium (*Lig.* 2.1 and
Att. 16.8.2), or they might write, reflect, or hunt. Travellers with more
leisure time, such as poets, were bound by no calendar, could take off
when they wanted to. Horace, for example, spent as much time as possible on his Sabine Hill estate (Suet., *Hor.*), and he and Vergil (Suet., *Verg.*
13) spent their winters on estates in Campania. Students also travelled
during their breaks from school; Aulus Gellius reflects on his escapades
with fellow students at Cephisia (Aul. Gell., *NA* 2.1–2), or when they
went to Naples to escape Rome's summer heat (15.1). Sources for aristocratic holidays include, for example, the letters of Cicero, Pliny the
Younger, and Sidonius Apollonius, or one of three surviving accounts
of personal journeys (see below). These sources rarely mention wives
or children, so it is unknown whether families travelled together, or
whether women and children were sent out of town on their own. For
the most part, however, the people who spent most of the time in such
posh holiday homes were the ones who maintained them during the
master's absence.

Some travelled either as part of their work or looking for work. These
include, for example, soldiers (on military manoeuvres and travelling on
leave), traders, and migrants trying their luck elsewhere. There were also
those on the road who worked for the government. The imperial post
travelling on the *cursus publicus*, for example, stopped at *mansiones*,
or stations, where they could change their horses. Others were VIPs

carrying diplomas of immunity and right of free passage and lodgings, endorsed by the local governor or even by the emperor himself. These documents were good until that emperor died, then such persons might be in a quandary if they were still on the road. For example, whose was the legal signature on these documents during the Year of Four Emperors (CE 69)?

Travel by road could be tiring and dangerous – there were robbers and brigands; inns were seen as dangerous, dirty places where unwary travellers were robbed (cf. Sid. Apoll., *Epist.* 3.2.3, 8.12.1). To compensate for this, Varro recommends farmers on land bordering roads to consider building a little hotel or even a restaurant on the property to lodge travellers safely, for a little extra cash (*Rust.* 1.23–25). Aristocrats could bunk with buddies at their country villas; this was good news for the friends of Cicero, who owned at least six. When travelling on the Viae Appia and Latinia, the orator could stop off at Arpinum (*Leg.* 2.1), Sinuessa (*Att.* 10.42.1; *Fam.* 13.20), Minturnae (*Fam.*,10.2.1), or Tarracina (*Att.*7.5.3), for example. One of Pliny the Younger's longer letters is a loving description of his country villa and his activities there (5.6). Such homes and retreats were bad news, however, for the servants, for whom life on these estates was no holiday. Juvenal describes slaves who were forced to sweep dog shit out of slovenly villas ahead of guests (6.59–66). Sidonius raves about the good times at the homes of his friends whilst his servants were forced to dig a bath (*Epist.*, 2.9.8), to run ahead of the travellers to clear the roads in gangs (5.13.1), to pitch their tents for them (4.8.2), and to catch breakfast while the travellers had a lie-in (4.3.24).

The best way to travel on the road was the slowest – by litter, accompanied by servants and slaves who could protect their masters – but others travelled by horse or mule, in four-wheeled carriages or sportier two-wheeled models. In theory, a traveller could sleep in the four-wheeled wagon, which covered about twenty-four miles a day, but, given that wheels were wooden and shock-absorbers non-existent, it wouldn't have been a very restful nap. Horace travelled with his pals around 37 BCE via carriage, getting into scrapes and drinking their way from Rome to Brindisi, on an embassy headed by Maecenas, Augustus's later minister for cultural affairs (Hor., *Sat.* 15). Horace's group met with the usual ups and downs of tourists. Some days were full of good travel and good fun; other days meant bad weather, dicky tummies, and a girl who promised to meet the poet for drinks, but stood him up (*Sat.* 1.5.82–83). Despite his complaints, Horace was quite lucky his group wasn't robbed on the trip back to Rome – four-wheeled carriages headed back to the City were prey as robbers knew that they'd be loaded with food and goods.

In addition to Horace's road trip, there are also two other real-life 'travel diaries' that survive from across our period, which are useful not only for travel times and conditions but also for descriptions of vehicles and baggage. One of these is the journey of Aelius Aristides, a Greek orator (Ael. Ar., *Orat.* 27.1–8) who travelled as part of the Second Sophistic. These were a group of orators-cum-entertainers who travelled around on the back roads of Asia Minor, telling stories to entertain one another while on their diplomatic journeys during the second century CE. His works are not readily available online in English, but they have been published as part of the Loeb series; the tale you want is found in his oration that covers his trip from Smyrna to Pergamum around 165 CE to take the cure at the Temple of Aesclepius (*Orat.*, 27).

The other account comes from Theophanes, a Roman official who travelled on official business from Egypt to Antioch and back. He is the original 'dad driver' whose relentless pace on the journey must have been a real trial of friendship to his companions. He's a little later than our period (his journey was some time in the early fourth century), but it is an example of how fast one could move across the land on imperial business and the efficacy of the imperial post during the reign (306–337) of Constantine. An older version of his account was published by Hunt and Roberts (1911) or you can read it in the summary by Casson (1994).

TRAVEL TIMES, MAPS, AND SOURCES FOR GUIDES

Casson's *Travel in the Ancient World* (1994) is an accessible survey of travel, lodgings, and tourism in the Classical world; the first section considers travel in the Classical Greek era, but the majority of the book focuses on Rome. Casson's style is conversational, but the notes are diligent in providing the original contemporary sources. An updated study and bibliography on this topic are much needed.

Travel times varied depending on the condition of the roads, one's purpose, and one's companions. The average, based on the texts above, is about twenty miles a day – these sample travellers managed to hoof it as much as fifty miles in a day on imperial business or as little as fourteen on a leisurely trip. Rome to Bridisium could be covered in about seven days, but in times of emergency the speed of the couriers was impressive: the news of the mutiny on the Rhine in 69 CE reached Rome in about a week, an average of 150 miles a day for the messenger (Casson, 1974: 188).

Things to think about here include road conditions (and perhaps the more perilous sea travel), travelling along the roads as tourists or on official business. Casson covers Roman roads and construction (debunking the traditionally held, somewhat erroneous views put forth in television documentaries and elementary classrooms), travel times, different types of inns and lodgings, and information on tourist sites, maps, and itineraries. He summarises key travel texts from our period – miscellaneous surviving itineraries, the major works of Pausanias and Strabo, and the Peutinger Table. Other immediate sources on Roman roads tend to focus on roads in Britain or Italy and include the Shire books, aimed at a non-academic, general audience who intend to walk or visit the roads (in person or virtually): see, for example, Davies (2008) and Bagshawe (2000). Much older is Stillwell (1981); the text has been superseded by later discoveries, but the maps and photos are still useful references.

There were milestones on all of the Roman roads – the most famous source for these is the Peutinger Table, a medieval copy of a map of the Roman world c. 100 CE – it lists the roads, cities, points of interest, lodging, and a host of other things (Casson discusses it generally). The *Periplus Maris Erythraei* (*Circumnavigation of the Red Sea*) is a first-century CE manual of sea and trade routes from the east and into the Roman Empire through Red Sea ports. Casson has written on the *Periplus* (1991), presenting the text with commentary well worth chasing up from the library. Complement your study here with Sidebotham (2011), whose professional life was inspired by reading about the *Periplus* as a young scholar. His work is an extensive but accessible case study of one of these major Roman sea-ports (Berenike) along this route.

BUILDING A ROAD

'But he [Gaius Gracchus, 160/153 – 121 BCE] busied himself most earnestly with the construction of roads, laying stress upon utility, as well as upon that which conduced to grace and beauty. For his roads were carried straight through the country without deviation, and had pavements of quarried stone, and substructures of tight-rammed masses of sand. Depressions were filled up, all intersecting torrents or ravines were bridged over, and both sides of the roads were of equal and corresponding height, so that the work had everywhere an even and beautiful appearance. In addition to all this, he measured off every road by miles [the Roman mile falls a little short of eight furlongs] and planted stone pillars in the ground to mark the distances. Other stones, too, he placed at smaller intervals from one another on both sides of the road, in order that equestrians might be able to mount their horses from them and have no need of assistance' (Plut., *GG* 7, trans. Bernadotte Perrin, Plutarch, *Lives*, vol. 10, Cambridge, MA: Harvard University Press, 1921, p. 213).

GETTING DIRECTIONS

Roman streets did have names, although directions might be provided only by description. For example, if you were sending a letter to someone, you might give the name of the person and a description of his house. If you wanted to make sure a lost (or runaway) slave was returned to you, you put on his slave collar your name as owner and a vague description of where you lived (with luck near or on a main street or near some well-known landmark). The Romans knew that this wasn't the most effective system, and they played it up in their comedies. For example, in Terence's play *Adelphi* (573–585), Demea just wants to find someone's house:

SYRUS   I don't know the guy's name, but I know the place where he lives.

DEMEA Then tell me the place.

SYRUS   You know the portico down here, just by the marketplace?

DEMEA How do I not know it?

SYRUS   Go straight past it, right up that street; when you get up there, there's a downhill slope right in front of you. Go straight down that. Past that is a little shrine on this side. Nearby is a little alleyway.

DEMEA Which alleyway?

SYRUS   The one nearby a big fig tree.

DEMEA I know that one.

SYRUS   Go through there.

DEMEA But that alley isn't a thoroughfare.

SYRUS   Oh yeah, that's true – Cuh! You must think I'm mental! My bad. Turn round and go back to the portico. Indeed, that'll be a much more direct route and less chance of getting lost. You know the house of ol' rich Cratinus?

DEMEA I know ...

SYRUS When you get past this, turn left, then go straight down the street. When you get to the temple of Diana, go right. Before you get to the city gate, just by the reservoir, there's a bakery – opposite there's a factory. There you go.

URBAN COLLECTIVES

Castellum (plural castella)

A general term that might cover a fort, fortress, or fortlet. These turned into fortified towns out on the frontiers; hence the many modern British -chester, -cester, and -caster place names.

Civitas (plural civitates)

This can refer both to an organised urban community and its surrounding territory, and to the populace itself, that is, the collective of the citizens (cives) inhabiting the space, and bound together by the same laws, institutions, and customs. The Romans also used the term to describe citizenship (specifically Roman citizenship) itself.

Colonia (plural coloniae)

A Roman colony of citizens or allies. It usually has an air of newness about it as either it's made up of people sent deliberately to establish the town or it's a retirement community created for former soldiers. There will be more of these in the West and North Africa than in the Eastern provinces. For a general, though older, discussion of the relationship between Rome and its coloniae (usually military retirement camps) see Smith (1875)'s description at Penelope online (link in bibliography), especially as a means to keep an eye on conquered people; this work cites references from Livy and Strabo on this Roman practice.

Municipium (plural municipia)

These were free cities in Italy, comprised of the Italian tribes whom the Romans conquered and were farther removed than the federated states and towns. Residents might receive the allowance of half-citizenship (which granted them tax relief, but also obliged them to serve in the army). *Municipia* could become full colonies in due time; they were permitted to maintain their own languages, laws, and customs. They were mainly answerable to Rome in foreign affairs.

Oppidum (plural *oppida*)

A walled town, usually in Italy; sometimes a protected town in the provinces, a place of sanctuary.

Vicus (plural *vici*)

A country village or hamlet; it might be a county seat out in the provinces. It could also be a cluster of houses and thus refer to a particular neighbourhood or street of associated houses within a larger town or city. *Vici* might form local administrative authorities within a city or town – the term is similar to 'neighbourhood' in that sense.

Urbs (plural *urbes*)

Used to refer specifically to the City of Rome (with a capital 'U') but can also refer to any major, large city. A capital city of a province. As with *civitates*, the *urbs* can be the physical place or the political entity of the city.

PUBLIC BUILDINGS AND SPACES

Not every city or town will have all of these buildings and structures. A number of these buildings can be multi-purpose – temples could house administrative records (e.g. the Temple of Saturn in Rome); a palace could also be open to the public and filled with monuments and park space (e.g. Nero's plan for his Golden House).

Ager publicus

Public grazing land – its appropriation by the aristocrats and then the state during the era of the Gracchan reforms caused rather a big stink – see Plutarch's *Life of Tiberius Gracchus* and *Life of Gaius Gracchus*.

Amphitheatre

An open, oval or circular building constructed from earthworks, wood, or concrete (often façaded with marble) with a central floor-space, surrounded by tiers of seats for spectators. These were sites for public display, entertainment, criminal punishment. Nearly four hundred amphitheatres sat across the empire, most of them in the west.

Baths and public latrines

Cramped houses rarely had decent sanitation. Public baths could be lavishly equipped with cold, warm, and hot baths; public latrines were also great hubs of social activity.

Brothels

Is it true that there is always a brothel near a library? Popular knowledge about Pompeii would have you think so … most of the information on the material remains of brothels will be from Pompeii and Herculaneum.

Circus

The Romans liked their spectacles, but they liked their horses even more – racing was *the* sport of the Empire. Rome itself had no fewer than five circuses at the time of the *Pax Romana*. The circus itself was an open-air structure surrounded by tiered seats for the spectators. The track was usually oval, and down its centre (the *spina*) might be found statues, structures, and other decorations.

Engineering works (above and below ground)

Aqueducts, roads, and sewers. Vitruvius and Frontinus are the main sources; see the chapters on construction, engineering, and hydraulics in Humphrey, Oleson, and Sherwood (1997) and Cuomo (2009).

Forum
The centre of town – the market (its original function) and the heart of public city life. Rome has several of them, as successive emperors attempted to outbuild their predecessors – till the money (and peacetime) ran out in the late second and early third centuries CE.

Government and administrative buildings
The Senate house, law courts, assembly buildings ... although sometimes trials were held in the public square or forum (cf. Apuleius's *Apologia*) and assemblies met in a temple (cf. the *concilium plebis* which met at the Temple of Ceres on the Aventine).

***Insula* (plural *insulae*)**
Apartment blocks; small rooms, few amenities, up to five storeys high. Could be cramped and dark fire traps – no wonder people lived mostly out of doors.

Libraries
Pompeii's layout tends to be the paradigm for libraries as many dot the city; the spectacular ones were in the East, where Hellenistic scholars admired the idea of cataloguing and speculated on historiography as much as they liked actually reading the books.

Monuments
These are your columns, arches, statues, inscriptions, tombs: you can put up any kind of monument to proclaim your achievements. Augustus encouraged public building on a grand scale, Trajan and Hadrian excelled at it; with his baths Caracalla created the last of the truly great imperial monuments of our period.

Palaces and homes of local officials
They've got to live somewhere – the imperial palace on the Palatine Hill, imposing villas in the provinces, large homes in the centre of town – walled up to create an oasis of quiet and peace away from the noise, dirt, and dangers of the streets outside. Fishbourne in Sussex is a good example of the palace of a provincial official.

Shops

Ubiquitous – on the ground floors of the buildings lining the street. Everything from food stalls to goods and services.

Temples

Public monuments dedicated to the gods, they also served as tourist attractions, museums, and even archival repositories. Shrines were smaller, more intimate places of worship, more hidden away and exclusive.

Theatres

The Romans built dedicated theatres (unlike the Greeks, who used natural hillsides). Roman theatre buildings were made from similar materials as amphitheatres. They were half circles or half ovals with tiers of seats for the viewers and a semicircular stage which was backed by the façades of stage-front buildings or houses.

Tombs

Tombs were most often found in dedicated necropolises alongside the streets that led into a city centre. Sometimes funerary monuments might be found inside the city-limits – the Tomb of the Baker in Rome is one example – and Trajan's ashes were placed in the base of his column. Don't forget *under* the city, where the catacombs lay – they would have been originally outside the city limits. Catacombs were used by both pagan and Christian Romans although they have become synonymous with the secret meetings of Christians in the days before the sect's legalisation.

ROOMS IN THE ROMAN HOUSE

Atrium

An entrance hall, but it can also be the centre of the house, open to the air, with gardens and decoration in it. The atrium at the centre of the house was an oasis away from the noise and crowds of the street.

Ala
'Wings' that lead off the atrium.

Cubiculum
Specifically, a bedroom; generally, any small room.

Culina
The kitchen. Some bigger houses might have a water closet off to one side of the kitchen; this was a cramped closet, not only a nasty little latrine but also a place to dispose of general waste. *Villae* or larger military forts might have their kitchens situated where there was running water. Caerleon in Wales, for example, had a channel running through it both as a source of water and for flushing away waste. The kitchen is a frequent setting in comedies as cooks were popular characters in New Comedy and then in Roman comedies.

Exedra
A garden room. Not every house had one; they are most likely to be found in larger city dwellings of aristocrats and wealthy freedmen.

Peristylium
The colonnaded garden around the *atrium*. The peristyle would be decorated and/or populated with things brought home from the master's travels or purchased to show off his travels, wealth, and [lack of] good taste.

Taberna
The shop which may make up the front or downstairs or street part of the house in town. To protect against crime, houses in towns and cities did not have ground-floor windows facing the street (shops were shuttered); instead there would be a blank wall – check out the houses on the street view in Pompeii. HBO's *Rome* renders well this look, placing high walls all around the outsides of the houses, especially of the aristos, and putting shops and taverns along the ground floors of buildings in the poorer quarters of towns.

Tablinum

An office or study; the houses of wealthier men would use these little rooms as libraries. A sort of Classical 'man-cave' where the man of the house could seclude himself from his family and his clients, in order to think or have some peace and quiet. Augustus hid from the public and his family in his library-study (Suet., *Aug.* 72.2). Small libraries have been found in the houses at Pompeii and Herculaneum.

Triclinium

The dining room. In a posh villa, these may also be outside in the garden. The Emperor Tiberius had a *triclinium* built in a grotto at Capri, with floating couches and tables and boy-swimmers as servers (Suet., *Tib.* 44).

Vestibulum

The entrance hall. The boys in the *Satyricon* remark on the *vestibulum* at Petronius's house and its décor (with its *canem cave* – Beware of the dog – sign) (Petron., *Sat.* 29). They are berated by a slave to enter with the right foot (*dextro pedo*) first, otherwise it will be bad luck (30).

4

THE SENATE AND THE PEOPLE OF ROME: LAW, ORDER, AND ADMINISTRATION

The Romans described their administration succinctly: *senatus populusque Romanus*, or the Senate and the People of Rome. In the early days of the Republic, that is, from the sixth through to the mid-third century BCE, the Romans met the challenges of administrative organisation by creating pragmatic institutions, magistracies, and legal concepts to deal with practical problems. Roman culture was conservative and somewhat old-fashioned in its value system, but, unlike a static state such as Sparta, the Romans folded change into their political development – sometimes through compromise, sometimes through violence. Rome's collection of social forces (as discussed in Chapter 1) and political institutions formed the basics of its constitution. It was a simple, but effective system as long as Rome was small and had contacts and allies that were close culturally. There are great complexities to observe in Roman administration between 200 BCE and 200 CE as the original constitution became stretched very thin. The old values and traditions of the early Republic simply were not nuanced enough to handle the effects of a growing, diverse empire on institutions such as jurisprudence, administration of the government, and the army. The social and political institutions that held together the government were affected by Roman imperialism, the assimilation of other peoples' practices and cultures into the Empire, and internal competition for glory amongst ambitious men. When Augustus (reigned 27 BCE–14 CE) finally calmed the issues that had caused discord during the last century or so of the Republic, he did so by drawing on the very traditions that had originally comprised the Roman constitution. The result was more or less an era of two hundred years' peace known as the *Pax Romana*, and it became an era in which the principles of the Republic were codified and cherished as political ideals, at least by the writers who chronicled the period.

How the Romans ruled themselves, and then their increasingly large and diverse empire, was based on allowing a certain amount of local autonomy. This was most obvious in the West, where rural provinces tended to be flat-packed into the Roman administrative system by locals eager to demonstrate their loyalty towards the centre. The administrative structure here, much like the construction of the buildings, indicates some planning from the start; this was in contrast to Eastern cities that had grown organically for centuries before the Romans came along. Not surprisingly, the Romans were often more brutal in the East than in the West when it came to establishing their rule there. One source of conflict in the East came from the difference between Roman and Greek political and administrative policies. For the Romans, *libertas* meant the freedom to maintain local authority and custom with Roman rule and custom on top. Local areas became clients to the Roman centre and owed political allegiance and military obligation in exchange for economic benefits, protection, and possibly the privilege of Roman citizenship. For many Greek city-states, especially Athens, *autonomia* meant complete freedom from rule by an individual or outsider. For them, allegiances, federations, and leagues were only stopgaps in the face of immediate danger and common enemies.

The Romans found the Athenian system of democracy a weakness: the general populace should not have equal opportunity to compete for political power. Allowing assemblies to discuss political policy led only to chaos and the rise of demagogues. Oligarchy and elected representative suited them better. Of course, the Romans knew that those in charge needed to be the *right kind* of oligarchs, and, initially, these were members of the old, rich patrician families. As a consequence, family factions appeared and competed for dominance in Roman politics and for the vote of the people. Adding to the tight competition for limited administrative positions was the rise of new men from amongst the plebeians – such competition led to a century of warfare between 133 and 30 BCE This strife is well documented, as contemporary writers and rhetoricians tried to determine what had caused the rifts in the Roman state, and why there were an increasing number of breaks in the traditional and customary means to gaining power. See, for example, Cicero (*Leg.* 3.6–9, 12) on the ideal constitution, or Polybius (Book 6) on the organisation of the Roman government and magisterial offices. When the plebeian Gracchi came to power in the second century BCE, for example, they insulted the Senate by using the popular assemblies to pass their reforms and laws, bypassing the usual practice of consulting the Senate on such matters (Plut., *TG* 11.2–3, 13.1–3, 14.1–3, and so forth). Whilst this wasn't completely unprecedented, it was highly unusual and deviated from normal procedure which showed deference to the Senate first. Subsequent political patterns showed further break from tradition as others followed suit to gain power through crowd-pleasing measures (the *Populares* faction) on the one hand, in conflict with conservatives and 'old guard' (the *Optimates* or 'best men') on the other. Alternative means to power in the late Republic included military gain and reputation: the general of an army gained the loyalty not only of his soldiers but of his retired soldiers as well. The *novus homo* or 'new man', such as Gaius Marius, was able to gain political power not necessarily with a patron but with their military might and client armies (cf. Plut., *Mar.* 7.2–4; after breaking with his patrician patron, 9.1–4, 11.1–2; cf. Liv., 9.46.1–15, on the career of a typical *novus homo*). Additional powerful individuals such as Sulla, Pompey, and Caesar appeared as the days of Republic waned, and the Roman state began to look more and more like a monarchy as these individuals competed for power.

ROMAN CONSTITUTION: INSTITUTIONS, ASSEMBLIES, AND ADMINISTRATIVE POSTS

The origins of government offices and assemblies are found during the time of the Etruscan monarchy and were formalised during the early Republic. As Rome got its government in order and consolidated territory in and around Rome (including most of Italy), its simple constitution did the job. Male citizens – free men – voted for officials to represent the interests of the people: the Roman 'constitution' during the early Republic was all about electability, collegiality, limited terms of office (Cic., *Leg.* 3.6–9, 12; Polyb., 6). The structural institutions of the government included the Senate, the assemblies, and the magistracies. Ideally, what kept the system incorruptible on paper was the Roman dedication to collegiality: higher offices in the government were held by two, four, or more men (and men only). Notice that only on rare occasions is there a single man occupying any position of power and all of these exceptional positions have some military purpose, especially during a time of crisis when swift decision by one individual was needed: dictator, *princeps*, *imperator* (all three were originally types of military commands; the latter two became synonymous with the emperor). Consensus was another failsafe built into the system; deference and respect of the *mos maiorum* and tradition were a third. Where the system shifted and changed was in Rome's policy of assimilation (addition of new provinces from the third century BCE onwards) on the one hand and its practice of reaching compromise rather than civil war (as with the Conflict of the Orders) on the other (on the early tribes of Rome, see Var., *De Ling.* 5.55–56).

When Roman interests were limited to the Italian peninsula, this system worked well: the local tribes absorbed into the Roman state had much in common with Rome in terms of language if not custom; the conflicts between the patricians and the plebeians, whilst hair-raising, were solved out of practical need: the patricians had the money to go to war, but the plebeians were the human resource. Initially, political offices of the *cursus honorum* and membership of the Senate were limited to the patrician class, but the plebeians fought for and gained the right of their own assembly and their own magisterial officier, the Tribune, during the 'Conflict of the Orders'. This was a series of clashes that took place from the fifth to the second century BCE between patricians and plebeians over the rights to hold political office, to intermarry, and to form their own assemblies. Sometimes the Conflict was violent, but more often issues were resolved through negotiation. Plebeians made up the bulk of Rome's army, and they threatened to withhold their military service when Rome needed it. When you've got Gauls pouring over the Alps and threatening the city, you compromise with the plebeian soldiers who are threatening to go 'on strike' (cf. Liv., 2.31–7 to 33.3). The Romans' respect of authority and strongly ingrained sense of hierarchy (*ordo*) were deterrent enough to resolve internal strife through discussion rather than through civil war between the social classes (cf. Liv., 4.1.1–3, 6.1–11 on the Canuleian laws; 6.35.1–5 on the Licinio-Sextian laws; description of the conflict and the evolution of the Roman government can be found in Books 6, 7, and 8 of Livy's history).

The rot set in especially from the second century BCE onwards: Rome initially struggled not only with how to rule all of the new provinces, especially in the East, but also with what to do with its newfound wealth. Competition for limited offices was fierce, and those who found themselves shut out of the traditional *cursus* turned to 'popular politics' (*Populares*) – not necessarily because they were 'men of the people', but because they were ambitious, and it was an excellent means to get ahead. Ambitious individuals not only bypassed the traditional respect given to the Senate as the older body but also claimed that the Senate in turn disrespected them, that is, publicly offended their *dignitas* or self-worth. The individuals at the centre of the civil war pretty much threw deference out the window, ignored consensus, and pandered to the popular assemblies.

Wars and military glory provided new means to power. Certain generals might snub their patrons and take political office on the strength of military exploits – as Marius, Pompey, and Julius Caesar did. New provincial positions out in the hinterlands opened up new opportunities to exploit the local populace and squeeze out extra taxes to keep for oneself (check out Cicero's prosecution of Verres, for example; see Chapter 5). Voting became a game of buying the urban mob through spectacle and food doles – and sometimes employing gangs of thugs to sway the constituents' votes in their favour. See Cicero, for example, on

Julius Caesar's henchman Clodius (*Har.* 57–59) and enmity between rival gang leaders Clodius and his rival Milo as they tore up Rome (Cass. Dio, 39.6.1–3, 8.1–3). When the Republic changed to the Principate (the first era of the rule of the emperors (27 BCE–284 CE), there was no longer a need to vote: appointments from the centre became key. The emperor became the biggest patron, but other officials could gain from political patronage. Administrative posts were still fiercely competed for, and a new class of politicians rose amongst the *equites* class, as they (and freedmen) became part of a professional, paid bureaucracy. These new men, however, maintained a loyalty to the ideal of the old offices and the traditions of Roman magistracy: even when emperors irritated the generals who supported them, the idea of a Roman aristocrat as the 'first man' of the state persisted. For example, the Gallic commander Vindex, who rebelled against Nero in 66 CE, supported a Roman aristocrat (Galba, governor of Spain) as a replacement rather than taking the job on himself (Suet., *Ner.* 40.4–44).

The Senate originated during Etruscan rule. *Senex* means 'elders,' and the *comitia* was originally a group of male citizens who came from the oldest of the patrician families in Rome. Acting as a council of elders, they evolved into an advisory body for the kings. They chose the new kings (as the monarchy was not hereditary) and acclaimed the new monarch. After 506 BCE, when the kings were driven out and Rome became a republic, the Senate remained; now they made decisions for the entire state. As a body Senators were regarded as experienced and knowledgeable, and their advice came to have the force of law during the Republic (Polyb., 6.13.1). They were regarded as the greatest institution of the Republic, as a symbol of stability. When the magistrates were elected annually, the Senate remained a respected body during the imperial period. Occasionally a strong leader would have a house-clean and purge their numbers as Sulla (Plut., *Sull.* 31.1–6) and Augustus did (Aug., *RG* 8). Even though they were weakened in power from the time of the reign of Augustus onwards, they still advised the consuls and other magistrates.

The assemblies included the *comitia curia* which had religious, political and military functions (Polyb., 6.14.1). The *curia* comprised the stronger families of the patrician class who organised themselves into groups called *curiae*. The assembly originated during the time of the monarchs, and a form of this assembly remained in place from the Republic through to the imperial period. Originally assemblies had no real authority as they were primarily units of defence and aid, but they could declare war or choose the new king. They were instrumental in times of harvest and emergency, and it is from these early practices that Rome developed its rudimentary political organisation. This assembly met occasionally to discuss matters that affected the entire community; their families (the *gentes* – see Chapter 1) strengthened their power through intermarriage. Roughly around 264 BCE, however, this original assembly was replaced by the *comitia centuria* (see Dion. Hal., *Ant. Rom.* 4.20.1–5, 7.59.2–8). The *comitia centuria* was supposedly created by an Etruscan king who organised the state into 193 centuries (military and political units). Voting on policy and legal matters was done by these assemblies, but only on issues put to them by the magistrates, and voting was done in groups in order by property class. Initially, the oldest families, the patricians, dominated the *centuria* because they shouldered the greatest burden of defence and because the voting blocks went in order of social rank and wealth: it took 80 votes to win a decision, and the first 80 or so blocks in the curia were all comprised of aristocratic and merchant-class voters. Consequently, they could outvote the plebeians and exclude the voices and interests of those who made up the majority of the population and who filled out the ranks of the army. In 471 BCE, however, the plebeians gained their own assembly, the *consilium plebis* (cf. Liv., 3.55.17–7, 13–15 on the tribune and the plebeian council). Led by the tribune, they won the right to meet in assembly and pass ordinances (Dion. Hal., *Ant. Rom.* 6.89). Eventually bills passed by the council of the plebeians were recognised as binding on the whole population.

Many of the higher offices (magistracies) were part of the *cursus honorum*, a political ladder that was assembled over the first couple of centuries of the Republic. There was a lower age limit on each office, and one was expected to hold each office in order. In the time of the Republic, candidates competed for votes via promises and entertainment; campaigns might be swayed through bribery and corruption. Additional civic positions that formed the Republican and imperial administration included the various priesthoods. These included the *pontifex maximus*, the highest religious office, and one indicating the remains of the religious rituals practised by the kings. Priesthoods were elected offices during the time of the Republic; like the other offices, they became appointed positions during the imperial era. One could start one's political career by being elected to a priesthood, as Julius Caesar did (Plut., *Caes.* 1.3–4; he eventually became *pontifex maximus*, 7.1–3). Finally, there were administrative offices that included judicial and legal positions, governorships, city officials (such as *duoviri*, tax collectors and decurions), and the increasing number of bureaucrats, office officials, and household managers ranging across the Empire.

PATRONAGE: HOW THE ROMANS GOT THINGS DONE

Patronage was how the Romans got things done. It existed from a personal level on up and permeated all aspects of society. Understanding of how people worked and got along and of the modes of social convention and institutions comes back repeatedly to the patron–client set-up. Quite simply, a patron is someone who can do a favour for you that you can never fully repay; a patron demonstrates his or her prestige and virtue by showing their beneficence. No one did anything in the pagan Roman world out of selfless charity: benevolence came with a price, whether it was to indebt others to you or to serve as a means of commemorating your deeds after death. The patron–client relationship was governed by tradition; there was no written contract between the parties. If you look at Roman myths and the history of their earliest society (in Livy's *History*, for example, Ovid's *Metamorphoses*, Apuleius's *Metamorphoses,* or Vergil's *Aeneid*), you'll see the patronage even of the gods in mortal life (see Chapter 7 on state religion). In real life, patronage existed at all levels of Roman society from the smallest household up to the actual state itself, including the relationship between Rome at the centre and its provinces and the Empire and its client-kingdoms. New citizens were patrons of the state; a strong man, such as Pompey the Great, might have a client army (Plut., *Pomp.* 6.3, 11.2). Clients, like a family reputation, could be inherited.

Patrons could give you a leg up on life – literally, in the case of a child's very first patron, his or her mother, for giving life and her family connections. The latter can lead to not a few complications in the mother–son relationships of politicians, especially when Mum won't let him forget just how much he really owes her for his life and pedigree (cf. Tac., *Ann.* 13.13). Fathers are important patrons as they connect the son to his tutors and mentors and then to employment via their own connections, clients, and friends. Patronage was also a way to improve one's social standing. Whilst family reputation was important, frequently the more important patrons in one's life were from outside the family. Note that the root of patron is *pater*: often a patron assumed the role of father where the actual father was absent or simply did not have the wherewithal to provide a son with a career. Other patrons include masters who free their slaves: both men and women are honoured in inscriptions by freedmen and freedwomen for the benevolence received from their former masters. A careful reading of a freedwoman's funerary inscriptions, for example, might reveal that her former slave partner, on gaining his freedom, went on to buy hers so that they could marry. In the provinces, patronage could help the local elite to gain attention and even better positions from someone at the centre. Local administrative offices could be rewarded with citizenship – and from there it was a step up into the equestrian class as a New Man – and who knows, maybe eventually a lofty appointment as the procurator (governor) or a province. It was, however, very difficult to gain the attention of someone who was at the centre, but to become a big fish in a small provincial pond was rewarding, as well. Cicero's and Pliny the Younger's letters are excellent sources for examples of patronage, requests for favours, and references written on behalf of others.

VOTE FOR ME! CAMPAIGNING AND ELECTIONS IN THE REPUBLIC

Campaigning, elections, and voting were increasingly more important for Roman men from the middle to the end of the Republic, especially as the drive for competition in political and public life increased and the number of available administrative offices decreased. Corruption, strong-arming, and mob rule affected the system from the beginning of the first century BCE, reaching their pinnacle in riots and violence during Julius Caesar's dictatorship. One result of courting votes was institutionalised spectacle and sport, especially in the first century BCE, as well as social relief such as bread doles as part of campaigning strategy. Under the emperors, of course, people were appointed into their administrative jobs both in Rome and in the provinces, so, whilst there was no more election campaigning after this point, similar strategies of display (games, *alimenta*, building projects) remained in place both to keep the crowd on the incumbent emperor's or local magistrate's side and to gain attention from the centre in hopes of a cushy promotion or further appointment.

Your fictive Rome during the Republican period may well include electioneering. Looking at the sources available during the period, say 70–44 BCE, you could piece together an active campaign or have one going on in the background. Here are some things to think about for your campaigning character.

- Who are his campaign managers – otherwise known as his clients? Who are his henchmen and toadies?
- What platform or faction does he represent? Where will he find his supporters – amongst the old aristocracy, the freedmen, the army, or the mob? How does he gain their support?
- Why is he the best person for the job? His military experience? Prior political work? Smooth and fancy talking?
- How does he court votes? Is he a general who demands perks for his soldiers and veterans, who in turn will repay him by voting

for his policies in the assembly? Does he have loads of money to spend on games, public works, and *beneficia* to keep the masses happy (as *Populares* did), or will he have to bribe, borrow, and blackmail to get ahead? Is he all about old-fashioned Roman values (like *Optimates*), which have been sadly undermined and imperilled over the past half century?

- Does your candidate see a new future for Rome based on the principles of Greek philosophy – or perhaps a future teamed up with the ruler of another power in the region, such as North Africa, Egypt, or even Parthia?
- What office will he campaign for? Is he aiming for a high magistracy or is he a petty little jobsworth desperate to have a foot up on an inconsequential step on the ladder? Think about his platform, his promises, and what he'll do for Rome if elected.
- Don't forget public debate. How will he craft his speeches? Know both sides of the issues so that your character can not only speak in favour of his platform but also be able to aptly denounce his opponents. Supporters can change sides at will – so how will your character gain their loyalty and keep it?

For inspiration check out the careers of politicians in Plutarch's *Lives* of, for instance, Fabius Maximus, both Gracchi, Marius, Sulla, Pompey, Crassus, Cicero, and Julius Caesar. Cicero's speeches are great models of declamation. See Chapter 8 for contemporary sources and modern scholarship to help shape the careers of your politicians – including scholarship on *losing* campaigns; learn from their mistakes!

LAW AND ORDER: THE *TWELVE TABLES* … CODIFICATION OF THE LAW

The earliest Roman law was civil law, *ius civis*, which governed the lives and regulations of citizens. These were the customs, statutes, and forms of procedure that were meant to protect property, lives, and reputation of citizens, and to give satisfaction to victims of injustice. Roman law was originally oral only; you were at the mercy of the law courts to read and interpret the law fairly in your favour. In the fifth century BCE, however, the plebeians insisted on more rights as there was no written law code, and they were aware that court decisions and penalties were weighted in favour of the wealthy classes. They might, for example, find themselves facing charges and punishments in court completely different from those faced by patricians in the same predicament. So around 450 BCE, the patricians chose ten men (*decemviri*) to codify public and private law. The result became known as the *Twelve Tables*, and it remained in effect as the basis of Roman law for about one thousand years (Dion. Hal., *Ant. Rom.* 10.55.4–5, 56.6–7). The 'tables' were the bronze tablets into which the law was inscribed and posted publicly for all to see. Oral contract was still the norm in the ancient world, so for laws to be written down was radical and showed just how serious the issue was.

Roman law was proscriptive (rather than *pre*scriptive), that is, it came after the fact: when looking at legal sources, you often have to work out what the original problem was from its solution. A good example is the *Urso Charter* of 44 BCE (*FIRA*, 122): from its contents, the problems and issues that beset the provincial town of Urso, Spain, have to be reconstructed, especially in terms of financial pressures, election fraud, and aristocrats attempting to purchase control of the town. This isn't to say that the Romans didn't add new laws to the books: they did, and in abundance, especially as they added new provinces. They allowed locals to maintain indigenous law while having the right to appeal to Roman courts. Consider the trial of Jesus in the Gospel of John; Pilate gets involved because the Pharisees want Roman law to condemn him to death (Jn 18:19–24). Pilate turns Jesus back over to the Jews because he argues that it's a local problem for them to sort out (Lk 23:4–12; cf. Jn 18:28–40, 19:16). Similarly, Philo, an ambassador from Egypt, arrived in Rome in 39 CE to petition the Emperor Gaius Caligula following the Alexandrian riots the previous year. Here the Egyptians invoked their right to have their case heard in Rome itself (cf. Joseph., *AJ* 28.8.1). Considering what Philo found in Rome and wrote about in his essay *Legatio ad Gaium*, Caligula's sensational exploits put the local legal troubles into some perspective. Roman law remained flexible and, as always, practical when it came to sorting out situations; this adaptability helped Roman administrators in the long run as they had to think of laws that would suit both Rome and local administrations overall and in maintaining the peace.

One problem was the Romans added new laws, however, was that they tended not to amend the old ones or strike them from the books. By the time of Hadrian's reign, the Roman law code was a sprawling, antiquated, contradictory mess. Hadrian ordered a revision of the law, specifically of the Praetor's Edicts (Gai., *Instit.* 1–9). This was an attempt to codify the principles and procedures of Roman civil law, and Hadrian, cosmopolitan emperor that he was, recognised that there was a need to consider new times and new precedent that might be affecting centuries-old – and very simple – legal procedures. Around 131 CE, he contracted Salvius Julianus, an influential legal writer, to tackle the task. Salvius gave it his best shot. All laws drawn up by the praetors were binding unless the emperor (or Senate) (Gai., *Instit* 1.48–49) decreed changes or alterations (Eutr., 8.17). Statutes of the emperor were an important source of law as well, including imperial edicts, imperial mandates, and administrative directives on the emperor's order. New judicial districts were created to make hearing cases faster and more efficient. Salvius wasn't entirely successful as it was a huge task, and it was more than one man could handle; further complicating matters was how citizens were treated in the eyes of the law (as compared to non-citizens) and maintenance of local law and custom. It wasn't until Justinian in the sixth century CE that a team of jurists was put to work properly to codify Roman law and to divide it into several major sections including the massive *Corpus Iurus Civilis*, or body of civil law.

CRIME AND PUNISHMENT

The world of ancient Rome was a violent one; behaviour that the Romans (and Greeks) took as an ordinary course of events would shock us in the modern world. Complementing your study of Roman law and order ought to be Reiss and Fagan's (2016) study, as they provide context for understanding how the Romans perceived different types of violent acts and behaviour, and how such attitudes were, as always, shaped by class and status. The Romans could be severe when it came to punishment, but, once again, status affected the nature of that punishment, even for the same crimes. *Honestiores* (patricians) and *humiliories* (plebeians) were treated very differently in court despite the social leveller that the *Twelve Tables* were meant to be. Poor Roman citizens could be executed for a number of crimes; wealthier citizens were frequently given the option of exile in place of execution. Punishment, as with much else, came back to status and *ordo*, even with the death penalty. If an *honestior* was sentenced to capital punishment, his or her execution was a comparatively quick and clean death. They could opt for the honourable way out of suicide before the executioner arrived, in the face of which they could win credit by exhibiting proper stoic fortitude. The Emperor Otho, for example, whilst otherwise a vile person, redeemed himself in Suetonius's eyes by committing suicide as an honourable alternative to being captured and ignominiously murdered by his enemies (Suet., *Otho* 93). Suetonius notes that nothing about Otho's bearing or character would suggest that he could be this brave (12.1) *Honestiores'* punishment, however, unless for crimes of treason, was usually expulsion, deportation and/or confiscation of goods – penalties that could be devastating, but ones that did not propel them into the public limelight, let alone humiliate them there.

The *humilior*, on the other hand, suffered humiliating and public capital punishment, usually in front of the mocking crowds in the arena as part of the entertainment. The Romans had absolutely no sympathy for those who suffered public humiliation as part of their punishment because it was an indication of their loss of status. This was considered entirely the fault of the victim whether through fate or poor moral character. By making certain types of punishment public spectacle, such humiliation reinforced hierarchy and adherence to authority (at least as much as an individual could – poverty or hardship due to fate were not preventable). So one day you might be cheering on the beasts against their victims, but the next day that could be *you* in the arena. To see the fate that awaited the traitor, the thief, the murderer was meant to act as reinforcement to keep to good custom and morality. Other examples of the social divide when it came to capital punishment include the Cornelian law on wills: 'Anyone who knowingly and with wrongful intent forges … a will is liable under the *lex Cornelia testamentaria*. *Honestiores* are to be deported to an island, *humiliores* are either sent to the mines or crucified' (Paul., *Sent.* 5.25.1) Then there is the Cornelian *lex de sicariis*, 'On murderers', which includes poisoning and assassination. Those of high status were exiled or had their property confiscated; those of low rank were sentenced to the mines, suffered crucifixion, or were thrown to the wild beasts (23.12–15). A third example, for the crime of removing boundary stones, saw slaves condemned to the mines, *humiliores* to hard labour, and *honestiores* to temporary expulsion with either one-third confiscation or full deportation (5.22.2). Finally, the *lex Julia de maiestatis*, 'on treason', laid down that *humiliores* should be thrown to the beasts or burned alive, *honestiores* more cleanly, perhaps by decapitation – a quicker and more honourable dispatch than becoming public entertainment (5.29.1–2). Paulus's *Sententiae* (*Opinions*), whence come these examples, can be found online in English translation; they are an excellent source for such regulations and how they are applied across the social hierarchy.

So when you are crafting the inevitable crimes or executions that liven up tales of Rome throughout this period, consider the sharp delineation between *honestiores* and *humiliores* (slaves were a separate category also covered by Paulus). Consider, too, how these punishments and distinctions affect or encourage Romanisation, how they might motivate the behaviour of the locals in the provinces, and where there is room for exploitation and corruption amongst officials. Robinson (2000) provides a seminal look in English at how Roman law was shaped not only by the nature of common crimes but also by the public's demands for protection against criminals. If you prefer a succinct overview, Harries's (2011) survey complements Robinson's. Both scholars consider not only major categories of crime and punishment but also the inextricable effects of social institutions and cultural traditions on shaping legal practices and perception of crime and bad behaviour.

SOME COMMON CRIMES

The Romans could be inventive with their punishments; after you study Robinson and Harries, check out any Christian martyrology for sensational tips and how-tos. Slicing people up with giant wool combs (St Blaise), roasting them on braziers (St Lawrence), cutting off various body parts (St Agatha), yanking teeth (St Apollonia) – it's a masochist's cabinet of delights. Then there are the punishments in the arena – criminals fed to starving beasts, criminals forced to act out myths that led to their deaths (Gaius Caligula and Commodus were especially fond of these displays), criminals forced to fight professional gladiators. In the case of the latter, these executions were scheduled during the lunch hour of the *munera*, as serious gladiator fans had no interest in watching terrified and untrained people attempt to ward off professionally trained fighters. Check out the recommendations in Chapter 8 under leisure, entertainment, and spectacle for current studies by Kyle (2007), Kagan (2014), and Fagan (2002), especially on punishment as public spectacle.

Robbery and mugging

Common in the streets, especially at night. Punishment varied from restoring costs (Paul., *Sent.* 5.3.5) and flogging and fines through to being sentenced to the mines or thrown to the beasts (5.19.1).

Burglary and theft

This is one reason why you don't see windows on the lower floors of building in Pompeii, and why the houses of the wealthy are behind such high walls in both country and city. Roman citizens were flogged for theft. Theft from sacred places was punished by execution. There are graffiti in Pompeiian baths cursing towel thieves; Juvenal comments that a slave stealing a bath towel would be branded as a thief (cf. Paul., *Sent.* 6.20–21); Paulus notes that bath thieves might be sent to the mines or forced to labour on public works (5.3.5).

Runaway slaves

Slaves wore iron collars around their necks with their names and owners' addresses on them. If caught, the slave might be branded on the face. See Paulus again (1.6a–1.7) on the fate of fugitive slaves.

Slaves who kill their masters (and free children who kill their parents)

Parricide was held as a horrendous crime, whether a slave of his master, or a child of his or her parent. The most famous punishment here was the *poena cullei* (*culleus* = sack). The convicted person was sewn into a leather bag along with cock, dog, monkey, and viper, and thrown into a river. The ritual persisted for centuries until the Romans swapped it for burning at the stake (possibly because of all of the pagan symbolism that the various animals represented). After Agrippina the Younger was assassinated in 59 CE, statues of Nero acquired leather bags over their heads – anonymous wits' ways of accusing Nero of ordering his own mother's death. Numerous Roman authors, including Suetonius (*Aug.* 33.1–2), Cicero (e.g. *Rosc. Am.* 71.26), and Juvenal (8.211–14), refer to this practice of executing parricides, and it was incorporated into Justinian's law code (cf. Paul., *Sent.* 5.24).

Fraud

Fraud covered counterfeiting coins and claiming wages for dead soldiers. Roman citizens were flogged for committing fraud (Paul., *Sent.* 1.8.1–2).

Arson

Fires were frequent and common in cities, and their origins were sometimes suspicious. It was commonly believed that Nero started the Great Fire of 64 CE to clear out space in prime real estate locations in Rome so that he could build his new palace (Suet., *Ner.* 37.1–3; Cass. Dio, 62.16.1–3; Tac., *Ann.* 15). Roman citizens were executed if found guilty of arson (Paul., *Sent.* 5.3.6).

Rioting

One of the reasons that there were no permanent or stone theatres and amphitheatres until the middle of the first century BCE was fear of having too many restless people in a confined space, worked up with frenzy and excitement – especially when most games, spectacles, and entertainments were sponsored by politicians garnering votes. Famous riots include the one at the Pompeiian amphitheatre in the first century BCE, which is depicted on a fresco – showing the rioters spilling out into the streets – and the Nika Riots in the sixth century CE (documented by Procopius in his *Anecdota*), a politically motivated and perhaps manipulated riot between chariot-racing fans and factions during the reign of Justinian.

Murder

Murder in antiquity was thought to bring bad luck on to a city. For a new perspective on murder as a tool of powerful families during the time of the Republic, see Gaughan (2010). The renowned Roman women's scholar Sarah Pomeroy (2007) focuses carefully on a case study of a woman called Regilla who was beaten to death by her husband in the late second century CE; this work is a blend of critical reading of the sources and historical reconstruction.

Treason

Crimes against the state and the head of state were treason; Tiberius was infamous for his paranoia and treason trials in the latter half of his reign (Suet., *Tib.* 61.2–6). Likewise Domitian set up many prominent men under charges of treason so that he could claim their estates (Suet., *Dom.* 11.1–3). Anyone who refused to swear allegiance to the emperors or, more specifically, to the imperial cult was held liable of treason, as such rituals were necessary to show devotion to the state and the state gods, and failure to carry them out would bring about bad luck and ill fortune (Paul., *Sent.* 5.29.1–2).

Slaves and punishment

Slaves who committed capital crimes, especially treason, murder, and rebellion, were crucified – as in the case of Spartacus: Crassus lined the *Via Appia* with six thousand crucified slaves in the 70s BCE after this revolt (App., *BC* 1.120). Crucifixion was public, humiliating, and led to a slow death – which made its victims an awesome public warning for others. Another way to keep slaves in check was to punish the entire household for the transgressions of one.

Military punishment

Flogging and execution were the main military punishments, the latter famously incorporated into Roman myth when Manlius Torquatus executed his own son with the axe from a *fascas* when he learned that his son had disobeyed a direct order and put the lives of the other soldiers in his unit at risk). The Roman army was also famous for *decimatio*, which Polybius describes in Book 6.38 of his *Roman History*. Livy describes an early example of it in the fifth century BCE as a punishment for desertion (2.59). Mark Antony also dusted off the punishment to use on his legions in anger after a defeat (Plut., *Ant.* 39). Everyone loves using the word 'decimation' to describe total destruction, but it means to diminish by one-tenth: it was a punishment rarely needed because of its consequences. If a soldier committed a crime, every tenth man in the unit was selected at random to be beaten (or sometimes stoned) to death by the remaining troops. The threat of executing one's best friend and innocent comrade drove home the importance of consensus and the safety of the group over the individual.

KEEPING THE PEACE: THE ARMY

The Romans never had a formal police force. The *vigiles*, or the Urban Cohort, were tasked with keeping order in the cities; they were originally organised by Augustus, comprising soldiers who were mostly on standby in case a riot broke out. In Rome itself, the emperors had the Praetorian

Guards as bodyguards, but outside of the City, in the provinces, and on the frontiers, the real peace-keepers were the army. As the character Loretta says in *Monty Python's The Life of Brian*, 'They're the only ones who could maintain order in a place like this, Reg' (cf. Larsen, 2018: 205–222). The Roman army was famous within and without the Empire for its discipline and training (e.g., Joseph., *BJ* 3.5.71–107; Veg., 1.1.9, 10, 19, 27; 2.23 and 25).

The army was a critical aspect of Roman life from early doors, and the army would always be the biggest financial burden on the Empire. Coinage was designed and taxes levied to help meet the army's needs; the military needed a huge supply of food to keep it running. Roads, way stations, ships, routes were all created with the army in mind. The cultural exchange between the Roman army and the locals was a two-way street, as soldiers on the move helped to carry ideas, custom, and religious practice (not to mention more tangible things such as luxury goods as well as disease) across the Empire. When the army became more static from the first century CE, barracks on the edges of the frontier became trading posts and drove the local economy; they were the foundation of little Roman towns. Resultant farming from these colonies and towns brought Romanisation to the far reaches of the Empire.

During the early days of the Republic, there was no real uniformity in equipment or organisation, and tactics were modelled on the old Greek phalanx. By the third century BCE, whilst they still maintained a civilian army, years of warfare had led the Romans to standardise their weapons and to develop versatile strategies with a great emphasis placed on training. As they consolidated the peninsula under their rule and then met with their first international foes up and through to the end of the Second Punic War, the Romans lost many battles but tended to win wars simply because they had a seemingly inexhaustible supplies of human resources – those allies and clients who stood to gain from *Romanitas*. The persistence of the Romans even in the face of defeat is one reason Pyrrhus of Epirus (318–272 BCE), who used the superior fighting tactics of his Macedonian cousin Alexander the Great, finally gave up even after handing the Romans a number of defeats in the early third century (hence 'Pyrrhic victory' – a win at great cost) (for more on Pyrrhus, see Plutarch's *Life*). Hannibal Barca (247–c. 183/1 BCE) wiped out entire swathes of Roman armies during his marches up and down the centre of Italy as recounted in Livy (21–22) and Plutarch's *Life of Fabius*. The formidable Carthaginian general used what we might call psychological warfare to lure the Romans into battles where they were soundly trounced by the tens of thousands – but because the Romans were on home ground, maintained the loyalty of their allies, and were determined protect their land and gain the *virtus* of military *gloria*, they were able to rally and come back for more. Generals such as Fabius Maximus were thoughtful and understood how to fight Hannibal with more effective tactics; Fabius resisted being drawn into battles that he knew the Romans could not win. Consequently Fabius was removed from command, replaced with machismo from the new consuls Paulus and Varro, and sat back to watch the enemy slice through the home team like a scythe. It must be remembered that at the same time the Romans suffered one of their greatest defeats (Cannae, 216 BCE), they were fighting in a major war in the Greek East and Macedonia (see Livy, 31–45). Where did these soldiers come from, and why were they so willing to fight for Rome?

Allies and conquered peoples added continuously to Rome's human resources from its earliest days, and the army became a means of Romanisation and advancement for a man politically and even economically. The army not only provided economic stability in the provinces and on the frontiers but also allowed a man a chance to learn a trade and eventually to gain citizenship in exchange for his services to the state (mooted after Caracalla granted universal citizenship in 212 CE). Officers were originally from Italy and the more Romanised provinces, but from the late Republic and especially through era of the *Pax Romana* and beyond, fewer and fewer soldiers were actually Italian Romans, and members of the legions and auxiliaries came from all over the Empire.

6 Detail of an armoured statue of Hadrian, Antalya,
second century CE

EMPERORS AND SOLDIERS

Any general who fought and slept alongside his men was extremely popular. Marius, for example, got right out there and hauled equipment with his men (Plut., *Mar.* 7.2–3); Tiberius was popular for sleeping rough on the ground with his soldiers (Suet., *Tib.*18.1–2). Hadrian was another man's man who toured his Empire (*HA, Hadr.* 12.1 and 6, 13.1–8, 23.1), staged personal inspections of the troops (10.4–6, 8; Cass. Dio, 69.9.1–5) and became incredibly popular amongst the soldiers (*HA, Hadr.* 10.2, 21.9). He watched all aspects of their drills and exercises, and, like Marius, also marched along with them bearing the same equipment as a common soldier (10.1).

MILITARY REFORMS: FROM CITIZENS TO PROFESSIONAL ARMIES

The nature of warfare and the composition of the army changed as Roman conflict moved out into the international scene. The result was a change from the citizen army of the early Republic, which fought to protect its land and homes, to a professional army which followed the power (and money) of a particular general. The first major over-haul of the army came with Marius, who initiated a series of military reforms in his second consulship around 100 BCE. The so-called New Army (or 'Marius's Mules') (Plut., *Mar.* 13) changed the army from a citizen army of conscript land owners to a professionally paid one. In addition to technical changes in weapons and the reorganisation of the cohorts and centuries, Marius created a fast, mobile army with uniform equipment. Land requirements for enlistment were waived, and the military accepted volunteers who would fight for pay and booty. The promise (and reward) of land and public positions after fighting meant that the general became a patron to his soldiers. These client-armies were soldiers who fought for personal reasons and were loyal to the general who might reward them the best, rather than loyalty in particular to the Roman state. These soldiers repaid their patron-generals by voting for their legislation and consequently helped to shape the course of *Populares* political factions in the civil wars of the first century BCE.

Further reforms came after the wars in the early days of the Principate as emperors enacted other changes in the army in the first two centuries of the imperial government. Augustus, for example, had all soldiers take an oath of allegiance to the Roman state (Aug., *RG* 3), effectively making him not only the sole head of the army (as consul) but also the patron of all the soldiers. He reduced the size of the army after Actium (31 BCE) and rewarded well those soldiers whom he retired (*RG* 3). Out of the remnants he created a permanent army of 28 legions of 5500 infantry and 120 cavalry each (cf. Cass. Dio, 55.23.1–7). The terms of service were regulated, as was payment: soldiers were recruited from citizen volunteers to serve for twenty years; retirement was rewarded with land, citizenship, and a retirement bonus from the treasury. In addition, there were auxiliary units of light infantry and cavalry who were drafted from 'warlike peoples'. Over the next two centuries, the emperor had carefully to placate the army and the Praetorians, who played an increasing role not just in protecting the emperor but in supporting candidates and evicting the current incumbent. In 69 CE, the legions across the Empire became divided in loyalty for whom they supported as the successor to Nero. When Vespasian finally won, he did not want to chance a repeat of civil war. He stopped stationing troops on the frontiers and in the regions where they had been recruited to avoid problems with loyalty and to prevent local strongmen from using the army as a support (cf. Suet., *Vesp.* 8.1–3). In addition, he formed new auxiliaries from a mix of tribal and national origins. The result was that large concentrations of legions were broken up and spaced more distantly along the frontiers.

Additional reforms came with Hadrian, especially when he let go of territories that his (economically) imperialist predecessor had acquired. Under Hadrian, the Romans had about four thousand miles of frontier to defend with only about two to three hundred thousand men. The army was again stationed in fixed camps and occupied walled forts and garrisons, partly to defend the frontiers but also to act as economic checkpoints and crossroads. Hadrian made further changes in the organisation of the army with the progressive removal of distinction between legions and auxiliaries. All soldiers now had more or less the same training and the same gear; the numbers in the army were made up of both Roman citizens and non-citizens, and many recruits came from the frontiers, born in or near the camps. Although the army became static during his reign, Hadrian created new types of troops: a small, mobile corps called the *numeri* and mounted scouts called *exploratores*. Both groups tended to be locals who knew the local languages and customs. Battle tactics, something the Romans adapted as they met new enemies and folded other cultures into the ranks, now included an improved version of the old Macedonian phalanx – even if the enemy attacked first, the *auxilia* were thrown at them, then the phalanges came in and mopped up the exhausted enemy.

The next real changes in the army and consequent effects on administration, economics, and society come after our period, with the Barracks Emperors in the third century, followed by the fundamental changes to the Roman government during the reign of Diocletian (285–301).

RESTORE THE REPUBLIC! ... OR NOT

Anyone familiar with *I, Claudius* or *Gladiator* knows that a theme running through the fictionalised reign of Claudius and the plot of *Gladiator* is the desire to overthrow rule by an autocrat and restore the good old days of the Republic. Rhetoricians since the days of Cato the Elder wanted to restore the old constitution of the Republic (see Plutarch's *Life of Cato*) and return to the collegiate rule of the Senate and assemblies. Dictators such as Sulla (Plutarch, *Life of Sulla*) and Julius Caesar (Plutarch and Suetonius, each one penning a *Life of Julius Caesar*) justified their one-man rule as a means to restore the

Republic. Then Augustus came along and built an entire propaganda machine around the notion that he *had* restored the Republic (Augustus, *Res Gestae*) – although he didn't step down and let the Senate and the people of Rome take over again. A generation or two later, the Praetorian Guard had had enough of Augustus's great-grandson Caligula and assassinated him – but *they* didn't restore the Republic then, either. Instead, they propped up Claudius as emperor (Suetonius, *Life of Gaius*; *Life of Claudius*; Cass. Dio, 63.22.2–6, 23, 24, 25, 26). The same thing didn't happen again during the rebellion of Vindex in 66, when he was fed up with Nero's handling of rule (Suetonius, *Life of Nero*; Tacitus, *Annals*). Then no return to the Republic following a rebellion in 68 or civil war in 69 … or after Domitian's assassination (96) and after Commodus's assassination (192) … or all the way through the era of the Barracks Emperors in the third century, or when the Germanic and Goth *magistri militum* ostensibly ruled the Empire in the fourth and fifth centuries while feeble men or children held the purple … until Odoacer got properly fed up in 476, retired the puppet emperor Romulus Augustulus (himself the son of a Gothic military commander) and declared himself King of Rome (*Anonymous Valesianus* 8.38; cf. Cass., *Var.* 3.35; Jord., *Geth.* 242). Even then it wasn't over, as the Gothic and early Frankish kings copied aspects of imperial life: Theodoric dressed as a Roman (Sid. Apoll., *Epist.* 1.2.6), Theudebert (d. 548) presided over chariot races (Proc., *Goth.* 7.33.6), and Chilperic (d.584) attempted to compose poetry and added (Greek!) letters to the alphabet (GT, *HF* 44). Then in 800 the Carolingian Frank Charlemagne had himself crowned 'Roman emperor' (after all, the current Byzantine emperor was a woman, and surely that didn't count; *RFA* 800; Ein., *VKM* 28 – a work supposedly modelled after Suetonius's *Life of Augustus*). If the romance of *Restore the Republic!* persists in modern popular depictions of Rome, why did no one seize the opportunity in these moments of rebellion, get rid of the emperors, and bring back the SPQR good and proper?

Up through Augustus, various individuals mourned the erosion or loss of the symbols of the Republic, those values and practices discussed in Chapter 1. Cato saw threats from aristocratic love of luxury and Greek ideas; Sulla feared corruption from the plebeian reforms of his predecessor Marius. Julius Caesar planned to reform all of the wrongs that had affected Rome throughout a century of civil war. Augustus ruled for over thirty years ostensibly as first citizen along with the Senate, even though he actually held all of the power. (To be fair, Augustus *had* restored peace and stability, after decades of terrible civil war.) By the time of Claudius (41–54), no one in their right mind wanted actually to restore the Republic as a form of government, as too many still remembered or felt the repercussions of the chaos and war preceding 27 BCE when Octavian, renamed as Augustus, became the first emperor. Claudius turned out to be a capable ruler who was very old-fashioned and keen on Republican tradition, but even he focused on stability and succession (the latter being the number one issue for every emperor from Augustus onwards – how can you have a successor in a government and not openly admit it's a monarchy?) By the time of Nero, it was the *idea* of emperor that was important and becoming symbolic of Rome, not the man himself. The original imperial cult focused not to the human being but on the *genius* of emperor, that is, his spirit or his embodiment of the position (see Chapter 7). The emperor had to be Roman: hence Vindex the Gaul not declaring himself emperor in 66 CE, the armies in 69 supporting Roman candidates as emperor, and the myriad of Germanic, Gallic, and Goth military commanders – who actually ran the Empire – supporting a Roman in the purple. The Republic as a political institution was finished by the time Julius Caesar declared himself dictator in 45 BCE, but the fiction persisted. Augustus ruled with his Republican façade, making himself a man of the people; Tiberius (ruled 14–37) attempted to maintain this early in his administration, but didn't have the strength (or interest) to keep it up. Vespasian (69–79) was too pragmatic to play the part, and Domitian (81–96), his son, ruled openly as an autocrat. Emperors were made outside of Italy of non-Italian stock. Military-careered emperors continued tightening the idea of emperor as autocrat; at the end of our period, Septimius Severus (192–211) restored rule after civil war not by playing the role of a traditional Republican but rather by clamping down with an iron fist and maintaining peace through martial law. His Syrian in-laws introduced new Eastern ideas about the image and persona of the emperor, and as we leave our period, from the time of Diocletian (284–301), the emperor as 'man of the people' and 'first citizen of the Republic' was replaced by a mysterious and remote figure.

Make 'Restore the Republic!' your theme if you like – but first read Syme's seminal work (1939, rev. ed. 2002) on Augustus and book-end it with McCormick (1990), who discusses how the emperor had become a remote, distant figure from the third century CE). For the Romans, remembrance of the Republic meant always trying to return to an idealised past and maintenance of cultural traditions that were constantly evolving – Cato the Elder would have been baffled by the fact that the rhetoricians of the imperial period such as Tacitus wanted to return to the 'good old days' of his era, as he himself longed for the 'good old days' of Brutus and other heroes of the earliest days of the Republic.

5

VENI, VIDI, VISA: ECONOMIC MATTERS

Rome was neither a capitalist nor a consumer economy in the modern sense; it was an agrarian society supported by a servile labour force. Land came first and foremost. The need for feeding the City, the Empire, and especially the army was of utmost importance. Land represented stability, and aristocratic wealth was tied up in agriculture and property holding.

The problem with a land-based economy, especially one in a culture as status-conscious as the Roman, was that there was very little incentive for technological advancement. Some of this had to do with the values of Roman civilisation and the curriculum of its education. Ancient education emphasised oratory, rhetoric, and philosophy – the key talents needed to succeed at public life. Graeco-Roman education did not foster scientists, technicians, or industrial engineers. Little value was put into industry, banking, commerce, or technology as a means of social advancement amongst the aristocracy. Business and industry did exist, but there was no such thing as a 'middle class' during this period. There was some support of contracts in public enterprise and shareholding, but laws made private enterprise illegal for the aristocracy (except for entering into business as a partnership). So, for the most part, commerce, business, and trade as vocations were considered vulgar pursuits best left to equestrians and freedmen.

Slow transport also inhibited any industrial process. It was cheaper and less risky to produce locally than to try to ship over long distances.

Only super-specialised luxury goods would be shipped far afield because they were unavailable elsewhere (and thus part of a limited market for such goods for the well-to-do). Small, local shops were preferred over factories although certainly factories and workshops existed, but not on the scale associated with the later industrial revolution. As slaves did most of the hard graft, there was no incentive to develop labour-saving devices. Consequently, innovations were limited to mining and military developments. Even if someone did come up with a new device, it was often seen as a novelty (cf. Cicero on an astronomical device, *Rep.* 14.21–22). There was no reward for such inventions, and there were certainly no concepts of patent rights – so no incentive to create a tool or device for profit. Ultimately, especially after the Empire ceased to expand, industry and commerce stagnated and did not keep pace with the increasing cost of government. This led to over-taxation to make up for the shortfall; then the peasant population (the majority of the population) became impoverished. Whilst poverty and wide economic gaps were endemic problems after our period, it is especially visible in areas such as Egypt in the first and second centuries CE (see, for example, L&R, 2: nos 77 and 85, for issues with poverty and taxation in that province).

Expansion was the key to Rome's great prosperity during our period because it brought wealth into the Empire in the form of new territory for farming, sources of minerals and ore for mining, and a steady supply of slaves to work the *latifundia*, the great landed estates that appeared from the late third century BCE onwards. Even though land remained the 'gross national product' in the *Pax Romana*, urbanisation (especially in the West) and spread of empire led to an economic boom in the first and second centuries CE as raw materials were procured from the new territories. When expansion stopped, as it did in the mid-second century CE, there were fewer new raw materials and the sources of slaves diminished. This is one issue that caused the economy to falter on a larger scale than before (issues with prices, inflation, and coinage debasement occurred even during times of greatest prosperity). Another effect of the cessation of expansion was that formerly underdeveloped areas began to create their own markets to supply their needs, undercutting suppliers who had previously supported them.

Cracks in the economy begin to show, ironically enough, at the height of greatest prosperity. Perhaps one cause of Rome's economic crisis from the third century CE wasn't the barbarians or the rise of Christianity, but the fact that the Romans were victims of their own success: peace and prosperity meant no new territories to conquer and to bring in more money. Many former frontier states became provinces and no longer functioned as buffers against Rome's enemies. Furthermore, it became increasingly difficult to pay the armies who were meant to be protecting the long frontiers of the huge Empire. With no understanding of how inflation worked, the Romans fell back on debased coinage as early as Nero's reign, but most notably from the third century CE (cf. Diocletian's *Edict of Maximum Prices*, excerpted in L&R, 2: no. 112: 398–400). Simply put, Rome ran out of places to conquer on the one hand, and it was living beyond its means on the other. As a consequence, Rome suffered from economic stagnation: as the crises of the third century CE began to mount, the Romans could not meet increasing military needs and simultaneously maintain civilian economy.

THE IMPERIAL TREASURY: INTERNAL FUNDS

The principal treasury in the imperial period (*aerarium Saturni*) remained at Rome, as established by Augustus (Suet., *Aug.* 32.2, 36.1, 41.1). Revenue from all of the provinces came into it. Our word *fiscal* comes from *fisci*, or chests, which refers to the local, provincial branches of the treasury. Money moved from the *fisci* to the central treasury (except from Asia and Egypt – they kept their surpluses). The central treasury was ostensibly under the administration of the Senate, and the emperor was obliged to ask their permission to take money from it. Augustus demanded strict accounts of these books, which were overseen by a freedman. In times of financial crisis, emperors could shore up government finances, especially in Italy. Augustus, for example, had enough money (from his personal bank account, that is the province of Egypt) to bail out the treasury several times when the Senate ran out of money (Aug., *RG* 17, 18). Tiberius was tight-fisted and had a habit of imprisoning wealthy senators on charges of treason (thus claiming their coffers by default) (cf. Suet., *Tib.* 34.1, 46.1, 47.1, 48.1–2, 49.1–2), but left a healthy legacy behind (Cass. Dio, 59.2.1–4). His successor Gaius Caligula frittered it away in no time (59.2.5–6) on grand spectacles (Suet., *Gai.* 18–20) and extravagance (37.1–3). This led him discovering a latent talent for auctioneering (38.1–4, 39.1–2), as he sold everything not nailed down in the Imperial palace when not demanding new, excessive taxes (39–42), or confiscating people's properties and inheritances, including his own nephew, Nero's. Vespasian knew his way around finances (Suet., *Vesp.* 19.2); he rebalanced the books after ransacking Jerusalem, re-subduing Egypt (cf. Cass. Dio, 65.8.3–5), and levying taxes on spending pennies that added up to larger account (Suet., *Vesp.* 16.1–3). His tax on public toilets (*Vesp.*, 23.3) might have offended his son Titus, but it put Rome back in the black after the costs of Nero's reign and the civil war of 69. Trajan and Hadrian also built up healthy treasuries through conquest and its immediate benefits. Antoninus Pius left behind the largest treasury (*HA, Ant. Pius* 7.8–11), but, with frontier wars, lack of booty from conquest, and increasing inflation, his successor Marcus Aurelius had to debase the currency to try to finance his campaigns up on the Danube. Aurelius further had to sell off everything in the palace to balance the budget (*HA, Marc.* 17.4–5); Rome's financial woes were not helped by his spendy son and successor Commodus who ran up imperial debts for sixteen years before his comrades had had enough and assassinated him (cf. *HA, Comm.* 9.1, 14.3–8, 16.8). Restoring peace to the Empire and establishing his own dynasty, Septimius Severus left behind a legacy of about seven years' savings of tribute and grain (*HA, Sept.* 8.5) – which *his* (son and) successor Caracalla quickly plundered (cf. Cass. Dio, 78.9).

LAND, GRAIN, AND PUBLIC DOLE

Landholding and farms were the backbone of the Roman economy, and Rome and its surrounding territory were made up of smallholdings until the end of the third century BCE Not only did land keep the populace fed, but its ownership was linked originally with military service. In the early days of the Republic, one couldn't join the army without specific property-holding qualifications. This land requirement for service changed with Marius and the New Roman army in the late second century BCE (see Chapter 4) as Rome needed more soldiers. The subsequent reward for service was land (the establishment of a colony or *colonia*) and retirement packages. This practice continued into the imperial era, and a number of *coloniae* flourished during the *Pax Romana*, spreading Roman culture and enabling the economy to thrive. That said, the conditions of landholding varied, of course, depending on the climate and conditions of the soil throughout the Empire. A year of bad harvests would be followed by famine – this was catastrophic in a subsistence economy.

Keeping the Empire fed (including Rome's cities and especially its army) was the top priority of any ambitious individual who wanted to get elected and then to stay elected (in the Republic) or (later) an emperor who wanted to stay popular. Areas that were Rome's 'breadbaskets' – Egypt and North Africa, for example – were fiercely protected from threats on the one hand (*HA, Sev.* 8) while being squeezed financially on the other (cf. Cass. Dio, 65.8.3–5). Further provision for sustenance came in the form of agrarian laws and in food doles called *alimenta* which catered to the hungry mobs who populated Rome from the late second century BCE onwards. Many of the urban free poor were former soldiers and their families who had lost their small farms during the very wars that had led to Rome's prosperity. During the days of the early Republic, the Roman army fought nearby the City or at least within the Italian peninsula. They, like other soldiers in the Classical world, tended to fight when it was convenient to the agrarian calendar, that is, during the summer months after planting but before harvest, returning after battle to pick up their lives as small farmers. By the third century BCE, however, the Romans were fighting much farther afield, for example in Greece against the Macedonians. As these wars dragged on and were so far away, soldiers were away from home for much longer periods of time. They left their families behind to maintain their land, but oftentimes they returned home to discover that their farms had been lost due to a financial crisis. Invariably, these little farms were purchased by wealthy aristocratic landlords and consolidated into the great *latifundia*, landed estates sometimes dedicated to one or another major type of crop (see Chapter 2 on the Mediterranean triad).

Returning soldiers came home to find not only their land gone but also their livelihood and their families. They couldn't even work as tenants on their own farms because they had been replaced by the slaves brought back from the East by their own conquering armies. As a consequence, the original farm owners and their families migrated into crowded urban centres. Amongst the free poor, they became a substantial body for officials and administrations to feed and to look after. Rebellion from the lower classes came not because of this type of land-grab or the unequal distribution of wealth – the social order was simply too well ingrained for that. Panic was the result of grain being in short supply or priced out of reach (Amm. Mar., 18.10.1); this led to civil violence and riots (Tac., *Ann.* 6.13, 12.43) – the Emperor Gaius thought it was hilarious to withhold grain and to watch the ensuing hysteria (Suet., *Gai.* 26.5). Sometimes simply a rumour of a shortage was enough to rile up the mob, ever fearful of famine. Demands were made on the consuls and Senate to do something; the mob pelted the Emperor Claudius on one such occasion with stale crusts (Suet., *Claud.* 18–20). During the late first century BCE, the mob threw stones at the politicians because they felt they weren't doing enough to keep the city fed. That particular riot, Cicero notes, was stirred up by Clodius, a leader of the gangs running roughshod in Rome during the civil war between Julius Caesar and Pompey (allegedly as Caesar's henchmne and capitalising on the constant fear of starvation in the City (Cic., *Dom.* 11–12). It wasn't only the urban poor who were a danger during grain shortages: Julius Caesar was well aware of the consequences on military morale of not only a grain shortage but also the ensuing panic – when prices went up, the army could become dangerous (Caes., *BC* 1.52). Other examples of leaders manipulating bread prices, leading to riots, are described by Dio Chrysostom (*Or.* 46) and Philostratus (*VA* 1.15).

For an indication of how desperate the land and food situation had become by the second century BCE, check out Plutarch's *Life of Tiberius Gracchus* and *Life of Gaius Gracchus*. The Gracchi rose to political prominence by embracing popular concerns; they passed reforms that included creating more public grazing and farmland (Plut., *TG* 8.1–4, *GG* 5.1), putting grain prices and distribution into the hands of the state (5.2), establishing new colonies (to relieve urban crowding) (5.2, 10.1–2), and using the money bequeathed to Rome by the wealthy state of Pergamum to relieve land and food crises (*TG* 14.1–2). Subsequent ambitious politicians focused on similar needs of the poor to keep them happy, fed, and entertained – and to keep them voting in favour of these same leaders (or husbands of munificent women) who provided these amenities. Hence many contemporary sources note occasions when Republican leaders and emperors lowered or adjusted the exorbitant cost of grain (or prevented riots by lowering grain prices), but also when they effected better distribution of goods (especially grain). Placating the urban poor and the soldiers to maintain stability did not cease at the end of the Republic. Emperors were preoccupied with grain and food distribution as well – for example, when Claudius enlarged and expanded the harbour at Ostia (Suet., *Claud.* 20.1), or when Nero cost the treasury with his boondoggle project to dig a canal through the Corinthian isthmus (Cass. Dio, 62.16.1–2). Other rulers tried to ingratiate themselves and keep their heads by distributing free or cheap grain. Probus (reigned 276 to 282) attempted to court popularity by increasing the amount of grain brought in from Egypt – a province already under enormous financial burdens from Rome (*HA, Prob.* 10.9). He tried to keep the soldiers up on the Rhine happy with grain supplies appropriated from 'the barbarians' (14, 15, 28). He had some success, as his reign was one of the few peaceful and stable ones of the era of the 'Barracks Emperors'.

LABOUR FORCE: SLAVERY

Slavery was a well-established institution in the ancient world and a part of the Roman economy. Throughout the four hundred years of our period, slaves probably made up nearly half the population. The major sources were from warfare and piracy (*nexum*, or 'debt-slavery' was outlawed before our period); Julius Caesar once boasted of enslaving an entire community of fifty thousand people at once (Caes., *BG* 2.33.1–7). There were laws pertaining to slaves in the *Twelve Tables*, but their numbers increased significantly in the Roman West, and especially Italy, as a result of territories freshly conquered, including the Greek East, then later North Africa, Gaul, and the German and British frontiers. The slave population comprised men, women, and children, the well-educated and skilled, captured soldiers, and those who happened to be in the wrong place at the wrong time – territories defeated or places levelled and their populations enslaved as a Roman object lesson (e.g. Corinth, Cass. Dio, 21.72.1). Slavery had nothing to do with race; there were few questions regarding morality amongst aristocratic writers of owning another human being or human rights. That said, issues about the treatment of slaves and their legal rights began to appear in legal texts of imperial-age jurists such as Paulus and Ulpian. From the era of early Christian *apologia*, discussion of the morality of holding and maintaining a slave became part of the dialogue. The pagan Romans resolved the issue by arguing that Roman citizens could not be slaves (there were similar laws in Classical Athens). Christians likewise got round the problem by enslaving non-Christians. For recent overviews on slavery in the Roman world, see Hunt (2017) and Joshel (2010); for a sourcebook, Wiedemann (1980) is still useful.

Whilst the wealthy might own a large cohort of slaves, slave-owning was found at all levels of the Roman economic hierarchy, including slaves owning their own slaves. Slaves could be owned as private property by a single master or they might be part of the public pool of slaves who maintained the temples and assisted the state priests or who worked the public farmland. Household slaves held a variety of jobs;

these ranged from basic tasks around the home to specialised skills. A number of slaves from the Greek East, for example, were valued as doctors, teachers, and secretaries. Depending on the needs of the owner, slaves might be housed in conditions that were actually better than that of the urban poor. Examples of exceptional household slaves include Tiro, Cicero's secretary, who became an accomplished enough writer and secretary to Cicero that the latter wrote a series of letters to him. Freedman Polybius, author of a history of Rome and friend to such intellectuals in high Roman society as the general Scipio Aemelianus and the poet Lucan, started his career as one of the young hostages brought from Greece to be raised in Rome in the second century BCE; he became part of the so-called Scipionic Circle of aristocratic Hellenophiles whose interest in Greek arts, literature, and philosophy in the second century BCE alarmed conservatives such as Cato the Elder. Another member of this group was, according to tradition, another former slave, the playwright Terence. For further examples of the types of jobs held by slaves in a multi-generational household over the course of several generations, an excellent source is the tomb inscriptions of the family Volusius (see Treggiari, 1973, 1975).

Talented slaves could be loaned out by their owners as craft workers or entertainers, for example, and made money for the household. Slaves were often permitted to keep some of the money they made in this capacity, and they might save up to buy their own remittance (and frequently the freedom of their partners – slave 'marriages' were not legally recognised, so once free, a man or woman might purchase the freedom of their common-law spouse and so legitimise their union). Becoming *liberti*, they gained legal independence and *libertas*, the right to vote. Others were freed as a reward or in their owners' will. In turn freedmen could themselves become prosperous and wealthy as merchants, businessmen, and craftsmen; others remained employed by the same household that once held them. The relationship between household slaves and their master or mistress could be very close – the *libertus* or *liberta*, that is, freedman or freedwoman, might actually remain within the household as an employee.

PATRONAGE

There are a number of inscriptions by freedmen honouring their former masters and mistresses as their patrons: for
example, 'To the spirits of the departed. [Remains of] Marcus
Canuleius Zosimus; he lived twenty-eight years; his patron
erected this to a well-deserving freedman. In his lifetime
he spoke ill of no one; he did nothing without his patron's
consent; there was always a great weight of gold and silver
in his possession, and he never coveted any of it; in his craft,
Clodian engraving, he excelled everybody' (from L&R, 2:
no. 48.6: 172).

LEGAL STATUS OF SLAVES

About half of the slaves in the Roman world were agricultural. Because
slaves worked on the farms as well as in other laborious industries such as
mining, the Romans had very little incentive to develop technology in the
form of labour-saving devices outside of developments in brick-making,
for example, or the use of water-wheels in mining. Consequently, having
an enormous number of slaves meant that, even in the busiest industries
or on the great *latifundiae*, labour was by hand. The lot of the field slaves
was brutal and backbreaking work; living conditions were crude and
basic. The same treatises on how a gentleman ought to manage estates
also reveal how brutally owners and overseers treated estate slaves. For
example, Cato, who was criticised for his appalling treatment of his
slaves by Plutarch, advised ridding oneself of weak, old, or sick slaves as
financial liabilities (Plut., *Cat. Ma.* 4.4–5.2). Columella and Varro were
somewhat more pragmatic and advised that caring for slaves the same
way one would look after – and breed – livestock was profitable and sensible for any good estate owner (Var., *Rust.* 17, 18). Pliny the Younger, by
way of contrast, writes to one of his friends (Paulinus), urging him to be
good to his slaves and to treat them with respect and care in their dotage
or times of illness in response to the hard work that they have done on
behalf of their owner (*Epist.* 5.19).

Slaves could and did run away, as evidenced by the remains of chains in their bunkhouses, surviving metal collars that had been riveted around their necks, and mentions in literature of the problems of escaped slaves. The legal status of Republican slaves was that they *had* no legal status as independent beings. Imperial jurists such as Paulus and Gaius commented on the legal status of slaves, and emperors such as Hadrian did implement laws to protect slaves from cruel and abusive owners (Suet., *Claud.* 25.2; *HA, Hadr.* 18.7–11; Gai., *Instit.* 1.53). Slave testimony was no good in court unless it was extracted under torture. Execution by crucifixion was a common way to punish criminous slaves (discussed by Paul., *Sent.* 5). When Crassus finally defeated Spartacus's army of slaves (no thanks to Pompey who showed up pretty much at the end, mopped things up, then took all the glory), he had them crucified all along the *Via Appia* as a warning and object lesson to any other slave who was considering rebellion (App., *BC* 1.120).

THE CLEVER SLAVE

So ubiquitous were slaves in Classical society that the relationship between slave and master (especially its inversion) was a staple of Roman comedy in the mid to late Republic. The plays of Plautus and Terence drew inspiration from Greek New Comedy plays, by Menander especially, which feature many servile characters; from the fourth century BCE onwards the political and economic situation had reduced many in the Mediterranean world to servitude and poverty. Plautus's plays are filled with stock 'clever slave' characters who constantly prop up their dim-witted young aristocratic owners or outwit their older, aristocratic masters – the world of Edmund Blackadder and Baldrick can trace its roots right back to plays such as *Pseudolous* and *Menaechmi*. Reversing roles, and having the master wait on the slave (or the parent on the child), was a big part of the Saturnalia rites (described in some detail by Macrobius in his sixth-century CE work *Saturnalia*).

7 The manumission of a slave

COINAGE AND MEANS OF EXCHANGE

The Roman word for money was *pecunia* (hence 'impecunious' as a synonym for 'poor'), derived from the word *pecus* which means herd (sheep or cattle). The Romans also used small bronze weights (*aes rude*) to measure out transactions. Coinage was invented originally in Lydia in the sixth century BCE as a means of paying soldiers and to give them some tangible reward aside from booty. The Romans didn't start striking their own coins until the early third century BCE to pay soldiers after the Pyrrhic Wars when the Romans were fighting farther afield and longer wars; coins were a more practical reward, indeed payment for service (rather than land). The Second Punic War (against Carthage) saw the

Romans diversify their coinage into silver and bronze coins to make transactions even easier; silver became the standard after the Eastern wars in the third to second centuries BCE, following the Greek model. Another coinage reform came when Augustus re-stabilised the currency after Actium and introduced a standard gold coin into circulation. Over the next two hundred years, the discovery of gold and silver veins in newly conquered territories helped to keep the metal content in coins high and consequently keep the economy stable. In addition to being a means of exchange, coins were a handy means of spreading the image of the current leaders, symbolic information on the authority, prosperity, and stability of the Empire, and reminders of *Romanitas*.

Keeping coinage (and prices) stable was always an issue for Roman leadership; there are numerous references to prices, reformation of prices, and coinage debasement even during period of prosperity. The Romans had no concept of compound interest, inflation, or credit as one might find on a Year 1 economics module. As far as the Romans were concerned, money and funds were limited only to the coins in circulation, and a coin's value was fixed and based on the actual content of precious metal. Even with new mines, supplies were limited. During Nero's reign (54–68 CE), for example, the productivity of Spanish gold and silver mines was falling, and he was forced to debase coinage to try to compensate (cf. Diod. Sic., 5.35–38, on Spain's mines). Eventually he did re-stablise silver coinage during his reign, setting what is called the *argentus* standard, and was publicly lauded for it (cf. Suet., *Ner.* 44.2).

The policy of boosting the American economy after the 2008 recession would have baffled the Romans: then-President Bush had 'economic bonuses' sent out to households across the United States, encouraging recipients to turn around and immediately spend the money on consumer goods to get the cash back into the economy. The whole idea of 'patriotic' consumer spending was a result of the industrial revolution or even the Cold War (both in the 1950s and in Reagan's 1980s) (see Taylor, 2012: 4). Instead, the Romans attempted to sort out economic crises by debasing their coinage to spread the amount of that metal in circulation. This led to more problems including inflation and runaway prices. Trajan didn't invade and conquer Dacia just for the scenery – there were a number of silver mines in the region (as well as an obnoxious client king whom he wanted to shut down). Trajan's aggressive economic imperialism helped to support the vast government *alimenta* programmes of Hadrian and Antoninus Pius, but it turned out to be a short-term solution. Loss of territory (as Hadrian pulled back the frontiers) and endemic warfare forced Marcus Aurelius to debase the coins yet again.

The practice of debasement, coupled with counterfeiting, only made inflation worse: at one point in the late third century CE, parts of the Western empire reverted to bartering. For about twenty years consequently, Marcus Carusius acted as a rogue emperor based up in Britain because he could pay his soldiers in gold coins – something no one in Western Europe had been able to do for a few years. Marcus had at his disposal the gold mines in what is now modern Lampeter, Wales. It was not the first time that British gold had played a role in propping up an ambitious Roman general, even if Plutarch had dismissed Britain as an island with nothing worth taking (Plut., *Caes.* 23.4). Three hundred years before Carusius, Caesar had rallied support for his expedition to Britain, pointing out that the gold torques worn by the barbarian locals were a sign that the island had untapped riches; the raiding party was disappointed to discover that the Britons used brass and iron rings as currency (Caes., *BG* 5.12) and that there was very little gold and no silver lying around (Cic., *Fam.* 7.7; *Att.* 4.17). Still, Britain had good farm and grazing land (Tac., *Agr.* 12.5), and its inhabitants became another source of slaves (Suet., *Iul.* 47.1).

Another drastic solution to curb runaway inflation was to fix all prices at wholesale rates uniformly no matter what the quality of the product and to make illegal (with capital punishment) any attempts at retail profit. This law was Diocletian's *Edict of Maximum Prices* (301 CE); it resulted almost instantly in black marketeering and was quickly struck from the books. The *Edict* was a response to almost half a century of dire financial crisis, but even during the heights of Rome's economic prosperity prices for even the most basic of goods remained high, if not out of reach, for the majority of the population. That said, however, the Romans did have public support programmes that worked – as long as the Empire was expanding and acquiring new sources of income (see below).

HOME ECONOMICS

In Classical Rome, *oeconomia* referred to overall household management (Greek *oikos* – household; *nomos* – law). Roman examples of such *oeconomia* can be found in those estate handbooks of Cato, Varro and Columella. The *Oeconomia* of Xenophon (d. 354 BCE) was a handbook on the practical matters of running the house; see, for example, his advice for young housewives (L&F, no. 319: 247–253). One sees praise for such management by the women of the household in the *Laudatio Turiae*, one of the longest surviving funerary inscriptions and one of the most detailed elegies of a woman from the period of the Republic (*ILS*, 8393 and in L&F, no. 191: 165–169), as well in Suetonius's *Life of Augustus*, where praise is given to Livia and even Julia for their running of Augustus's household as a model for other households throughout the empire (Suet., *Aug.* 73.1). Women who looked after their home were praised by the rhetoricians as the ideal wives and mothers, but slaves and servants would also be tasked with the basic chores of acquiring goods (mainly food) for the home.

HALF A *DENARIUS* FOR ME LIFE STORY? THE VALUE OF MONEY

My students often ask, 'What are these coins worth in modern money?' A better question is, 'What is their contemporary buying power?' Prices could vary depending on where and when you are in the Empire – the highest being in Rome, and the lowest away from the centre. In the first century CE or so, a loaf of bread cost about two *asses*, and a *modius* of wheat (enough to make 16 to 20 loaves at a pound each) was worth about 7 HS. Soldiers made about 3 HS a day; an adult slave could be bought for a little over 6,000 HS at around the same time in Pompeii. A handy online source, via the internet Wayback Machine, is a now deleted page of comparison prices and values at Ancient Coins, http://web.archive.org/web/20070113183811/http://www.ancientcoins.biz/pages/economy/. The author provides no references to ancient sources specifically, but pulls information from general surveys on daily life in Greece and Rome. It's a useful tool to crunch numbers for setting your fictional scenes if they include budgets and shopping, but as always with this type of source *caveat emptor*.

A detailed contemporary source that might be of some use (with caveats) is the *Edict of Maximum Prices* (301 CE). This edict attempted to do exactly what it said on the tin; it's useful because it also provides examples of wages, at least in the fourth century CE, and some details about relative pricing of foodstuffs, goods, wages, and slaves. Sear's survey (2000–14) may be of some use; for a more recent English translation of the Edict, see Kropff's 'New English Translation of the Price Edict of Diocletian' (link in bibliography). His introduction includes a survey of contemporary Roman coinage and buying power, at least in the later era of the Empire. He also includes a table of weights and measures – also useful for picking your way through the Edict. A less academic but useful source for piecing together a fictional look at consumer Romans would be Falka's *Coins for Education* website (link in bibliography). It's aimed mainly at teachers who wish to put together school lessons on the Roman economy and not the kind of source you'd cite in an academic paper, but he includes a number of handy charts and graphs that lay out the prices of basic goods, services, and wages. Ditto for Matyszak (2007) which considers throughout expenses for the tourist time-travelling to the second century CE.

CAVEAT EMPTOR

Markets (*marcella*, singular *marcellum*, or permanent markets), *nundiae* (which were markets held every ninth day, and when the freshest produce was available), and shops (*tabernae*) were ubiquitous in Roman towns and cities. Surveys of excavated cities such as the usual suspects of Pompeii and Herculaneum are good sources of the kinds of shops and services available on a Roman high street and, in the cases of the Vesuvian towns, surviving examples of perishable items.

A recent study that considers the idea of Roman shopping and 'retail' and how it compares to modern understanding of economics is Holleran (2012). She fills a gap in the scholarship of Roman economy which generally looks at trade, industry, coinage, and the big picture of the city of Rome as an urban market centre. Holleran emphasises the diversity of the retail trade in Rome and the central role it played in both the infrastructure of the city and its urban economy. Her work isn't so much about actual shopping, as the sources are so scarce, but rather, as Beard notes in her review (2013), it is a careful study of retail trade. Holleran highlights the relationship between the retail trade and the wider social and economic environment; her approach is useful for the author of historical fiction because she frames her discussion of Rome's retail culture in the context of modern retail and its definitions (especially against the capitalist retail revolution of the late nineteenth century). The full study is available as an ebook; she has also written a digest version for *BBC History* reprinted at *History Extra* (link in bibliography).

Holleran is one source to help you create the ambience of shopping and running the household. Matyszak notes in his popular surveys of life during the *Pax Romana* (2007) and of a day in the life of the city (2017) that it can actually be a bit difficult compiling a 'typical' household shopping list because specific written sources just don't survive. There are a few floating about, mostly from the pens of comedy and satire writers. For example, Horace moans about high prices turning his gourmet dinner plans into a night in with lentil soup (*Sat.* 1.6.111–19). Because so many goods were produced via private enterprise, inexperienced shoppers or rubes might find themselves purchasing inferior goods at the market whilst the merchant or the farmer's regulars got the prime stuff. Shoddy goods were sold for high prices, and sellers, then, as now, had unctuous sales pitches for the gullible. Still, one can piece together the general staples the average household might need. Matyszak (2007) provides a neat summary on shopping (types of shops, words and terms for the different markets), exchanging money, and what to buy, and gives ideas for the value of money. Other contemporary sources for shopping include Apicius's cookery books, the tablets from Vindolanda, and the *Edict of Maximum Prices* – again, later than our period, but also representative of the various staples, basic goods, and services available in the marketplace.

SHOPPING LIST FROM VINDOLANDA

'Bruised beans, two *modii* [a measurement of about 6.6 kg]; chickens, two; a hundred apples (if you can find nice ones); a hundred or two hundred eggs, if they are for sale at a fair price; 8 *sextarii* of fish-sauce; a *modius* of olives …' (Tablet 302) (transcriptions and translations of all of the letters are online with indexes, keywords, and explication at http://vindolanda.csad.ox.ac.uk/index.shtml).

FOREIGN TRADE

Foreign trade flourished during our period. Pompey and then Augustus's navy cleared up the piracy problem in the eastern Mediterranean and allowed ease of trade across the sea. Other factors that contributed to trade networks included the extensive road network, Roman currency as an acceptable single currency across the Empire, and low duties on customs and taxes on the provincial frontiers – not to mention the overall peace during the first two centuries of the Principate. Land routes also benefited from the road system and general peace, and the caravan trade brought goods into Rome from as far away as India and even China (McLaughlin, 2010 and Arkenberg, 2000). Traders from all part of the Empire converged on Italy and Rome with very little regulation from the government on productions and distribution.

Large cities, including Rome, also saw myriad goods coming in from the provinces; Rome's reputation as a consumer parasite on the Empire has been re-evaluated by scholars recently, but there is no denying that balance of trade between Italy and the rest of the Empire was unequal. The centre, for example, demanded foodstuffs, raw materials, and manufactured luxury goods that far exceeded the value of its own exports. Scholars now argue that urban growth, and Rome's (and Italy's) demands helped to stimulate the Roman economy. With the establishment of cities came peace in the surrounding countryside so that trade and commerce could flourish; cities created marketplaces to distribute surplus wealth. This is turn helped to fund the purchase and transport of goods (especially food supplies) where needed. The demands of Rome and Italy soon made the provinces and territories even wealthier as provincial trade and manufacture surpassed Italian trade and manufacture. The huge demand for food in Rome also helped foster the economy in Egypt, North Africa, and other grain-producing regions.

Aristocrats, Senatorial and equestrian, could become wildly prosperous during this era, especially in the provinces, where they might get stuck into moneylending, then gobbling up estates when the borrower went bankrupt. Much trade was private enterprise – trade and success in trade were not a means of elevating one's social standing or social respect so those in the old patrician hierarchy would not be so concerned about such hustling as a means of social competition or increasing their own status. Those who mostly participated in trade and business were the equestrians. They were a subclass in the Roman gentry, but not prohibited by law from trade as the Senatorial aristocracy were. Freedmen and former soldiers might also become active in trade and business; veteran soldiers frequently opened shops and taverns in the *coloniae* on the back of their retirement bonuses. Senatorial aristocrats were more restricted in their financial schemes. Some might bid on contracts for public buildings, operation of mines (e.g. in Spain and Macedonia). They collected rents from public lands in Italy (competing with local, native, and provincial tax collectors: refer to the *Urso Charter* for an example of how a *municipium* sought to protect itself from such predatory aristocrats (*FIRA*, 122).

The table below shows a selection of provinces, goods, and contemporary sources (based on L&R, 2: no. 23: 76ff). For an overview on the major provinces' economy, administration and cultural life during the height of the *Pax Romana*, see *CAH*, 11: 405–678.

PROVINCES AND THE GODS THEY SUPPLIED TO ROME

Spain
Spain was noted for mining (lead, tin, silver, gold); the Rio Tinto mine in Spain predates Roman times. Parts of Spain were also turned over to large-scale olive production. On Spain's ores, see Diod. Sic., 5.35–38.

Gaul
Gaul was a source of grain; farmland was one of the main profits of Caesar's conquests and the subsequent pacification of the province. Also ore, pottery, and textiles. On the general benefits of farmland and mining, see Strab., 4.1.2; 2.1–2 (abridged in L&R, 2: no. 23: 78–79).

Italy
Italy exported olive oil, wine, and livestock. Strab., 5.1.12.

Greece
Greece produced marble and honey. Strab., 9.1.23.

Bithynia and Pontus (Black Sea)
Bithynia and Pontus produced timber and grain; Strabo discusses the wool industry from the area's sheep. There was some mining; Strabo remarks on its horrific conditions. Strab., 12.3.12–13.

Asia (modern-day Turkey)
Asia was renowned for its olive oil, marble quarries, and black wool. Strab., 12; 8.14, 16.

Syria and Judaea
The expensive and famous purple Tyrian dyes come from Syria. So does asphalt. The Syrians were stereotyped for being hustlers and sharp traders. Strab., 16.2.23, 42.

Egypt
Egypt produced papyrus, grain, and gold – it had special status amongst the provinces in terms of taxation and autonomy (Strab., 17.1.12; *FIRA* 1.99 in L & R, vol. 2, no. 79: 298–302). Augustus kept a tight grip on the province as it was the source of his vast personal wealth. According to Pliny the Elder, by the reign of Nero, the place was already crushed under untenable taxation: only six landlords controlled the entire province (*NH* 18.7), and stories came out of the area of people abandoning their homes and villages to avoid taxes. See also Pliny, *NH* 13.22–23.71–77 on the making of papyrus.

North Africa
North Africa produced grain – more or less Rome's Kansas. Pliny, *NH* 28, 29.

Britain
Britain had farmland and produced tin, lead, some gold, and cheap blue and grey pearls. Tac., *Agr. passim*; Strab., 4.5.1–4.

TAXES AND TAX COLLECTION

Imagine a map of the Roman Empire as having Rome and Italy at the centre, ringed by a band of civilised (in the sense of urbanised) provinces, and then ringed again by client-states and the frontiers where the army was stationed. Taxes came in to the centre, then Rome redistributed them back out on to the frontier as these funds went primarily to support the army. Certain taxes went specifically towards the wages and supplies of active soldiers and towards funding soldiers' pensions; this tax was the *stipendium*, noted for becoming a fixed rate from 180 BCE. There was compensation – protection by the army – for these payments but at the same time other provincial obligations could be more burdensome than direct taxation. The middle band of provinces was hit the hardest in terms of contributions.

Taxes fell into two main categories, direct (*tribute*), which included tribute and land and personal taxes, and indirect (*vectigalia*). It was a complex system, as direct and indirect taxes were inextricably linked. Direct taxes included the annual tribute of grain expected from areas called the *annona;* such tribute was paid in kind rather than coin, as this grain usually went to feed the army. Provinces were also expected to furnish supplies to the troops and officials, for example animals (particularly horses) for imperial messengers or post, or to perform personal services (*munera*) for the state. *Vectigalia* could take any number of forms, including, for example, local taxes (poll taxes). Other indirect taxes included taxes on goods (which in turn affected prices) and payments from travellers moving through customs checkpoints and tolls at Roman harbours and along Roman roads. Industries related to and affected by the tax system also included minting coins, how silver ore was used in currency, and regulation of the coin supply. The mines which supplied the materials for coinage were themselves taxed; for example, in 195–194 BCE Cato the Elder levied *vectigalia* on some of the mines.

There were great regional differences in levies and collection across the Empire. One example comes from the *Tariff of Coptus*, from c. 90 CE in Egypt. It set the tolls for various categories of travellers and goods at the port of Coptus where merchants, traders, and travellers arrived at the Red Sea. In the local Greek currency a ship's captain might pay 8 drachmas and his sailors 5; 2 obols would cover a donkey permit (*Tariff of Coptus*, L&R, 2: no. 18: 66). Another example of imperial levies came when Tiberius divided the Empire into ten customs districts. At the borders of these districts, a merchant was taxed around 2 per cent of the value of the goods he was carrying, but slightly less at the tollbooths within the districts themselves. Luxury goods coming in from the East, however, were hit up with a tax of up to 25 per cent of the value of the goods (L&R, 2: no. 18: 65). Citizens paid less tax than inhabitants of client-states, and those living in the Eastern provinces, which were wealthier, were subsequently slammed with higher taxes. When Caracalla enacted universal citizenship in 212 CE (Cass. Dio, 78.9.4; for the law itself, *FIRA*, 1.88, in L&R, 2: no. 106: 380), it wasn't out of civic generosity, it was because the emperor was broke. With this law, suddenly all of those Eastern inhabitants of the Empire had to pay up overdue inheritance taxes as well as taxes due on first becoming a citizen.

There were plenty of opportunities for corruption, exploitation, and profiteering in the Roman financial system. Roman proconsuls (governors), especially in faraway provinces, had a habit of skimming off the top for themselves, especially in the later Republican period. As for the proconsular assistants, many of them were drawn from the local area and plenty keen to exploit their own neighbours. Sometimes, the local governor or magistrate wasn't even present as taxes were levied and paid in, leaving his property (or province) vulnerable to the whims and temptations of the bailiffs and accountants left to do these jobs in his place. The locals could always file a complaint against these factotums, or even appeal to Rome directly; they could request an investigation and to have the magistrates brought up on charges in court for unfair treatment. The problem was, of course, that the aristocrats and their cronies usually won these cases: they had influence, they had powerful associates, and they could offer patronage and advantage to the adjudicator. *Usually* does not mean *always*, however: a case of a powerful proconsul being brought down on charges of corruption (and for setting precedent for checks and balances on similar provincial strongmen) was young Cicero's career-making court case against one of these proconsuls, Verres in Spain. Cicero faced the top lawyer of his day, and, as the rookie, he was expected to take a sacrificial loss for the experience. Instead, he won brilliantly. His prosecution exposed the corruption of tax-collecting under Verres's jurisdiction, including selling the job of tax-collector (Cic., *Ver.* 3.8). Cicero's career was established, and the Roman centre narrowed its sights on corruption in the provinces, putting into place the means to alleviate future cronyism. If you wish to see someone cut loose on the uses and abuses of the *vectigalia*, check out Cicero's speeches on the Agrarian law, *De Lege Agraria*.

Even with such precautions against individuals profiteering off a province, taxes could squeeze the life out of certain regions. For example, Egypt, kept by Augustus as the source of his personal fortune, was just about ground down by the levies imposed on the locals, especially from the third century CE onwards. Egyptian census records are filled with details that reveal devastating poverty because of overtaxation. For example, during the reign of Nero, there are accounts of villagers so poor that a single person might own only one-sixth part of an olive tree and one-tenth part of a house (in which twenty-six people might be living). One group of tax collectors contacted the prefect of Egypt c. 55 CE to report that they couldn't collect tax because there simply *wasn't* any money or property that they could take from the inhabitants of the village (*Select Papyri*, 281).

Debt collecting (a job of the decurions) was consequently one of the most dangerous to hold, especially in the eastern part of the Empire. Tax collectors had a terrible reputation; Plutarch remarks that it was considered a disgraceful occupation (Plut., *De Vit.* 829C). So terrifying was the taxman that, for example, in 57 CE, one man fled the decurion because he could not pay his poll tax, pig tax, or dyke tax (an annual levy to maintain the waterways) (L&R, 2: no. 85: 317). Other tax dodgers fled into the desert – this is why St Antony, considered the first of the eremitical monks, was believed by the locals to be a tax dodger (Athan., *Vit. Ant.* 44, 46). Antony sought the solitude of the desert to contemplate God

(Book 3), and there he discovered among the dunes that he had loads of neighbours who actually were on the run from the tax man (cf. 49; see L&R, 2: no. 85: 316–318). Other decurions who were sent out to collect taxes from certain areas (such as Egypt) sometimes never came back; follow-up investigations often learnt that the locals had despatched him (if they admitted anything). Even the tax collectors themselves would run away rather than face villagers and demand money from them; decurions who couldn't collect the taxes were expected to make up the shortfall (Berlin Papyrus, no. 372, in L&R, vol. 2, no. 77: 294–295).

SOURCES FOR TAXES AND TAX COLLECTION

These sources, usually in the form of census records but also papyrus tax receipts, survive in abundance from Egypt from the first century CE onwards; L&R, 2, includes a selection of documents (nos 308–318) which include census records, tax privileges (held in both Judaea and Egypt), and reports of 'fugitive paupers'. A sift through the Loeb volumes of *Select Papyri* will also yield up a number of census, tax, and other economic records – mainly from the Eastern side of the Empire, given the ephemeral nature of the papyrus and the caches of documents discovered at sites such as Oxyrhyncus in the twentieth and twenty-first centuries. These volumes are also terrific sources of letters, wills, contracts, and other administrative business.

POVERTY: VIRTUE OR VICE?

Poverty and misfortune, for the Roman rhetoricians, was the result of personal failing, laziness and/or simply fate; there was no pity for those fallen on hard times. Frugality, on the other hand, was seen as a virtuous choice (provided one wasn't frugal to the point of being a miser). Plutarch, for example, commented on Aristides' famous poverty: 'Only those who were poor in spite of themselves should be ashamed of their poverty; those who, like himself, chose poverty, should glory in it. And surely it were ridiculous to suppose that the poverty of Aristides was due to his sloth, when, without doing anything disgraceful, but merely by stripping a single barbarian, or seizing a single tent, he might have made himself rich' (Plut., *Comp. Aristid. Cat.* 4). Cato the Elder was another admired for his frugal lifestyle (Plut., *Cat. Ma.* 1.3–4, 4.3–4, 5.1, 6.1–3, etc.); Cornelia was lauded for treasuring her sons, rather than baubles, as her jewels (Val. Max., 4.4). Anyone could practise such traits; Livy notes that, during the wars of the third century BCE, even women and children gave up to the state any gold or silver that they had, following the model of the Senators, because to live simply demonstrated 'modesty and purity' and virtuous living – especially amongst Roman women (Liv., 34.6) As Sallust warned Caesar, 'In no other way can any mortal exalt himself and touch upon the divine unless he casts off the delights of wealth and bodily pleasures and devotes himself to his soul, not by giving in to and indulging its cravings, thereby allowing it a perverse gratification, but by exercising it in labour, in patience, and in virtuous precepts and brave deeds' (Sall., *Epist. ad Caes.* 7).

FINDING THE LOWER CLASSES AND POOR PEOPLE IN THE SOURCES

Ordinary people can be glimpsed in the letters of Cicero and Pliny the Younger, as well as in a few surviving land registers (noted in this chapter) or in the *Urso Charter* (Chapter 4), or the practice court cases in Quintilian's handbooks on education. Although letters suggest a degree of literacy that poorer people might not have access to, collections of tablets from Vindolanda and papyri from Egypt offer insight into everyday matters; funerary inscriptions, while formulaic, also indicate household and family situations that mattered enough to pay for the tomb. The lower classes populate Roman comedies; they populate the satires of Apuleius and Juvenal. The truly poor are the mob mentioned in passing in the histories and biographies of Tacitus, Suetonius, Josephus, Plutarch, and Christian scripture, amongst other places. Scholarship on 'the ordinary' and lower classes really began in the 1960s with the advent of sociological studies in general; combined in the past thirty years with archaeological studies, this is a growing field. A good study on poverty in the Roman world is a collection of essays on attitudes towards and political and social influences of the poor in Rome in Atkins and Osbourne (2006), and on daily life as found through inscriptions see Harvey (2004).

THE *ALIMENTA* SYSTEM – THE PUBLIC DOLE AND BENEFACTION

That said, it was well worth the while of government to look after the (urban) poor, if anything to keep them fed and entertained (Juvenal's *panem et circenses*, bread and circuses) and on the side of the current leaders. There were government schemes in place to relieve the problem of food shortages, all of which depended on the wealth coming into the Empire, or the largesse of wealthy individuals, to work. These schemes fell in general under the heading of the *alimenta* system, a type of public dole that existed from the time of the Republic as part of a system of greater social welfare that saw both distribution of grain and gifts of money at intervals to the urban poor (examples can be found in L&R, 2: no. 70: 255–259, and Parkin and Pomeroy, 2007: 211–212). The land registers discussed above include information on the practical working of the *alimenta*. Livy remarks, for example, that a large proportion of Rome's grain dole came from the tribute of conquered and client-states (Book 23). Other contemporary sources that mention the *alimenta* include Sallust, Augustus, the *Historia Augusta*, and Ammianus Marcellinus. Augustus maintained a public grain dole, a result of his both reorganising the shambolic system of the late Republic (Aug., *RG* 5) and paying for a grain dole out of his own pocket (from Egyptian revenues) (15, 18; Suet., *Aug.* 40, 41). Other emperors who standardised public distribution included Trajan. His aggressively imperialistic policies saw Rome annex Dacia with its silver mines, and Mesopotamia and parts of Parthia with their markets and trade routes; it was all income that helped to pay for Hadrian's generous imperial dole. Septimius Severus was another emperor in our period whose conquests and forward planning had allowed for the system to thrive (*HA, Sev.* 8; *Heliog.* 27). Additional imperial funds included assistance for women who were left both widowed and childless or spinsters (for example, Liv., 24.18; *HA, Hadr.* 7) and for orphans.

Other funds went towards keeping the mob entertained; spectacles, for example, functioned as a medium to demonstrate publicly the power and authority of the Empire at both the state and local level. Entertainments, gladiator matches, spectacles, chariot races, were held at great expense from the time of the *latifundia* movement onwards through to the imperial period and really didn't come to an end in the West until quite late in the fifth and sixth centuries, despite the efforts of Christian emperors to suppress pagan fun. Some spectacles and entertainments are discussed in Chapter 6, but they are relevant here in terms of the economy, as they could be big business. Not only did they keep the unruly city mobs occupied, but they also employed quite a number of people – trainers, costumers, grooms, vets and doctors, musicians. Much of this was paid for by the upper classes: senators and new men who wanted votes in the Republic, and emperors and local administrators who wanted to show off their largesse as well as keeping everyone in line during the imperial era. Such displays could lead to corruption, as the *Urso Charter* of 44 BCE demonstrates: this decree warns off aristocrats who might splurge on entertainments and amenities to try to control voting in a neighbouring city. Spectacle could also impoverish a local area, when provincial administrators splashed out extravagant shows as they emulated life at the centre; Trajan and Hadrian had to send word to the provinces that local authorities had to rein it in as the town locals were being crushed under the financial (tax) burden of paying for it all instead of using the funds to pay Roman taxes or to support the army (*ILS*, 5163 = *CIL*, 2.6278, in Mahoney, 2001: 97–100).

Despite such programmes, Rome was not a 'welfare state' as you might consider Britain in the late twentieth and twenty-first centuries. Roman *alimenta* schemes and spectacle were extremely expensive to maintain, and they worked only as long as the Empire was thriving in terms of property and wealth that had been brought in via conquest and not because of any regulated study of economics in the modern sense. The underlying purpose behind these programmes, whether enacted by the state or by an individual, was as always a show of patronage and the abilities of an individual to act as a patron to impoverished clients, as well as a means of crowd control. 'Distribution of bread', for example, could include flinging loaves into the crowds at spectacles as part of the entertainment (Cass. Dio, 62.18.1–3; Suet., *Ner.* 11.2; Suet., *Gai.* 18.2, 26.4). Public assistance would be redirected if there was a military crisis; funds would be diverted from the poor and into the army. And despite being 'state' programmes, the *alimentae* were at the mercy of the person at the centre of that state: Emperor Elagabulus subverted the entire system by diverting an entire year's worth of the dole to all the harlots, procurers, and rent-boys who were kept within the walls. He promised an equal amount to those without, for, thanks to the foresight of Severus and Trajan, there was in Rome at that time a store of grain equal to seven years' tribute (*HA, Heliog.* 27).

Public benevolence was another means of patronage. *Caritas*, the Christian idea of giving – of money, or favours, of help – with expectation of no return, no repayment, and no consequences was a baffling and alien idea to the Romans, who saw all gifts as reciprocal in some way. Pagan Romans practised civic euergetism, that is, displays of munificence that made them patrons of their city and memorialised their reputation. These actions were an excellent way for individuals to contribute to the building and maintenance of public roads, buildings, and markets. Tax collecting was driven from the centre, but so much of the economy was kept running at the local level through individual contribution. Many inscriptions survive of (especially) women and freedmen leaving to their towns legacies and trust funds not only to help with food shortages but also to see to the education of children (e.g. in L&R, 2: no. 71: 259–272). Such acts seem to modern eyes acts of charity and kindness, and there surely was some sense of civic pride and giving back, especially in the case of *liberati* (freed men and women) who made good. Civic responsibility went hand in hand with the patron–client relationship. If you did well for your town or city, or its inhabitants, you not only became a patron of your city (and elevated in status) but also gained glory and remembrance for the good of the state.

This is by no means to disparage the work or gifts of any of these benefactors, nor should they always be viewed with cynicism – although you might be able to read desperation in the largesse of some of the less popular emperors, especially the ones who foolishly emptied the treasuries for but a moment's pleasure. Working towards public munificence, for example, Hadrian made loads of financial gifts and payments to help impoverished Senators, to relieve people suffering under crushing debt, and to provide for widows and orphans, or, as the anonymous author of his life put it, 'he used every means of gaining popularity' (*HA, Hadr.* 7: '*ad colligendam autem gratiam nihil praetermittens*'). Instead, it must be kept in mind that everything the Romans did had some contractual effect and frequently reflects the strong institution of the patron–client relationship. Spending one's wealth recklessly was criticised as vulgar: Trimalchio is mocked for his ostentatious display of new-found wealth as well as knowing the price of everything on display in his house – and for bragging about it to his guests (cf. Petron., *Sat.* 34, 67). Conversely, giving away one's wealth as an act of patronage towards one's city or town was greatly admired. Gillias of Agrigentum was so wealthy, for example, that he single-handedly organised banquets for the poor when the price of grain went up, gave food to the poor, provided dowries to girls with no means, and assisted those who found themselves suddenly in debt. Notes Valerius Maximus, not only his town but the surrounding neighbourhoods too admired Gillas for his benevolence (Val. Max., 4). Another example is of the wealthy Junia Theodora, who died at Corinth in 43 CE. She was honoured on her tomb for all of her contributions to the city and all of the patronage that she offered the citizens of Corinth. Her monument states that she should be honoured with the glory that she deserved and 'that our people would not cease in their good will and gratitude toward her' (L&F, no. 225: 192).

PUBLIC BENEVOLENCE

Sources for public benevolence include inscriptions found on the University of Fordham's site at https://legacy.fordham.edu/Halsall/ancient/romancharity.asp, which is taken from Davis (1912–1913). Other useful caches of public inscriptions especially related to freedmen and freedwomen can be found in L&F, 190–194. Caelia Macrina (L&F, no. 221: 191) is one of the more famous; she left behind not only enough money (300,000 HS) to construct a public building in Tarracina but also a stipend of a million HS to be doled out annually to feed one hundred boys and girls each year. Another trove of public inscriptions that includes municipal gifts and grants such as this can be found in *ROL*, vol. 4; the volume is divided into sections including funerary monuments, honours, and public benefaction (*euergetism*). Check out also Lomas and Cornell (2013) which addresses topics on both civic building projects and entertainment, and Hemelrijk (2015) on women, civic life, and public benevolence.

A SELECTION OF ROMAN MAGISTRACIES

Each of these officers would have been accompanied by a *lictor* (a servant carrying the *fasces*); the number of *lictores* depended on one's rank. Private citizens might also be wealthy enough to warrant a *lictor* or two.

Consuls

The highest office of the *cursus honorum* (Polyb., 6.12.1). Two were elected annually, and the year was named after them. They could not hold consecutive office but rather had to wait ten years between terms (cf. Cic., *Leg.* 3.9) (Marius blithely ignored this, Plut., *Mar.* 12.1, 14.6–8, 22.3, 28.1.1–6). One could be consul only after having held the other positions of the *cursus* (which Pompey ignored; cf. Plut., *Pomp.* 14.1–2). The consuls were at first only patricians, but, after the Licinian-Sextian laws were passed in 367 BCE, first one, then both consuls could be plebeians (Liv., 6.35, 6.38ff). Amongst their duties, they commanded the army in battle, administered Senate business, convened the *comitia centuriata*, and supervised financial affairs. Consuls led the army, whether they had military experience or not – and whether they liked each other or not (see the Battle of Cannae, 216 BCE, for an example of how well that went; Liv., 22.46-50). If a consul died during his term, a temporary consul filled his post, as Octavian did after Pansa and Hirtius were killed at Mutina in 43 BCE (Suet., *Aug.* 10.1-4; App., *BC* 3.51.1 – cf. 3.73.1).

Praetors

An office created in 366 BCE to take the place of the consuls if they were away at war (cf. Var., *De Ling.* 5.80; Cic., *Leg.* 3.6). Two praetors were elected annually. The praetor was a military commander and awarded *imperium* by the Senate, that is, the right of command over a particular area for a designated time. Pompey managed to snag a series of *imperia* which resolved certain issues (piracy in the Aegean, for example) and gave him continuous power of martial law, for example the *lex Gabinia* (Plut., *Pomp.* 25.1.7, 26.4) and the *lex Manilia* (30.1ff). Sometimes praetors acted as treasurers; they also had some duties as administers of justice, especially to clarify areas were the law was vague. Part of the *cursus*.

Aediles

Four *aediles* were elected annually (Dion. Hal., *Ant. Rom.* 6.90.2-3). They were temple wardens originally but ended up in charge of records, files, and other documents which were stored in the temples for safe keeping. They also supervised public markets and street maintenance, and organised public festivals. Part of the *cursus*.

Quaestors

Eight quaestors were elected annually from 264 BCE (Tac., *Ann.* 11.22; Var., *De Ling.* 5.81). Their role was mainly financial, and they controlled the treasury. Part of the *cursus*.

Censor

An office created in 443 BCE; censors were elected every five years and stayed in office 18 months (Liv., 4.8.2; Cic., *Leg.* 3.3.7; Var., *De Ling.* 5.81; Plut., *Cat. Ma.* 16.1–3). The censor figured out who would pay what taxes on a quota system. The censor also supervised public morals, determined who could lawfully sit in the Senate, registered the citizens, and leased public contracts. Augustus, amongst others, became censor as it was also a great way to work out which people he could get rid of and thus confiscate their estates (cf. Plut., *Cat. Ma.* 16.3).

Tribune of the plebeians

There were ten tribunes of the people (i.e. of the plebeians) who were charged to protect the lower classes. The *tribunus plebis* (494 BCE) and the *concilium plebis* (471 BCE) allowed the plebeians to elect their own tribune(s) and to hold their own assembly to represent them. The tribune became a representative of the people and acted as a go-between for the Senate and the plebeian classes. In return, the plebeians promised military protection (a promise which, made on temple grounds, was considered sacrosanct). Eventually the tribune would gain enough power not only to have a voice in the Senate but also to veto Senatorial decisions. The *lex Hortensia* in 287 BCE finally ended the patrician–plebeian struggle as it gave the *concilium plebis* the force of law over patricians and plebeians (Gai., *Instit.* 1.3; Aul. Gell., *NA* 15.27.4; cf. Liv., 3.55.1–7, 13–15, on the *Lex Valerio-Horatio* of 449 BCE).

COINS: SPOTTER'S GUIDE

These are some of the main coins found in our period (c. 250 BCE to 200 CE). If you're looking for the bronze *nummus* or the gold *solidus*, they came into circulation later. In a cosmopolitan empire, there were, of course, loads of other coins floating about, especially

Greek and Egyptian. The value of a coin was its weight in metal, and this is sometimes reflected in the coin's name.

as

Bronze. One of the oldest coins, it derived originally from the bronze bars used to measure transactions. There were a number of smaller fractions of *asses* in circulation.

sestertius

Silver in the Republic, brass (*orichalcum*) from the reign of Augustus. Abbreviated HS, a version of which was adopted about two thousand years later for the dollar ($) sign. One of the coins that 'everybody knows'. Augustus set the qualifications that a Senator needed a million of them to qualify for his status and an equestrian at least 400,000. A soldier's wage was around 3.5 HS a day (and, like today, a lot of that went into their supplies at the camp commissary). The Praetorians made more, and might demand – and get – more (Tac, *Ann.* 1.17.4 and 1.17.5) The donative was a bonus (later bribe) given to the Praetorians on the accession of new emperors and varied from a year's worth of wages through to Didius Julianus's generous bribe of 25,000 HS to every member of the Praetorians in 193 CE if they would make him emperor (the rival bidder maxed out at 20,000) (*HA, Did. Jul.* 3.2, 4.6; Cass. Dio, 74.11.2–5). He lasted nine weeks, after which time the Senate stripped him of his imperial title (Cass. Dio, 74). The coin, on the other hand, lasted until the late second century, and then as a debased version through to the end of the third (when melted down).

denarius

Silver compound. Originally worth 10 *asses*, then readjusted to be worth 4 *sesterces*. The most common coin in our period and the most often debased. First went into circulation in the late third century BCE.

antoninianus

Silver. The latest coin in our chronology: from the era of Caracalla, it replaced the *sestertius* and *denarius*. It was increasingly debased throughout the third and fourth centuries as inflation went out of control.

aureus

Gold. Used by Augustus to raise the standards of coinage; not commonly in circulation. It was worth 25 *denarii* and usually reserved for ransoms, booty, and tributes. Debased over the next two hundred years to about half its value, it was replaced by Diocletian's *solidus* c. 284.

6

ROMANS JUST WANT
TO HAVE FUN:
LEISURE AND ENTERTAINMENT

Roman sports were called the *ludi* (singular *ludes*), and these games and entertainment existed primarily for the spectators, unlike the Greek *agones* (sing. *agon*) or contests in which participants themselves were honoured. The *agones* were contestants who strove to gain honour (*arête*) and public recognition (*timē*) for their achievements from the audience in order to gain *kleon* (fame). The Roman *ludi* existed for the spectators, a possible leftover from Etruscan military celebrations (Nic. Dam., 4.153; Liv., 1.35) or from religious mourning when people watched competitions to appease the gods, another Etruscan tradition. Large-scale public entertainment came to Rome on the back of expansion into Greece in the third century BCE. Livy notes that the first athletic competitions were exhibited in Rome around 186 BCE (39.22), and by the first century BCE such events had become a way for politicians to gain public recognition and votes. Lucius Murena, for example, was accused of bribing voters with games (Cic., *Mur.* 38–40, 67, 72; other examples in Futrell, 2006: 11–18, 24–29). Other events such as wild animal shows (Livy, 39.22; Plaut., *Poen.* 1008–1013) and mock sea battles soon followed. These were increasingly popular and spectacular throughout the late Republic and into the imperial period beginning with Julius Caesar (cf. App., *BC* 2.102), and a sea spectacle by Claudius involved draining a lake (Tac., *Ann.* 12.56). Cultural activities such as literary composition and reading, musical events, and theatrical performances also coincided with the influx of Greek culture and activities from the third century BCE onwards.

Unlike the Greeks, the Romans remained spectators; they appreciated skill and flair, athleticism and talent, but woe betide any free Roman citizen himself or herself who participated in athletics and sport or who sang, danced, or acted on stage. Whilst superstar charioteers (Juv., 7.105–114) and gladiators (cf. Tert., *De Spect.* 23.3–4) were well paid and well sought after as guests at all of the best aristocratic parties, it was disgraceful for a Roman citizen to be one or to marry one. It was a common insult to accuse an aristocrat, especially a woman, for spending too much time with any sort of athlete or entertainer (cf. Juv., 6.102–112; Mart., *Epist.* 5.24). Emperors with a taste for singing and poetry composition, acting, or athletics were regarded by conservative Romans with especial horror (Juv., 8.183–210; Tac., *Ann.* 14.14, on Nero's habit of forcing Senators into the gladiatorial arena and on to the stage). Such practices smacked of the perceived effeminacy and servility of the Greeks (which is why these same emperors for the same reasons were wildly popular back in Greece). It was one thing for an emperor to be a huge supporter of a chariot team, such as Caligula and the Green chariot team (Suet., *Gai.* 55; Cass. Dio, 59.14), but to want actually to get into the arena and compete (in any capacity) was viewed with distaste (Juv., 8.183–210). It was, in fact, illegal for a Roman aristocrat to tread the boards (cf. Suet., *Ner.* 51.5.1–2) or to fight in the arena. Laws were passed to prevent senators or *equites* (and at least three generations of their children) from becoming gladiators (*Tabula Larinas* from 19 CE).

Another reason why the Romans tended to scorn athletes socially was the nudity. The Romans were prudish: 'to strip naked among one's fellow citizens is the beginning of vice' (*flagiti principium*, Enn., *Trag.* 158, quoted by Cic., *Tusc.* 4.70). Athletic prowess and practice for public honour just weren't part of the Roman psyche; the Romans lacked heroic competition as part of their upbringing. The Greeks were raised on the Homeric epics of the *Iliad*, the *Odyssey,* and other poems now lost to us, where men strove to the heights of personal glory in order to attain immortal glory (through epic verse) or wished to emulate their heroes such as Herakles (Sparta) or Theseus (Athens). The Romans did not have a similar tradition. They were not involved in the interconnected polity of the Greek city-states that required professional armies or even complex civic diplomacy where one needed to stand out from amongst one's fellows in order to achieve any political or military glory. The Romans saw exercise such as riding, hunting, and boxing as a means to a more practical end, for good health or farming, or military training.

Competition designed simply to make one stand out as the faster runner or highest jumper simply for the sake of it seemed a waste of time. The closest you'll get to athletic training for the sake of athleticism amongst the Romans were the *iuventes*, associations sponsored by Augustus and supported by subsequent emperors. These associations functioned as ancient youth clubs and provided athletic exercise as a form of military training (Kyle, 2007: 292). Only aristocratic boys and youths were members; they would have had a patron deity whose name was reflected in their particular society. For example, there was one at Pompeii called *Iuvenes Venerii Pompeiani*, or 'The Youths of Venus of Pompeii' – Venus being the patron of Pompeii. Ultimately, however, the activities of these clubs were meant to train youths for military or civil service in Italy. Very little is known of their specific activities although there is some indication that their instructors were former gladiators.

Nevertheless, the Romans were passionate about their entertainment, leisure pursuits, holidays, and hobbies. The official divide was between conservative Romans of taste who (said that they) avoided such low-rent occupations as games and spectacle, theatre, or gambling, and the common mob who couldn't get enough. Aristocratic writers sniffed that such diversions were useful only for keeping the mob occupied. There were enthusiasts amongst the poets and intellectuals, however, and contemporary sources include a detailed description of the excitement of a day at the races (Sid. Apoll., *Epist.* 23.307–427), Martial's glowing series of epigrams commissioned for the opening of the Colosseum (*Spect.*), and Ovid's advice on how to pick up girls at the races (Ov., *Ars* 1.135–176; *Am.* 3.2). Other intellectuals looked down on sport as the pastimes of the yobs and regarded the mob's passion with distaste and as immoral (cf. Sen., *Epist.* 7.1–5). Cicero speaks despairingly of the idlers and indolent who attend the games (Cic., *Fam.* 7.1); Sulla was mocked by *Optimate* peers for choosing the company of actors, dancers, and singers down at the local taverns over time with his Senatorial colleagues (Plut., *Sull.* 2.2–4, 33.2). Furthermore, there were fears of passion leading to riots in the enclosed spaces of the arena or circus (cf. Cass. Dio, 39.7; Tac., *Ann.* 14.17, on the riot at Pompeii). Even at their snobbiest, the complaints of the intellectuals belie the enormous popularity of these activities and the relief they provided from the drudgery of the day-to-day that they afforded.

CHARIOT RACING

Chariot racing was known in Greece, but it was *the* Roman national sport as attested by contemporary writings, art, and the size of the circuses. They lasted long after the Christian emperors had banned or attempted to ban them because horses and horse racing maintained an association with royalty and hunting that superseded their pagan antecedents, so chariot racing wasn't as readily condemned as other spectacles were. The Byzantines in the East were still packing out the circus (see Proc., *Arc.* 7.1–41, 24, specifically on the Nika riots in the sixth century CE) long after the Empire became officially Christian. In the West, Gothic (Cass., *Var.* 3.51.1–2) and Frankish kings (GT, *HF* 6.2), acting as successors to the Romans emperors, hosted chariot racing into the sixth century (Kyle, 2007: 346). In the imperial Roman era, everyone from slaves to aristocrats was an enthusiast; the imperial family had their own boxes (Aug., *RG* 19), and the Julio-Claudian emperors built a causeway that led directly from the imperial palace into the Circus Maximus (cf. Suet., *Ner.* 25.2). A number of chariot-mad emperors, for example, Caligula (Suet., *Gai.* 55) and Caracalla, spent more time at the races than they did on administrative business (Suet., *Gai.* 18.3; cf. Cass. Dio, 78.10.1, 17.1–4). The Circus Maximus was only one of five circuses in the city, but, as its name denotes, it was the largest of them; sources claim it held from fifty thousand to three hundred thousand spectators (Pliny, *NH* 36, 24.103; cf. Suet., *Iul.* 9.2–3; Dion. Hal., *Ant. Rom.* 3.68.1–4, although the general consensus is that one hundred thousnd was its maximum capacity). It was free to attend the races, and there was no assigned seating, so one could be mixed with all levels of society. Despite the size and social mix of the crowds, there are virtually no descriptions of disorder (aside from the Nika riots).

Circuses appeared all over the Empire, even in its most remote corners. The largest was the same Circus Maximus in Rome; Carthage had the second largest. Constantinople also boasted a large circus, although all that remains now is its *spina*, the long, dividing spine down the centre of the track. The *spina* might be decorated with statues and obelisks (Pliny, *NH* 36.71), and here is where the lap counters were frequently placed. These counters might take the shape of eggs, representing the Dioscuri, or dolphins, representing Neptune – that is, gods associated with horses (cf. Cass. Dio, 49.43; Tert., *De Spect.* 8.3–6). People stood on the *spina* and tended, unfortunately, to fall off into the path of the chariots; these accidents were popular with the spectators. At the ends of the *spina* the chariots swept around the bend; the ends were marked with posts called *metae*. At these ends stood slaves who could throw water on the chariots passing by; as the wheels and axles were made out of wood, friction could set the chariots on fire. A contemporary carving shows a slave and his jug here; note the slave who has fallen and been run over (www.vroma.org/images/mcmanus_images/chariotaccident.jpg). Chariots also crashed and overturned at the *metae* due to the tight corners and the unwieldiness of the chariots; this made the ends prime places for spectators to sit (Cass., *Var.* 3.51). These accidents were called *naufractae* ('shipwrecks'). In the first century CE, Pliny the Elder wrote in some detail about the crashes one might see at the races: while spectacular, not all of them were fatal (*NH* 8.159–160, 28.238).

During the imperial period, there were four major teams, Blue, Green, Red, and White; there were Violet and Yellow teams (Cass. Dio, 67.4), but these were short-lived. It was fine to be an imperial fan but considered a disgrace for an aristocrat of any stripe actually to drive a chariot (cf. Juv., 8.142–182). Caligula and Nero were fanatical Green supporters (Suet., *Gai* 55, Cass. Dio, 59.14; Suet., *Ner.* 22.1); Vitellius (Suet., *Vit.* 7.1; Cass. Dio, 5.1) and Caracalla, the Blues (Cass. Dio, 78.10, 17.4). Caracalla used to dress up as a Blues charioteer (78.17.1) and once had a famous retired charioteer called Euprepes executed – simply because the guy had been on the Green team during his career (78.1.2). Team factions developed among supporters, and these factions took on political significance especially in the later Empire when the teams were reduced to the Blues and Greens only. Chariots were divided up into teams of individuals not unlike modern Formula 1 racing, and fans of one team might become political rivals of the other and could have great influence over political, social, and economic decisions within the government (see Futrell, 2006: 210–218, on the fans and fan unrest, including the Nika riots of 532 CE). It wasn't unlike the cultural and political divide one finds in Glasgow between modern Celtic and Rangers supporters.

Charioteers could race on their own (on behalf of a sponsor, usually the man – or woman – who owned the horses and paid for the chariot and the driver's gear); individual, unique sets of chariots could also be entered, but that was rare. More than one chariot could be entered for each team up to a total of three for each colour. Chariot teams ranged from *bigae* (two horses) to the more common *quadrigae* or four-horse teams; in the case of the latter, the well-matched team of horses was actually driven by the lead horse, and the other three followed. For novelty, chariots might be drawn by eight and as many as twelve horses. The Romans always harnessed horses side-by-side, however; these larger arrangements were difficult to manage and such chariots were for display or parade purposes mainly. Mosaics and illustrations sometimes depict whimsical chariot teams of cats, goats, and flamingos, usually driven by goddesses, women, or children. Nero supervised a race that featured camels (Suet., *Ner.* 11.1). Driving professionally was a dangerous business; a charioteer carried not only a whip to keep his horses moving and to warn off opponents who got too close but also a knife – charioteers wrapped the reins around their waists, and in case of a wreck or a spill off the chariot they had quickly to cut themselves free or be dragged or battered to death.

A day at the races was colourful and exciting; the crowd would be pumped up from seeing the horses as well as the vehicles themselves thundering down the track. To keep everyone at a fever pitch, cheerleaders called *hortatores* ran around in the midst of the action to get particular factions and sections of the audience whipped up in a frenzy of chants, especially to shout *Nike!*, Greek for 'Victory'. The races would begin with a parade of all of the participants going once around the track. After they were lined up at the white line to begin (Cass., *Var.* 3.51), the presiding official – the big man (*sponsor*) who was paying for all of it, whether local official or the emperor himself – would step forward from his special box seat (*pulvinar*) to raise and drop a white cloth called a *mappa* (cf. Tert., *De Spect.* 16.2–3). Races lasted fifteen to twenty minutes. The fifth-century writer Sidonius Apollinaris described in verse a seven-lap race at the Circus Maximus as his pal Consentius was a dramatic winner on the day (*Carm.* 23.307–427); Silius Italicus (Sil. It., *Pun.* 303–456) also provides a vibrant description of a race day in a third century BCE verse. By the time of Gaius Caligula (37–41 CE) the day's programme lasted from sunrise to sunset (Suet., *Gai.* 18.3) and could include up to twenty-four races a day (Cass. Dio, 59.7.2–3, 60.27.2); Nero (54–68) tried to extend the racing day even longer (Suet., *Ner.* 22.2).

Chariot racing was a big business, with vets, stable boys, accountants, team managers associated with the sport. Charioteers might have short life expectancies, but despite their low social status they were mobbed as celebrities and lauded on funerary monuments (cf. a selection of inscriptions translated by Mahoney, 2001:30–34). The winner was granted an official prize of a palm branch and a wreath as depicted in the mosaics at the Piazza Armerina; additional prizes included prestige and cash. A good winner at Constantinople could make in a year a hundred times as much as a lawyer did (Juv., 7.112–114), much to the annoyance of those aristocratic moralists who held the races in low esteem. Crescans, for example, was a famous charioteer who made over a million sesterces over the course of his career (*ILS*, 5285 = *CIL*, 6.10050, in Mahoney, 2001: 31); Diocles also made a fortune over the lifetime of his astonishing winning career (*CIL*, 14.2884, in Futrell, 2006: 200). The horses could become just as famous as the athletes; there are mosaics that depict winning horses with names such as *Volucer* ('Flier', owned by the Emperor

Lucius Verus, *HA*, *Ver.* 6), Corax ('Siege-engine', commemorated on a lamp, *CIL*, 25.6250; cf. Pliny, *NH* 8.160), *Tuscus* ('Etruscan boy', who won 386 times, *CIL* 6.10048) and *Victor* (who won 429 times, *CIL*, 7.10047). Horses were imported from breeding areas including North Africa, Spain, and Italy (Juv., 8.57–63) and delivered to the race tracks via special cargo ships (*hippagos*).

Much money was also made via gambling on the outcomes of the races; Martial hints in his epigrams that some teams may have thrown races on behalf of high-rolling gamblers (including the emperor) (*P. Oxy.* 2707, in Futrell, 2006: 198; cf. Mart., 10.74). Good sportsmanship at the races was unknown. Bribery to fix races was rampant (Juv. 7.105–114); there were also rivalries between drivers (*Planudian Anthology* 374, in Futrell, 2006:

8 A day at the races: depiction of a chariot race on a small medallion

198) – and rivalries between fans, who frequently wrote curses on lead tablets against drivers and fans they disliked (e.g. *SEG*, 34, 1984, no. 1437, in Futrell, 2006: 203–204).

GLADIATORS

Gladiators and gladiatorial combat are inevitable signposts in Roman historical fiction, and they remain ever popular there and on film. Most modern depictions are themselves inspired by earlier popular culture rather than academia: Ridley Scott's *Gladiator* in 2000, for example, owes as much of its storyline to *Spartacus* and *The Fall of Rome* (it is a remake of the latter) as it does to Scott deriving his original inspiration for the film from Jean-Léon Gérôme's nineteenth-century paintings such as *The Death of Caesar* (1867), *Pollice Verso* (1872), and *The Christian Martyrs' Last Prayer* (1883). Whilst the Romans themselves never really wrote specifically on gladiatorial combat, gladiators and the games were wildly popular throughout the period covered here, as seen from many references in literature, poetry, letters, inscriptions, medical texts, and material remains. The games were banned several times in the West during in the late fourth century CE once Christianity became the official religion of the Empire. Honorius, for example, banned the games in 404, but they persisted outside of Italy for a few more centuries (Theod., *Eccl. Hist.* 5.26; cf. August., *Serm.* 198.3, *Conf.* 7.8; Kyle 2007: 346). They continued officially in the East until the sixth century CE. Many images (of participants and equipment as well as graffiti) and material artefacts, including the arenas themselves, survive due to the great popularity of the sport. As with chariot racing, the terminology and language of the games persisted in idiom and metaphor long after the end of the 'official' era.

Gladiatorial games were referred to as *munera*, which means 'gifts'; their origins may lie in Etruscan funeral ritual as a means of sacrificing to the gods at the death of a loved one or significant personage. Livy notes that the earliest recorded games were held at the Forum Boarium (the 'cattle market') in Rome in 264 BCE as part of a private funeral (*Epit.* 16; Val. Max., 2.4.7). For about two hundred years, games were small affairs sponsored by private individuals. During the era of the Republic, the games were expensive; politicians such as Julius Caesar sponsored games as part of funeral commemorations (e.g. Tert., *De Spect.* 12.1–4; Liv., 39.46, 41.28) and military celebrations (e.g., Liv., 9.40), but also to entertain and to bribe votes from the urban mob and soldiers (e.g., Pliny, *NH* 33.53; Plut., *Iul.* 5.9; Cicero, *Mur.* 37–39). The *Urso Charter* (*Lex Ursones*), written around 44 BCE warns specifically against aristocrats attempting to bribe votes out of the citizens via entertainment and spectacle (71; cf. *CIL*, 2.6278, lines 29–37, in Futrell, 2006: 49). In the imperial period, when the games were used to impress the people with the might of the Empire (and of individual emperors), events could become extravagant and costly. Titus, for example, ordered one hundred straight days of games to launch the inaugural games at the Colosseum (Cass. Dio, 66.25), commemorated by Martial in a series of epigrams (cf. Suet., *Tit.* 8); Severus splashed out on costly games to reward the populace for supporting him (Cass. Dio, 77.1). Pliny the Younger notes Domitian's lavish extravagance and indulgence when it came to games (*Pan.* 33). Political leaders sometimes tried to curb such spending as it could be a burden on local economies (cf. Livy, 40.44). Julius Caesar, for example, limited magistrates to only one annual *munus* each (*CIL*, 1².594), and in 27 CE Tiberius forbade anyone of less than equestrian rank to put on shows (Tac., *Ann.* 4.63). In the early second century CE, Trajan and Hadrian passed laws in the provinces to protect local economies against native administrators who wanted to spend lavishly on games and entertainment venues in order to impress the Roman authority and perhaps receive benefits from the centre (*ILS*, 5163 = *CIL*, 2.6278, in Mahoney, 2001: 97–100; see Chapter 5). Marcus Aurelius also tried to curb spending on games and gladiators as the money could be better used elsewhere. During the *Pax Romana*, however, successive emperors upped the ante of how spectacular their particular games were – not only could this become very expensive, it also had the effect of depleting the local wildlife (cf. Kyle, 2007: 323–327). A number of species of European animals became extinct during the imperial period due to the increasing extravagance of not just the gladiatorial games but the attendant exhibitions, staged beast hunts, and other forms of animal savagery in the arena; already in the first century BCE, Cicero noted the shortage of animals, in particular leopards (*Fam.* 2.11.2). Nevertheless, gladiators gave good value for money: there was specialisation among the professionals, as noted especially in funerary descriptions, and different types of fighters were paired up for novelty and interest. Many artworks and surviving artefacts provide evidence for a wide variety, even though it is not known exactly what some of the types of gladiators actually did.

If the games were expensive, they were also as big a business as chariot racing: there were agents who acted as go-betweens as the *lanistae* (trainers) were considered too vulgar and lower-class for the emperor or his own agents to deal with directly – especially if they were known price gougers (cf. *CIL*, 2.678, in Futrell, 2006: 85). In addition, both the games and the schools in which gladiators were trained employed doctors, trainers, administrators, accountants, tailors, musicians, dancers, acrobats, and so forth (*ILS*, 5156 = *CIL*, 6326; *ILS*, 5150 = *CIL*, 10.4195, and *ILS*, 5157 = *CIL*, 6227, all in Mahoney, 2001: 23). Other costs to factor in included *sportulae*, that is the gifts flung into the audience; freebies might include loaves of bread or delicacies such as fresh fruit (Stat., *Silv.* 1.6.9–50; cf. Suet., *Claud.* 54, *Ner.* 11.2; Cass. Dio on Titus, 66.25 and 67.4 on Domitian). The gladiators themselves were costly, and some sources provide information on the cost of a gladiator's life down to the *denarius*. As a consequence more fighters survived than popular fiction would have modern audiences believe; for example, there are inscriptions noting wins, losses, and draws (Mahoney, 2001: 21–22). Many gladiators received the *missio* or permission to live after a defeat; they were an investment for the owners and trainers at the school and not to be used up lightly. Even though the games were sponsored, admission was not free: prices were based on the value of the gladiator, and the sponsor(s) of the games could make a profit. Tickets were usually pottery shards or small inscribed slabs; as today, there were scalpers and touts, and for a particularly important match or appearance of a celebrity gladiator there was price-gouging (cf. *CIL*, 2.6278, in Futrell, 2006: 133). Advertisements noted who was sponsoring the games, highlights of the event (for example that there might be an animal hunt), and if *velae erunt*: 'there will be awnings' – meaning that some shade would be provided to at least part of the arena, as noted in a surviving ticket inscription from Pompeii (Pliny, *NH* 19.23–25; Matyszak, 2007: 125). Bouts were advertised through word of mouth as well as posters and billboards; fragments of such programmes survive from Pompeii (*CIL*, 4.2508, in Futrell, 2006: 85–86). Gladiators themselves endorsed products for sale (examples found in Mahoney, 2001: 18–19). Plutarch describes admission and seating (*GG* 12.3–4); the 'wedges' of seating areas fell under the domain of the *duoviri* (*CIL* 10.855, 856, 857, in Mahoney, 2001: 83). Marks on the rows and seating areas of surviving arenas still show where particular sections of seats were, and presumably the holder's ticket was marked accordingly. Unlike at the races, seating in the arena (and theatre) was strictly regulated (cf. Martial's comments, in Mahoney, 2001: 84–86) according to one's place in society (cf. Tac., *Ann.* 4.62–63, on the problems of overcrowding).

GAMES AND SPECTATORS

Fans took the games very seriously and would frequently leave the arena during lunchtime (*meridiam*) when criminals were executed – as they saw no sport in watching amateurs being quickly despatched (Sen., *Epist.* 7). Fans of all types were caught up in the excitement and bloodlust of a good match; as much as the strictly segregated seating reminded them of their place in society, so, too, did the fighting and humiliating executions in the guise of play-acting myths (Tert., *Apol.* 15.4.5): Tertullian was an eyewitness to people forced to be sacrificed to the gods as part of the execution play-acting (cf. Plut., *Mor.* 5546, Mart., *Spect.* 9); Martial mentions a criminal forced to play Prometheus (Mart., *Spect.* 7); and Ps. Lucian's novel *The Ass* depicts a man who was forced to have sex with a condemned woman as part of her execution (Ps.-Luc., 53). Such 'shows' on the arena floor reminded all in attendance how quickly their status could change. If there was admiration for the winners, there was no sympathy for the losers, as the Romans generally felt that anyone who was poor or who had become enslaved had no one to blame but himself or herself, as pointed out in scholarship that discusses both Roman economy (see Chapter 5) and the Roman fascination with blood sport (see Chapter 8 for resources). Fans were passionate about their favourite performers; Nero took advantage of this and for his own amusement would bait factions in the audience until fights broke out amongst them (Tac., *Ann.* 13.25).

There were about four hundred amphitheatres built across the Empire, mostly in the West; the Colosseum (properly known as the *Amphitheatrum Flavium*) is the most famous, but the arena at El Djem in Tunisia is the best preserved. Originally, amphitheatres were temporary wooden structures out of fear of mob violence (cf. Tac., *Ann.* 14.20–21; Pliny, *NH* 36.15.117–120). The first permanent stone amphitheatre was built at Pompeii in the 60s BCE – and this particular arena was indeed the scene of a riot that spilled out into the streets almost a century later (Tac., *Ann.* 14.17). Amongst the features of the arenas were trap doors that might bring different fighters or animals to the surface floor of the more posh arenas. Other, smaller amphitheatres, such as the ones in modern Caerleon and Dorchester, were adapted from extant pre-existing earthen structures that were reinforced with wooden siding and wooded bleachers placed on top of the earthworks. In the case of these more primitive structures, gladiators, animals, and other entertainers might have only a small niche in which to cluster while waiting their turn to come on to the main stage. Musicians played rousing music as the combatants fought human or animal opponents; cheering sections called *claques* sat scattered throughout the arena, clapping in particular rhythm as a way to show support for their heroes (cf. Suet., *Ner.* 20.3). While there aren't many literary descriptions of the gladiatorial games (especially as compared with images), a good account of a day at the games was written by the so-called Pseudo-Quintilian; Martial composed a series of epigrams specifically for the opening of the Colosseum in 79 CE, amongst which is the only contemporary account of a gladiatorial match – for all of the excitement of the games re-created in popular memory and culture of the clash between these fighters, Martial's account depicts a rather tepid draw (*Spect.* 31).

'WE WHO ARE ABOUT TO DIE ...'

There is only one recorded instance of the famous 'We who are about to die, salute you!': Suetonius records that a group of gladiators so greeted the Emperor Claudius, who, jaded by too many gladiators who only pretended to die or to be hurt, sarcastically replied, 'Or not!' (Suet., *Claud.* 21.4–6; Cass. Dio, 60.33.4).

Gladiators were widely admired and could become very rich if they were big winners; Futrell provides a number of examples (2006: 146–147) of popular gladiators celebrated in graffiti. Men were warned by poetic wags to take care that their wives didn't run off with handsome gladiators (Juv., 6.102–112). At the same time, however, gladiators had very low social status; aristocratic women who *did* run off with them could lose their own legal, free status. The status of most gladiators was low from the start: recruits might come from amongst condemned criminals, from prisoners of war, from people who had sold themselves to the schools to escape debt, and free rogues who were simply filled with bloodlust. There are a few references to women as gladiators (e.g., during the reign of Septimius Severus, Cass. Dio, 76.16), but mostly in terms of laws forbidding it and writers condemning it as vulgar (cf. Juv., 6.246–67). When Spartacus rebelled in 73 BCE, he led an army of escaped slaves against the legions of Rome (App., *BC* 1.116, 1.117, 1.118), defeating them until Crassus (Plut., *Crass.* 10, 11) and then Pompey stepped in. These desperadoes were seen *not* as underdogs and heroes as one might expect in a modern Western film or story but rather a source of terror and a danger to civic life. Hence the famous punishment of Spartacus's men: six thousand of these slaves were crucified along the Appian Way (App., *BC* 1.120). Thus emperors such as Nero, who forced Senators (and their wives) to fight as gladiators (Tac., *Ann.* 14.14, 15.32; Cass. Dio, 73.17.1), or Commodus (161–192 CE), who dressed up as one and fought them in the arena (usually with real swords against the gladiators' wooden ones) (Cass. Dio, 73.16–17), were viewed with distaste by the aristocracy (although loved by the common mob for it) (Cass. Dio, 19.4, 21.2, 73.17). Commodus in fact went too far by planning to accept honours in the Senate dressed as a gladiator (73.22.2); the long-beleaguered Senate had him assassinated by bribing the wrestler Narcissus to strangle the emperor the day before he could humiliate himself, and, by extension, them (Cass, Dio 73.22.5).

GLADIATORS

Gladiators could and did look after their own; they organised themselves into *collegia*, like a modern trade union, and inscriptions provide evidence of how these groups helped to pay for the funerals of their fellows and the well-being of the widows and children left behind. See Futrell (2006: 148–153) for examples of funerary inscriptions which include mention of a gladiator's wife and children.

BATHS AND SWIMMING

A healthy mind in a healthy body – '*Mens sana in corpore sano*' (Juv., 10.356–364). Public baths (*thermae*) were a Roman institution; they were places to hang out, relax, and gossip. *Thermae* were ubiquitous throughout the Roman world: they appear in colonies and in military encampments across the Empire, and the locals may or may not have been allowed to indulge. That said, there are very few contemporary descriptions of what visiting the baths was like; see Fagan (2002) for a survey of the experience. Evidence for private baths, or *balnea*, date from the third century BCE. Austerity during this era due to the simultaneous wars against Hannibal and in Greece, and prudery about nudity, meant that initially bathing was a private activity restricted to the upper classes (for a description of a private bath, see Fagan, 2001; cf. *LTUR*, 4.13.421–443). Small bathrooms, for example, have been found in the luxurious homes and villae of the wealthy in places such as Thermine,

Buccino, and the Piazza Armerina. The Roman love of cleanliness and the so-called 'breakdown' of public morals after the introduction of Greek culture, however, led to the first public bath in Rome in the second century BCE. The Romans associated cleanliness with intellectual pursuits, beauty, and physical fitness, and public baths included galleries of artwork and libraries, plus exercise rooms to encourage good health (e.g. Mart., 6.42; Sen., *Epist.* 86.4–13; Stat., *Silv.* 1.5). For example, artwork discovered at Caracalla's baths included the Farnese Bull, a statue of Flora, one of Herakles, and the Belvedere Torso. Trajan's bath featured that famous statue of the doomed Trojan soothsayer Laocoön wrestling the sea snakes, a character familiar to students of Vergil's *Aeneid*. Martial makes extensive allusions to the cultural amenities and luxury of the *thermae* throughout his epigrams, and Seneca describes the 'lush surroundings' of the baths (Sen., *Epist.* 86.1–7).

Building public baths was the prerogative of wealthy patrons. According to Agrippa, who built the first free, public bath in 33 BCE (Cass. Dio, 43.27, 54.29), there were 170 public baths across the Empire (Pliny, *NH* 36.121), and by the fourth century CE nearly a thousand. There was a small entry fee at first; the rate was a quarter of an *as* (children got free entry) (Sen. *Epist.* 86.9; Mart., *Epist.* 3.30.4). Women had to pay more than men (Juv., 6.447; cf. *CIL*, 2.5181, 1.19), but imperial baths were free and open to all, paid for through government funds. The Julio-Claudians put up a number of public baths, with each emperor trying to outdo the extravagance of his predecessor. Later emperors down through the age of Diocletian and Constantine built larger facilities (with a gap in the middle during the crisis of the third century, when funding monumental buildings was often beyond the budget – the best Severus Alexander could do, for example, was a tiny fountain that was turned on only when he was around to see it; see Chapter 5). Trajan built a large public bath in Syria (*AE*, 1976, nos 677 and 678). Caracalla's enormous bath works clocked in at 11 hectares or 27.5 acres; Diocletian's public baths covered 30 acres (cf. *HA*, *Tyr. Trig.* 21.7).

The baths stayed open most of the day. Opening times, signalled by a bell, were around midday (the 'fifth hour', Juv., 11.205; Mart., *Epist.*

10.48.3, 14.163), and the facilities were available through to sunset (*HA, Sev. Alex.* 24). Initially men and women were completely segregated (Vit., *De Arch.* 5.10.1; Aul. Gell., *NA* 10.3.3) in the bathhouses by law (cf. Pliny, *NH* 33.153; Quint., *Inst.* 5.9.14), but by the late first or early second century CE there were some mixed bathing facilities (Pliny, *NH* 3.3.153, and elsewhere, e.g., Juvenal and Martial). We know about the latter because Hadrian put an end to them by imperial decrees in 117 and 138 (*HA, Hadr.* 18.10, *Marc.* 23.8, *Alex. Sev.* 24.2; cf. Cass. Dio, 69.8.2); then men and women had separate hours, also signalled by ringing a bell (*SEG* (1976/77), 1043/44). There were plenty of things to do, and the baths were associated with exercising as well as socialising. For example, customers might fence (Veg., 1.11 and 12), lift weights (Juv., 6.421; Mart., *Epist.* 7.67), or play ball games prior to bathing (cf. Mart., *Epist.* 7.32, 12.83, and Petron. *Sat.* 26–28). Martial, who lived over a bath, complained about the noise the ball players made (56.1–2); Seneca concurred that they were awful places to live above (*Epist.* 56.1–5).

Most bathers went in three stages: a hot steam bath, then a warm bath to cool down, and then either to the coldest bath or the *piscinae* for a swim. The Romans weren't very happy sailors, but they were good swimmers – whether it was at the bathhouse, in the sea, or in the chilly Tiber River. For example, Cato the Elder taught his son to swim (Plut., *Cat. Ma.* 20.4). Caesar was also a strong swimmer (at Alexandria) (Cass. Dio, 42.40.4; Plut., *Caes.* 49.7; Suet., *Iul.* 57.1) and expected his soldiers to be so that they could extricate themselves from danger in the water (cf. Plut., *Caes.* 16.6; Cass. Dio, 37.53.3). His descendant Caligula, however, was remarkable for his inability to swim (Suet., *Gai.* 54.2), but according to anecdotal evidence he sentenced his sister Agrippina to exile on an island to dive for sponges with slaves, as punishment for her alleged involvement in a plot against him. This stood her in good stead years later when her son Nero tried to drown her by giving her a collapsible boat (Tac., *Ann.* 14.3–4), and she swam to safety (14.5).

Bathhouses were an essential part of everyday life. A lot of maintenance, fuel, and resources were needed to keep them running unless you took advantage of natural hot springs, as in Bath (Roman Aquae Sulis) or

Budapest (Roman Aquincum). The Romans built many aqueducts just for the baths. Most aqueducts ran underground; the high, arched ones marching across the countryside were expensive to build and maintain, but they were needed to cross gorges and streams. Both Vitruvius and Frontinus detail the structure of those aqueducts for baths and building baths in general (Vit., *De Arch.* 5.10). Vitruvius, writing around the time that Agrippa was building his bath, explained the best way to maintain the water channel at the top (the *specus*) and where to place climbing holds as well as drainage tanks to remove debris and dirt (6.5–9, 8.3.1, 8.6.2). Frontinus, who wrote later in the first century CE, was a commissioner of public waterworks, and he wrote two books on the capacity of the various aqueducts, the work crews, and the annoyance of pressure dropping as people tapped into the mains and stole water for their private homes (2.97).

COMEDY THEATRE

The Romans had indigenous theatre and dramatic performance before adapting Greek dramatic arts; the various Italian tribes contributed to Roman culture mime, pantomime, an early form of sketch and variety shows called the *fabulae togatae*, and what became known as the Atellan plays after the local entertainment in the city-state of Atella, in Campania (Liv., 7.3 on the history of Atellan plays). There were street performances, usually short sketches that lampooned current events. There were also travelling entertainers who might set up stalls in the marketplace side-by-side with sellers and merchants. Formal theatre was performed at set times of year, usually between April and November, and then only during particular festivals and competitive occasions; plays didn't run continuously as they might in the modern West End or on Broadway.

Roman comedy became especially refined during and after the third century BCE as the Romans came into contact with the Greek world and brought home to Italy Greek literature, drama, and comedy. Two principal comedy playwrights from the period were Plautus (254–184 BCE) and Terence (c. 195/185–159 BCE). Twenty or so of Plautus's plays have survived, and they are an excellent source for slang and wordplay for both comedic and everyday dialogue – Plautus was keen on the super-superlative, so you can blame him for the enduring 'Boaty McBoatface'-type jokes. Plautus adapted many plays by the Greek New Comedy playwright Menander (342–291 BCE). As he felt his Roman audience might not appreciate all of the nuances of Greek comedy, he binned anything that he felt distracted from the funny (romantic stuff, long swathes of dialogue), focused on everyday situations, and added many musical interludes. Terence's six plays reflect the tastes of a more sophisticated audience, and frequently involve natural-sounding dialogue and double and triple plot strands before everything comes together for a happy ending. Terence eschewed using his prologues to tell the audience what was going to happen in the play – the audience and the characters find out and react to the comic situations simultaneously to heighten the tension and the humour. Both playwrights folded into these performances the familiar forms of indigenous Italian theatre, creating works that became distinctly Roman. Their plays' structure and comedic themes influenced subsequent comedy playwrights including Shakespeare, Molière, Gilbert (of Gilbert and Sullivan), Ben Elton, and Richard Curtis.

SO SORRY, HE'S FROM BARCELONA

Roman comedies reveal how rigid and conservative Roman society was: the mad antics and situations of the characters on stage provided a release from the tension of strict social norms and hierarchy of the audience. Plautus and Terence deliberately cast many of their main characters as Greek (or at least gave them Greek names), and set most of the plays in Greece. This way the playwrights could mock Roman behaviour and the audience could happily laugh at the characters and situations as the silliness (and release) was attributed to the behaviour of outsiders, that is Greeks, Carthaginians, or others. Not only was such attribution an acceptable way to poke fun at Roman conventions, it also spawned the Latin verb *pergraecari* or 'to Greek around'.

TRAGEDY

Don't overlook Roman tragedy! Fragments of early Republican poets Ennius (239–169 BCE) and Naevius (270–201 BCE) have been published in the Loeb series; complete examples of tragedy come from Seneca the Younger in the first century CE. Some are adaptations of bloodcurdling Greek tragedy toned down for Roman audiences, but Seneca's original pieces, such as *Octavia* (which is attributed to him, anyway) reveal much about the atmosphere and sensation surrounding Nero's court in the middle of the century.

Most of the Roman theatres that survive from antiquity were purpose-built or modified by the Romans from those already extant; the Greek theatre at Epidaurus is one of the few that has not been changed. What distinguishes Roman theatres from Greek is that the Greeks built their theatres into hillsides for natural stadium-style seating; Roman theatres were free-standing structures with enormous backdrops erected to represent houses or buildings. During the middle period of the Republic when these theatres begin to appear, they were wooden, temporary structures (in the West) or commandeered and renovated Greek theatres in the East. As with the *munera* and other spectacles, Republican Romans were hesitant to create permanent structures out of fear of mob violence and problems with crowd control. The first permanent, stone theatres, such as the Theatre of Pompey, do not appear in Rome until the middle of the first century BCE. Seats were arranged in tiers in a semicircle around and in front of the stage. The seating arrangement in the Roman theatre (both in Rome and in the provinces) represented a microcosm of Roman social order (and as such, reinforced one's understanding of one's place in that social order), as the various classes were separated into specific sections. The best seats at the front were for the Senators and visiting foreign dignitaries; the Vestal Virgins sat behind them. Next were seated soldiers, both veterans and those on active duty; behind them would be freeborn Roman male citizens, then freedmen and the poor, then women, gladiators, and those in debt – the standing-room-only at the very back was for the poorest and the slaves.

Viewing a show was not a passive activity: the actors frequently broke the fourth wall, and the crowd shouted back. There could be much competition for the audience's attention. Terence complained that it took three attempts to stage *The Mother-in-Law* (*Hecyra*) as the play was interrupted first when the crowds raced out to watch tightrope walkers (*Hecy.* 33–36), then a second time by a mass exodus to go to see gladiators (39–41). Still, despite regarding theatre and shows with distaste, authorities recognised the need for them in times of crisis: Livy notes that the first performers to come to Rome for public *ludi* were Etruscan actors enlisted to boost public morale following a plague in 363 BCE (Liv., 7.2).

As for the actors themselves, the appearance (and sex) of actors depended on the type of play; following the Greek models, comedies by Plautus and Terence and adaptation of Greek tragedy were all-male casts even in female roles, usually in formal masks; mimes and street sketches and plays (Atellan, and so forth) could feature female actors. The reputation of actors and actresses among the Romans was both great admiration and vulgar distaste; actors and actresses in Rome were not given the same respect that they would have found in Greece. While the Romans enjoyed comedy and drama and lavished actors with praise and admiration (e.g. Suet., *Claud.* 21.2), it was distasteful, even illegal for a Roman aristocrat to appear on stage in any entertainment capacity (Juv., 8.183–210). Even spending too much time with actors and performers, most of whom were Greeks, was viewed with distaste. Plutarch's *Life of Sulla* (*Sull.* 2.3, 33.2) and Suetonius's *Lives* of Gaius Caligula (*Gai.* 54), Claudius (Messalina and Mnester, Cass. Dio, 60.22.3), Nero (on stage, Suet., *Ner.* 22.1–2; Juv., 8.211–230), and Commodus (Cass. Dio, 73.18–21) provide many examples of the havoc that actors and love of the stage could wreak in the lives of politicians.

WHAT AN ARTIST DIES IN ME!

Nero horrified Roman conservatives (and soldiers) by treading the boards, but he thrilled the mob and his Eastern audience (compare contemporary reaction to Bill Clinton playing sax on the DMZ, or Tony Blair inviting Oasis to 10 Downing Street). Upper-class Romans were disgusted with his behaviour partly because it was distasteful for a man of his position to be an actor, and partly because he was simply so terrible at it; he had groupies-for-hire (cf. Suet., *Ner.* 25.1) positioned throughout the theatre to clap and cheer for him (20.3; Cass. Dio, 62.20.3–4). Allegedly, people would feign death (Suet., *Ner.* 23.2) to escape the theatre during his performances; he made it illegal to leave even if a woman went into labour (Cass. Dio, 62.9.4).

Knowledge of Greek drama and comedy was an important part of a Roman youth's education, especially as a source for pithy expressions and phrases to be folded into one's speeches in the law courts or political speeches. Whilst study of and enthusiasm for Greek tragedy were popular amongst (especially) early imperial Graecophiles such as Tiberius, Caligula, and Nero, there wasn't as much indigenous Roman or Latin tragedy. Some Latin tragedies are dry adaptations of Greek tragedy written by Nero's mentor and tutor Seneca the Younger (c. 4 BCE–65 CE). Seneca's version of *Medea*, for example, is rather dull compared to Euripides' (c. 480–c. 406 BCE) blood-curdling original. Nevertheless Seneca was a renowned Latin rhetorician who, like Plautus, felt the need to adapt Greek tragedy so that it was more in character with how he and other conservative Roman orators of that era felt best served ideas of Roman *dignitas* and *gravitas*. Seneca's personal motivation might have also been a response to Nero's insatiable (and socially unacceptable) Graecophilia and love of music, dance, and stage performance, all pursuits considered unseemly and unmasculine for a Roman politician and statesman. Still, the *Octavia*, a tragedy attributed to Seneca, is a good source for a contemporary response to the death of Nero's mother Agrippina (15–59 CE) and his beleaguered wife Octavia (c. 39–62), both of whom Nero ordered to be executed; Nero was publicly mocked for his hand in their deaths (Cass. Dio, 62.6.2). *Octavia*'s pathos wouldn't be out of place in *EastEnders*, and it features Octavia as a Little Eva or Mary Pickford-type tragic waif and Agrippina as a vengeful ghost. Nero didn't help matters by being a huge fan of the tragedy *Orestes* and insisting always on playing the matricide in the play himself (62.9.4).

DINNER PARTIES

Meals and feasting were an important feature of Classical society. The Greeks called the honourable behaviour between a guest and a host *xenia*, meaning guest-friendship: you didn't ask your guest's name when they appeared on your doorstep if you were a good host; you took them in and fed them. In return they would tell you a tale to earn their supper – and the friendship you forged was not only for life but inherited from one generation to the next (cf. the meeting on the battlefield of Diomedes and Glaucus in Book 6 of the *Iliad*). For the Greeks, dinner parties (*symposia*) were men-only activities where well-educated aristocrats got together to debate politics, recite poetry, and discuss philosophy. The only women present were highly paid prostitutes called *hetaerae*, who were also well-educated as they were expected to converse about art, literature, politics, or philosophy. As the evening wore on, participants played drinking games; the evenings eventually ended in the orgies so beloved of modern blockbuster directors. Recent scholarship in both Classical and medieval studies has focused on the importance of meals and eating as a social event; not only were political deals forged over food, but the association of the sensations associated with eating helped to reinforce the memory of the event and any promises made there.

Unlike the Greeks, the Etruscans and then the Romans allowed women as guests at their dinner parties (*cenae*). Dinner, taken in the evening, was the most important meal of the day, and, when not a part of a formal event, was a private, family affair. Nevertheless, freeloaders hung around public places, such as the baths, all day, hoping for an invitation (Mart. 82). As Ammianus Marcellinus notes, to refuse a dinner invitation was a great insult: it was considered better to kill a man's brother than to refuse his dinner invitation (Amm. Mar., 28.4.17; cf. Hor., *Epod.* 1.7.62–64); see Lendon (2002), who explains in some detail the labyrinthine ritual associated with invitations, dinner parties, and the social minefield to be navigated. When the Romans did splash out, they did so in style: Apicius allegedly spent 25 million *denarii* on entertaining and committed suicide when he found he had only 2.5 million left of his fortune to budget on food (Sen., *Cons. Hel.* 10). Gaius Caligula supposedly spent 10 million on a single dinner party (Sen., *Epist.* 95.41). Although Elagabulus spent only pocket change (HA., *Heliog.* 27.4–6; cf. 29.9) – a mere 25,000 per dinner – many times the food he served was deliberately inedible (for laughs, at the diners' expense). It puts Cleopatra and her pearl-earrings-into-the-wine-cup (also attributed to Gaius Caligula, Suet., *Gai.* 37.1) into perspective.

Roman dinner parties were defined by etiquette and ritual. When you showed up, you swapped your shoes for slippers; your host should provide you with a decorative wreath for your head (see Juv., 6). During the Republic, drinking before you got to dinner was rude; after the reign of Tiberius, it was not uncommon to prime the pump before showing up. Juvenal describes a woman who greeted her guests by drunkenly vomiting on them (6.431–432). Once you arrived, you were shown to your couches, and you got stuck in – those three to seven courses might take anywhere up to eight to ten hours to polish off. Trimalchio's party has been fodder for fictional excess for centuries (one Carolingian monastery had a partial copy of Petronius stuck amongst its otherwise religious holdings (see Reynolds, 1983: 295), but there were real-life gluttons – the emperors Vitellius (just look at his statues) and Domitian, for example. The sheer quantities of food and drink at a large meal meant that belching and farting were inevitable:

Claudius seriously considered passing a law making such natural functions acceptable as he feared people were making themselves ill holding it in (Suet., *Claud.* 32.1). Trimalchio encouraged guests to urinate on the floor rather than to waste time (cf. Petron., *Sat.* 27) – and, in case that *wafer-thin* peacock tongue was the breaking point, slaves might appear at your elbow with a bucket if you couldn't make it or couldn't be bothered to go out of the room in time to puke (see Chapter 2 on the *vomitorium*). In the meantime, your host provided toothpicks, napkins (unless you wanted a doggy bag – then you brought your own napkin to wrap up the leftovers), and cutlery – with the exception of forks, which first appeared as novelties during the Renaissance (even if Agrippina feeds Claudius his poisoned mushroom off one in the BBC's *I, Claudius*). So if it wasn't eaten with a spoon or knife, the Romans used their fingers and consequently washed their hands throughout the meal.

Ostensibly, dinner time was a time to talk, tell gentle comedy stories, and write and dictate letters. Rude jokes at the table were considered vulgar; authors such as Aulus Gellius, Valerius Maximus, Plutarch, and Cornelius Nepos wrote miscellanies of more appropriate dinner-party conversation. There might be music, entertainers, actors (it was a cool excuse to invite celebrities to your dinner parties), or readings. Then, like the Greeks, the Romans might just get drunk. The initial drinking was polite, but you might participate in a ceremonial drinking match called the *commissatio*: supposedly Novellius Torquatus was a champion at this game and could knock back three *congi* (or about ten litres!) in a single go (Pliny, *NH* 14.144–147); a mere amateur, Cicero's son could chug only two *congi*, or about five and a half litres, in a single swig (Cic., *Fam.* 16.21.6; Plut., *Cic.* 24). Tiberius was such a consummate professional in his youth that his nickname was Biberius Caldius Mero ('Boozy Hot Strong') (Suet., *Tib.* 42). The same emperor and his son Drusus could outdrink everyone (cf. Suet., *Tib.* 42.1–2; Cass. Dio, 57.14.10) except the family physician, who used to chow down on almonds to soak up the plonk before he set off to his host's party. The evening's festivities might well degenerate from there. Caligula was famous for abusing men's wives during the drunkenness (cf. Cass. Dio, 59.28.9); most guests had to be carried home in litters or by slaves at the end of the meal, except for Lucius Cornificius (consul in 35 BCE), one of Octavian's generals, who rode home on his pet elephant (49.7.6). Cleaning up for the servants and slaves afterwards was a magical wonderland of wasted food, vomit, urine, and other rubbish. For more on eating and drinking, see Chapter 2.

TRADE GUILD BANQUETS

In stark contrast to the dinner parties of the wealthy were trade guild banquets. These, and especially meals sponsored by burial societies, were sedate affairs. These modest get-togethers were sponsored by clubs of poor people who combined their lot to help pay for a decent burial amongst their associates. In between funerals they had small dinner parties that reinforced their camaraderie and companionship. These meetings and meals were eventually a model for Christians who met and dined together in quiet ritual and commemoration (see Wilken, 2003).

MUSIC AND DANCE

Music and musical performance were linked closely to poetry and recitation, and, even though no scores from antiquity survive, we know that the most famous of the poets were accompanied by music (even playing their own instruments). Music was also a prominent feature during festivals, games, spectacles, and plays. Plautus, for example, plugged into his plays lots of musical interludes and songs; Atellan plays seem to have been a mix of sketches, music, and comedy. Instruments ranged from stringed instruments (e.g., the lyre, *cithara*, and a monochord), horns (the *tuba* and *cornu*) to percussion (such as drums, clappers, and the *sistrum*, a rattle used most often in religious ritual), woodwind (for example, the *tibia*, a double-reeded horn, and flutes), and the water-driven (such as the hydraulic-organ). Musical accomplishment was an acceptable part of a young Roman lady's refinements, and, like the Greeks, the Romans admired professional musicians the same way they did athletes. Unlike the Greeks, however, who considered musical talents an honourable part of an aristocratic young man's skill set, Roman men preferred to watch and listen, as musicians were seen as lower-class, or indeed servile. A Roman aristocrat (such as Sulla) who hung out with them (in any capacity other than to have them decorate his parties) or, worse, wanted to *be* one of them, was regarded with distaste. Nero, nevertheless, didn't give a toss about Senatorial contempt for musicians, and he became an enthusiast of the *cythera*, a challenging stringed instrument. He doggedly practised the thing (Suet., *Ner.* 20.1), and, when he entered into competition (cf. 20.2, 21.1–3), he demanded that he be judged equally with all of the accomplished players (23.3, 24.1). He always won. Go figure.

The Greeks saw dancing as an integral part of life and a gift from the gods; the Romans, again, remained more reserved. Cicero, for example, expressed open contempt for dancing (cf. Cic., *Brut.* 224–229). They did observe ritual forms at dinner parties, and at weddings, funerals, and other religious occasions, but it was nothing like modern ballroom or formal dancing: dancing as an art form or entertainment was the domain of slaves and prostitutes. Other forms of dancing such as the stylised movement that accompanied poetry readings were also the practice of foreigners (inherited traditions from the Etruscans, for example, or practised by the Greeks), and were for viewing, not active participation. Conservative Romans were also scandalised by the public and wild dancing that accompanied processions of mystery cult adherents. Other forms of dancing, especially by specialists (usually prostitutes) at dinner parties became increasingly erotic over the course of the imperial period; the Christian emperors put a stop to this (and many other forms of entertainment). Such prohibitions come after our period, but is something to keep in mind if you have prudish Romans or early Christians amongst your characters. The

Christians in fact deliberately rejected dancing, music, and singing in their rituals not only to separate themselves from pagan practice but also to avoid confusion with some of the noisier Jewish or mystery celebrations.

MUSIC

In antiquity, especially amongst the Greek philosophers, music was both a science and a philosophy. Only intellectuals could comprehend the rhythm of the spheres and the harmonics of the universe. Popular music, for singing, for dancing, or for plunking away on cheap (especially stringed) instruments was the domain of drunks at aristocratic parties, children, or apes (Arist., *Pol.* 1339a–4161d). Boethius claimed that only a learned man could understand the ratios between intervals and how music works on a philosophical level, but a monkey could be trained to strum a guitar (cf. Boet., *De Instit. Mus.* 1.34.224).

SEX AND PROSTITUTION

Literature, plays, and illustrations often suggest that Rome was one big sex orgy and the Romans sexually liberated: they were *not*, no matter what Hollywood would have you believe. The Romans were prudish and conservative. But because they enjoyed inversion of social norms in their comedies, art, and rhetoric (either for amusement or to teach sombre moral lessons), however, they exaggerated sexual excess, poked fun at those who over-indulged, and expressed outrage at the alleged debauchery of those in authority. Attitudes towards sex (and gender roles) in the Roman world were complex, and its study is currently a vibrant one in scholarship. Roman authors wrestled with the concepts of 'masculine' and 'feminine': defined not by what bits one might or might not have tucked into the lower regions of one's toga, but whether one was the person of action (not only sexually but also in one's public behaviour in general) or the submissive, passive partner. A woman could have 'masculine' traits, to a point – how she conducted herself with dignity in public, for example, and to show a strong, noble face during times of adversity was admired. Men, on the other hand, were expected to be initiators and the active partners. When it came to sex, maidens remained untouched and chaste; virtuous wives lay back, thought of Rome, and produced sons.

Young men enjoyed a sexual double standard. On the one hand, they were expected to resist sexual temptation: Roman authorities in Pompeii ordered that brothels should remain shut until 3 pm, so that young men could attend to their morning exercises (*Schol. ad Pers.* 1.33). On the other, they were indulged if not encouraged to sow their wild oats: taverns in the same town offered women to any comer, any time of day (for prostitutes at inns, cf. *Cod. Theodos.* 60, tit. 7; Ulp., *Reg.* 54.23; Hor., *Sat.* 1.5.82). It was also not uncommon for an aristocratic young man to keep a mistress until it was time for him to put her to one side and marry a 'respectable' girl, and even then it was acceptable for a man to dally with prostitutes or 'unsuitable' women to spare his wife. For example, St Augustine's son was the result of his relationship with the companion of his youth (*Conf.* 4.2); Nero's mistress Acte seems to have been the love of his life (Suet., *Ner.* 28.1) and arranged his funeral (50.1); Livia procured sexual partners for Augustus on a regular basis (Suet., *Aug.* 71.1). Most famously, the Emperor Titus was a notorious playboy in his bachelor days, dallying with Berenice. On the one hand, he gained social admiration from all by putting her aside on becoming emperor. On the other, together they earned romantic immortality from the Middle Ages through to modern historical bodice-rippers because of the ill-fated romance between imperial Roman son and the beautiful Jewish queen (Suet., *Tit.* 7.1–2; Tac., *Hist.* 2.2; Cass. Dio, 75.18.1–2). Society indulged young men's premarital sexual escapades, but absolutely not young women's. Hence comedy plots feature virginal aristocratic women ruined because they went out alone (at night), were raped, and became pregnant, whilst their young men are lauded for their sexual roistering. Fortunately, there are happy endings all round when it turns out the young man who dragged that gal down the alleyway one night for a bit of fun has actually raped his fiancée – so the child is his, her virtue is intact, let's have a big wedding, huzzah! (and there's the plot of Terence's *Hecyra* for you).

Any woman who initiated sex or used sex as a business or a means to get ahead (whether as prostitute or imperial wife, such as Agrippina the Younger) was regarded as 'masculine'. Hence prostitutes and women who divorced for adultery were the only women in Rome to wear the toga in public (cf. Serv., *A.* 1.281), to indcate thet they were the opposite of other women (cf. Paul., *Sent.* 2.26.1–8, 10–12, 14.17, on the consequences and penalties of a woman caught committing adultery, or *sturpro*, amongst imperial women it could be tantamount to treason). Prostitution in Rome, however, was legal, and prostitution guilds were regulated by the government. As with Vestal Virgins who were at the other end of the social scale, prostitutes were financially independent of a man – making them a rare subset of Roman women. Expensive prostitutes were amongst the few women who wore elaborate make-up, hairstyles, and luxurious clothing as it was important that they be readily identifiable in public. This attire made them exotic creatures at once admired for their beauty but also scorned for flouting the virtues of a good Roman woman (cf. Dio Chrysostom., *Or.* 7.133–139).

There were a number of dedicated brothels (*lupinares*, or 'she-wolf houses') throughout the Roman Empire; Messalina, according to Juvenal (6.124) took the pseudonym 'wolf-girl' when she played the whore. The best surviving structures are found at Pompeii (cf. the *Curiasum Urbis et notitia de regionibus*, online at the Lacus Curtius website under a discussion of the brothel *vicus* or neighbourhoods in Rome), and there was a large facility at Ephesus. Most brothels were much smaller, even sordid affairs (cf. Sen., *Con.* 1.2; Hor., *Sat.* 1.2.30). In Rome and in other towns, squalid baths and nasty restaurants and bars were often fronts for brothels; the squeamish could simply hang out at the Circus Maximus and hook up with a *lupa*. Prostitutes' fees varied; the highest-paid were far out of reach for the ordinary man and soldier; one woman charged a heady two-months' worth of wages for her services. Seneca comments on the careful keeping of a brothel's books in his *Controversies* (1.2). These latter women, like their Greek counterparts, could be well-educated and become wealthy enough themselves to operate their own brothel or retire securely; see Athanaeus (*Deip.* 13.590d–91d) for the example of Mnesaretel and other anecdotes about famous courtesans. The harsh reality, however, is that many women turned to prostitution out of desperation. Most common were the *pornai* (from the Greek for 'to sell') who might charge a mere two *asses* (about the cost of a loaf of bread) (cf. Lucil., 9.1.359–360). It was not uncommon for poor free women and freedwomen occasionally to turn to the practice to supplement their income in times of economic crisis, especially if they were left widowed. Many slaves doubled as prostitutes; one inscription tells of a man who stayed at a small inn and was charged eight *asses* for partaking of the services of a maidservant who doubled as a prostitute (*CIL*, 9.2689). There were also state-owned slaves who acted as temple prostitutes, that is, slaves who performed sex as part of religious rites. This could include sexual acts that were part of fertility rituals or 'marriage' to the deity (*hieros gamos*).

HIGH-CLASS PROSTITUTES

Famous, higher-status women who worked as (or with) prostitutes include Claudius's third wife Messalina, who dressed up in a toga and gilded her nipples (Juv., 6.121), then defeated the head of the local guild in a sex competition; her nickname was *Meretrix Augusta* or 'The Imperial Whore' (cf. Juv., 6.115–132). Another was Cytheris, the muse of the poet Gallus (and a mistress of Mark Antony and Brutus) (Verg., *Ecl.* 6) – her actual fate is unknown, but she was so famous by reputation and legacy that many later actresses took her name (Cytheris/Lycoris) in admiration of her.

SEX AND PROSTITUTION

The prostitute is a stock character in a number of Plautus's comedies, usually as the 'prostitute with a heart of gold', although you'll also find the typical hag bawd who runs the brothel and embarrasses inexperienced young men. Pimps (*lenones*), that is, slave traders who dealt with the sale of young girls and female slaves for the sex industry, were regarded as among the lowest in society, and their characters are treated with contempt in Roman comedy. Other sources that describe prostitution include legal texts and medical textbooks, as these women had many concerns about their health, including issues with pregnancy, preventing pregnancy, and disease. Exact details of the brothel activities are sometimes difficult to find in the archaeological record, but there are many material depictions in pottery, paintings and frescos, and other souvenirs of the trade. See Chapter 1 for additional discussion of sex and prostitution.

GAMBLING, DICE, AND BETTING

Both the Greeks and the Romans loved gambling and betting (e.g., Juv., 1.87–93); Suetonius published a now-lost book on dice, for example. The Romans played especially during the Saturnalia (see Macrobius) when all laws against or regulating gambling were off (Mart., *Epist.* 2.9, 11.9). The rest of the year there were restrictions on gambling except in sports, and you faced either a fine of up to four times the value of the wager or exile (*Digest* 2.5.2 and 3). There's very little evidence, however, that such laws were upheld (cf. Cic., *Phil.* 2.56; Hor., *Carm.* 3.24.58; Ov, *Trist.* 2.9, etc.).

Gamblers could range from high rollers who lost as much as 25,000 *denarii* in a single night (or bet their clothing when they ran out of dosh; cf. Juv., 1.87–93) to others who played using children's stakes – i.e., gambling with nuts (Ov., *Nux* 75–86). Ammianus Marcellinus, writing in the fourth century CE, noted that there was a 'gambling mania' that cut across all social classes in Rome – although upper-class players sniffed at being called 'gamblers' and preferred the term 'dicer' (cf. Amm. Mar., 28.4.21). Emperors who enjoyed playing included Augustus, who loved to play dice (Suet., *Aug.* 71). He would not only supply people with money from his own pocket so they could keep playing, but also deliberately lose so that the game could continue. Gaius Caligula scandalised society by gambling with dice at his sister Drusilla's funeral; here's a surprise, he was a known cheater. Claudius was so well-known for his distraction with dice (he even wrote a book on the subject) that he was condemned, in the *Apocolocyntosis*, to an eternity of placing dice forever with a bottomless cup (*fritillus* or dice-box) (Sen., *Apocol.* 14; cf. Suet., *Claud.* 33 on the emperor's addiction to dice).

Gambling was an activity that cut across age and status lines, and plenty of dice and knucklebones made from bone or wood (*talus* or *tali*) survive. Wealthier people played with dice (*tesserae/tesserae*) carved from bone, ivory or precious materials such as gemstones. They were marked 1–6 on their sides (although, unlike modern dice, opposite sides did not have to add up to 7). Dice were thrown in sets of three; the highest score in six throws was a *venus*. Poorer people made due with knucklebones: workmen would play indoors when the rain kept them from their work. Gambling was a popular pastime of the elderly and children, who risked being beaten if caught. Even the Christian Romans loved playing at their dice games. Sidonius describes the Gothic King Theodoric's fondness for board games (maybe an early form of backgammon) and gambling with dice (Sid. Apoll., *Epist.* 1.2.7) and people playing dice at a bath-resort (2.2.13). When Theodoric played these games, he let his hair down a bit and encouraged people to have fun (1.2.8). Sidonius himself encouraged students to play with dice and the dice-box as a break from their studies (5.17.1).

POPULAR BOARD GAMES

Games and board games (*abacus*, *alveus*, or *alveolus* are all names for a game board) were popular throughout the Empire: there are lines for gaming cut out on steps of public buildings all over the Empire, for example (e.g. the Basilica Julia, the Parthenon, the baths at Carthage, the synagogue at Capernaum, at Abu Sha'ar). *Tali* were also used as tokens or markers on game boards. For descriptions of these and other board games, see Owen (1924), Austin (1934, 1935) and Schadler (1995).

Twelve Lines (*Duodecim scripta*)

Described by Ovid, *Ars* 3.363ff). Super-popular board game, but difficult for us to work out exactly what all of the rules for playing were. Boards were marked out in twenty-four squares, and each player received fifteen pieces. Moves were determined by throwing three dice. Enthusiasts took the game *very* seriously. Mucius Scaevola was so upset on losing a match that he went over the game in his head, analysing each move … and once he realised which one had cost him the match, he asked his opponent to reconstruct the game with him and demonstrated that he'd been right (cf. Val. Max., 8.8.2). Other fanatics were renowned for having photographic memories when it came to remembering games move-by-move (see Quint., *Inst.* 11).

Robbers/Soldiers (*Latrunculi*)

Described by Ovid, *Ars* 3.359 and *Trist.* 2.479). Popular but complex game; Isidore of Seville, an author from seventh-century Spain, was an enthusiast who wrote about the game (*Etym.* 18.60ff) – he was, in fact, buried with his gaming pieces. Opponents played with different coloured pieces and moved around the board, attacking opponents. Some played with stones (Ov., *Ars* 2.208) or bone; real enthusiasts might play with tokens made from precious stone or metal. Julius Canus, a philosopher sentenced to execution by Gaius

Caligula, was playing the game when the soldiers came to fetch him. He demanded that the guards should double-check the state of the game and note that he was winning, in case his opponent claimed the opposite after Canus's death (Sen., *Tranq.* 14.7).

OH DEAR,
I'M BECOMING A GOD:
RELIGION IN THE
ROMAN WORLD

STATE RELIGION

The Roman state religion comprised a number of public rituals dedicated to the worship of a particular set of gods, and, in the imperial age, worship paid to the *genius*, or life spirit, of the emperor. Whilst communities, towns, and cities might have their own patron god or gods, across the Roman world could one find temples dedicated to the principal Capitoline triad of Jupiter, Juno, and Minerva – their temple in Rome is one of the oldest and its construction dates back to the time of the Etruscans. State cults were largely impersonal, ritual-bound, and publicly practised to reach the maximum number of people possible who might otherwise have worshipped their local gods. Whilst the various aspects of worship of the state gods demonstrated *pietas* and public devotion, this practice was closer in tone to civic duty and civic pride than a personal or spiritual relationship with the gods.

The relationship between the Romans and their gods was contractual, along the lines of the patron–client relationship (see Chapter 4). Rather than *orthodoxy*, which is believing in the right things, the Roman practice was about *orthopraxy*, which is doing the right (*orthos*) practice (*praxis*), especially in public, that is sacrifices, rituals, and showing respect for the old ways and traditions (cf. Plaut., *Poen.* 253–254). Respect for the state gods or the imperial cult through sacrifices and prayer would ideally be rewarded through good fortune, prosperity, and peace. Therefore, if you did your duty towards the state gods (*pietas*) then you were rewarded with good fortune (*felicitas*). Because *pietas* was about public and civic display of loyalty to the gods, the Romans prayed to their gods for material rather than spiritual blessings. You prayed for health and wealth (for yourself, your family, your city) rather than for personal virtue or goodness. It is essential to remember that this state ritual or contract doesn't just affect the individual: orthopraxy was a public, community affair. The state had to conduct rituals as a whole (or with the representation of the emperor) with as much scrupulous care as the individual. Notes Pliny the Elder, sacrificing to or consulting the gods without prayer did no good (*NH* 28.11). Failure to perform one's duty left not only the individual but also the entire state vulnerable to the gods' displeasure. So important in fact were sacrifices that they were performed when swearing oaths or completing oral contracts and promises: to break such an oath or contract would then be considered perjury (cf. Liv., 10.19.17–18, which describes a promise of building a temple in exchange for a military victory).

THE ROMAN PANTHEON

As with their approach in just about everything else, the Romans were magpies when it came to collecting gods for their pantheon. They worshipped a number of nature gods and believed that there were powerful, malicious spirits who ruled the underworld. During the Etruscan period, the Romans had no organised collective of gods or indeed even gave individual names or attributes to their gods. Once they began to trade with the local Italian tribes and with the Greek city-states in southern Italy, however, the Etruscans adapted into their religion names and attributes which they assigned to indigenous spirits. The Etruscans also gave to the Romans an interest in divination and augury.

The Romans added their own spin on to these Etruscan foundations. They had a general belief similar to animism: that there were spirits in everything, living or inanimate, but with no names or specific attributes. They believed that these spiritual beings were more powerful than humans, and that they inhabited all the phenomena and processes of the natural world (cf. Sen., *Epist.* 41.3). These spirits were numerous and impersonal, and their power was called *numen* (plural *numina*) (note that the Romans' second king, the one who invented all of their religious practices, is called *Numa*). As Roman culture developed and the Romans came into contact with other tribes and cultures, the individual gods of the Roman pantheon began to take shape, and specific powers or forces became identified with particular gods. Originally their gods were associated simply with a place as the Romans themselves weren't given to images or temples; this practice would come from the Greeks and Etruscans.

The Romans subsequently shared many of the gods, goddesses, and myths from the Greek pantheon, albeit adapting or completely changing their names; well-educated and aristocratic aficionados of Greek literature and drama preferred to reference and identify with the Greek gods rather than the Roman. The Romans also borrowed other gods from various peoples who became part of the empire, as they allowed local practices to continue. In some provinces of the empire, one sees gods and goddesses with the merged characteristics, attributes, and iconography of a local and a Roman god; one example is Minerva Sulis, the patron goddess in what is now Bath. Finally, the Romans had deities unique to themselves. Your best bet is *not* to try to reconcile any Roman (or Greek or Egyptian) myths –the overlap and contradictions are simply indicative of ancient cults adapted and modified over time.

ETRUSCAN GODS AND GODESSES

The Etruscans borrowed names and attributes from the Greek pantheon; names for the oldest Roman gods were: Tin (Sky god) = Jupiter; Uni (his wife) = Juno; Menrva (Minerva from Greece) = Minerva; Aritimi (Artemis) = Diana; Pacha = Bacchus (from Dionysius).

FOUNDATION STORY: HEROES AND MYTHS

Unlike the Greeks, the Romans didn't have a cycle of epic poetry or indigenous myth to explain their origins or to provide role models. Nevertheless, they did develop their own foundation story out of bits of the Greek Trojan cycle, distancing themselves from the Greek heroic tradition by pulling Rome's founding hero out of the wreckage of Troy. This character, the greatest warrior in Troy after Hector, is Aeneas, who flees the city with his family eventually to fulfil his destiny: he lands in Italy where his son's line will eventually produce the famous founder of Rome – Romulus.

The story of Aeneas and the story of Romulus and Remus are two separate foundation myths. They were part of oral tradition codified most famously by Vergil (Aeneas) and Livy (Romulus and Remus) in the first century BCE, and Plutarch (*Life of Romulus*) in the second century CE. Both authors drew on oral tradition and earlier, lost accounts to shape their stories. Livy and Vergil were both supported by Augustus, who patronised poets and writers of verse and prose to reinforce his programme as restorer of the old traditions that made Rome stable. Aeneas and Romulus also embodied those qualities that made the Romans Roman (see Chapter 1). Thus the activities of these heroes demonstrate a love of farming, warrior ethic, family responsibilities, and duty towards the state.

Livy tells us that the king of Alba Longa, a city-state to the south of where Rome would be built, had a daughter called Rhea Silvia. Rhea was a Vestal Virgin, who attracted the attention of Mars. He had his way with her, and she gave birth to twins. Rhea's children were Romulus and Remus – their names are Etruscan, *Romulus* being 'Roman' and *Remus* an old word for Rome. She placed the children in a basket and sent them off down the Tiber for safety. The basket landed on a bank, and the children were rescued and adopted by a she-wolf and a woodpecker (animals sacred to Mars). In turn they were rescued again by a shepherd, raised by him, and grew up to found a pair of city-states (Liv., 1.6.3–7.3). Remus failed to complete construction on his, as, when visiting his brother one day, he leapt over the low foundation of the *pomerium,* or wall that marks the sacred boundary of a city, teasing Romulus that his new city had been invaded. Before Remus could shout, 'It's a prank!' Romulus killed him, noting, 'So perish all who breach Rome's walls' (Ov., *Fast.* 4.807–859). Romulus finished his city and became the first king of Rome (Plut., *Rom.* 11.1–3). In a nutshell then: the Romans have as part of their character the sacred vows of the Vestals, who protect home and hearth, the warrior blood of Mars, the ferocity of a wolf, and the values embodied in caring for the land courtesy of their step-father.

So where does Aeneas fit in? Vergil had other fish to fry than to bolt together the two myths, but here's his take on the story. Unlike the cycle of epic Homeric poems, which grew organically via oral tradition during the so-called Dark Ages of Greece – the *Iliad* and the *Odyssey appear* to be about the Bronze Age or Age of the Heroes (c. 1600–c. 1400 BCE), but they reveal instead characteristic life during the Dark Ages (between 1200 and 800 BCE) – Vergil created the *Aeneid* by assembling stories and myths into a purpose-built epic poem. Aeneas is definitely not a Greek hero. He panics when things get rough on the trip from Troy (*Aen.* 1.91–101, 208–209), and he gets distracted from his duty (*pietas*) by a woman (and a foreign queen at that) (starting from 1.494, but especially as the focal point of Book 4; cf. 4.259–267 when Aeneas has become Dido's blissful minion – *uxorious Aeneas*). Finally, he gets a divine boot on the backside to wake up and get moving (4.267–278, 619–20), and, terrified that he's been caught out dawdling, ditches Dido and heads over to Italy. At the end of the day Aeneas is a mighty warrior with a destiny, the son of a goddess (Venus), persecuted by Juno. He is famous for his *pietas*, his duty to protect his elderly father (*mos maiorum*) and his young son Ascanius (also known as Iulus).

Vergil (70–19 BCE) was Rome's greatest poet and a celebrity in his own lifetime. We know more about him than any other poet in antiquity. He was born into a time of civil wars and grew up in an Italy devastated by war, famine, land forcibly expropriated: the very survival of Rome seemed to be in doubt, and this is what forms the central theme of the *Aeneid*. Augustus commissioned Vergil to write an epic in the style of the *Iliad* about Octavian/Augustus (cf. Suet., *Verg.* 21–24; *Vita Servii* 27; Ov., *Trist.* 2.533; *Vita Donati*) and the triumph at Actium against Antony and Cleopatra in 31 BCE. Vergil felt that the event was still too recent and that it simply wasn't dramatic enough: Agrippa shows up with the fleet, outnumbers Antony and Cleo and they split, and the Romans win. The battle is exciting on film in *Cleopatra* and *Rome*; see Velleius Paterculus (2.85), Appian (*BC* 61–66), and Cassius Dio (50.13.32) for the historical accounts, which are more straightforward and less cinematic. Vergil just wasn't feeling it and didn't think Actium would work as the setting for the epic. Even if Augustus had made Cleopatra the centre of his propaganda to justify his war against Antony (seriously, when it comes to of all things detrimental to the Romans, she's scored a hat-trick: Eastern influence … a monarch … a *woman* …), Vergil was concerned – and rightly so – that Dido would become a figure of pity and tragedy for the audience. His compromise was that Aeneas receives a shield from Vulcan that depicts future events including Augustus's defeat of Antony and Cleopatra (*Aen.* 8.626ff; Actium is at 685–728).

Homer's *Iliad* starts with the word *menin* or 'wrath' and is about the consequences of the anger of one man, Achilles, at public loss of face. The *Aeneid* opens with '*arma virumque cano*', 'I sing of the arms and the man', and it is about a man who must fight in order to restore peace and found – or *re*found Rome, in the case of Aeneas's descendant Augustus (through Julius Caesar, whose Julian *gens* traced itself back to Venus). It is Venus and Juno who cause Aeneas to fall in love with Dido, the Queen of Carthage. Venus's motivation is that Dido will be nice to Aeneas; Juno's is that she supports Carthage and wants to thwart Aeneas from getting to Italy (cf. Juno's schemes at 4.90–128). Dido is overwhelmed by her love for him, but she doesn't understand why she behaves as she does. But Aeneas must leave her (4.393–396), and she kills herself (4.450ff., 663–705). Aeneas moves on and visits the underworld to meet his father (6.679ff.) as well as other Greek heroes, including a mournful Achilles, who wonders if anyone still remembers him up top (6.168). Aeneas also receives a vision of the future of Rome (6.57ff). In the second half of the poem Aeneas becomes more and more violent and is frequently described in terms of storms or frenzied animals, especially throughout Book 12. He's given a young man to mentor called Pallas (8.514ff), but Pallas is killed by Turnus (10.453–489). Forced into a battle with King Latinus, Aeneas has had enough, goes right over the swings and slaughters the Italian tribes in Latinus's army. The Italian champion, this same Turnus, is the former suitor of Aeneas's Latin-intended bride Lavinia. The pair meet face to face, and Aeneas and he fight (from 12.697ff) a passionate hand-to-hand battle reminiscent of the battle between Achilles and Hector. Aeneas defeats Turnus; Turnus begs for his life. Aeneas decides to spare his foe because he's so weary of war and fighting. At that moment, however, he sees that Turnus is wearing Pallas's belt, realises Turnus was the one who killed his protégé, flips out, and kills Turnus (12.940–952). The end.

Despite the violent end, the *Aeneid* ultimately has an optimistic outlook for the Romans. The poem is pragmatic and not the overblown exaltation of individual glory found in the Greek epics. It illustrates Rome's mastery of the Mediterranean: the Roman Republic is willed by heaven and the gods to impose peace and civilisation over the world. The *Aeneid* was a contemporary hit; entire lines of the poem would appear in highly abbreviated versions on coins and inscriptions for the next four hundred years. It remained continuously 'in print' as the verses were studied as a model of poetry and emulated throughout the Middle Ages and into the Renaissance; Purcell immortalised their story in his enduring opera *Dido and Aeneas* (c. 1688). Countless works of art have taken inspiration from it over the past twenty centuries. It's what second-year Latin students still study as a model of Latin poetry (you know, the first-six-books version with the purple covers, originally edited by Pharr, 1930; from where I'm currently sitting I can see my 1964 edition on the shelf). Vergil himself moaned that he was nuts to have taken on the task; the work was unfinished when he reached the end of his life, and his dying wish to his friends was to burn it (Suet., *Verg.* 39–40). The ancients believed in perfection, and he did not want a half-finished work published. Vergil's pals ignored the request; there are half-finished lines which are actually quite effective, even if that was not his intent.

VESTAL VIRGINS

One of the oldest and most sacred Roman cults (Ov., *Fast.* 6.249–298), the Vestals guarded the sacred fire of the hearth which Aeneas carried from Troy. Vesta was the goddess of the hearth; she is related to Hestia, the Greek goddess of the hearth and fertility. Her consort was Priapus, a fertility god borrowed from the Greeks and the would-be lover of Vesta. This pairing displays an example of typical Roman humour and love of inversion: Priapus's main attribute was his enormous erect phallus; Vesta was the eternal virgin. Her totem animal was a donkey, a mean-spirited and protective animal in real life; Vesta's ass would bray in alarm if Priapus was near and bite him if he got too close.

The Vestals' ranks were filled usually by the daughters of the oldest patrician clans; the girls were given to the temple at around the age of seven to begin their training (Aul. Gell., *NA* 1.12.63, 5.10, 13–14). They could retire and marry after the age of forty (Plut., *Numa* 9.5–10), but many did not; men found them too intimidating to marry as they were regarded as having extraordinary power and influence (see Suet., *Iul.* 1.2). They oversaw the Temple of Saturn, which, because of the Vestals' sanctity and trust, became the repository for public documents and wills (cf. Suet., *Aug.* 101.1). The Vestals were amongst the truly financially and legally independent women in Rome because of their sacred vows and duties (*ROL*, 3.444–445). These women were so important to the Roman state that they could sit in the imperial box at games (Suet., *Aug.* 14.3); amongst other rights they were permitted used of a special sporty chariot to make their way around town (see Tac., *Ann.* 1.14; Cass. Dio, 49.38). Certain imperial women were allowed the privileges of the Vestals, including Livia and Agrippina the Younger (Cass. Dio, 59.3.4), giving them financial emancipation and the right to sit in the imperial box along with the emperor. If a Vestal broke her vows of celibacy, this was a calamity for the Romans. So if, for example, she committed adultery, the traditional punishment was to bury her alive by sealing her up in an underground room with a candle and enough food for a week (see Dion. Hal., *Rom. Ant.* 2.67; Liv., 22.57.2–6). Domitian revived this punishment (Suet., *Dom.* 8.3–4; Cass. Dio, 67.3.4; cf. Pliny, *Epist.* 4.11), as did Elagabulus, who married a Vestal called Aquila Severa (Cass. Dio, 80.9.3–4). Hence Rhea Sylvia, raped by Mars, kills herself to redeem her honour and to avoid a punishment that would have brought dishonour on her descendants. The cult was established by King Numa in the seventh century BCE (Liv., 1.20), but the Emperor Theodosius had the Sacred Fire extinguished in 394 CE. The last Vestal, Coelia Concordia, stepped down, and the era came to a close (*CIL*, 2145 in L&F, no. 553, p. 390).

THE IMPERIAL CULT

Everyone has a picture in his or her head of a mad emperor (usually Gaius Caligula) bringing down the house because he demands to be worshipped as a god. This image, derived from Christian stories and propaganda, is perpetuated by Hollywood stereotypes: eventually the evil pagan emperor gets his comeuppance at the hands of the One True God. Check out, for example, Eusebius's (*Hist. Ecc.* 352–56) or Lactantius's (*De Mort. Pers.* 33) history of the death of Galerius, the last emperor really to persecute the Christians, and his horrendous dying hours. In hope of placating the Christian god and to relieve his suffering, Galerius passed the Edict of Toleration in 311 (Lact., *De Mort. Pers.* 34); it was too little, too late, and Eusebius is just a little too gleeful in his descriptions of the dying emperor's rotting and maggot-filled genitalia. To be fair, the imperial cult was sometimes appropriated by megalomaniacs, from Caligula (who insisted he was actually Jupiter: cf. Suet., *Gai.* 22.2–3; Cass. Dio, 59.28.3) to Domitian (who demanded he be addressed as 'Dominus' in all oaths sworn to the emperor: Suet., *Dom.* 13.2; Cass. Dio, 67.13.4), to the teen-emperor Bassianus, who was considered to be the living embodiment of the god Elagabulus (*HA, Heliog.* 3.4, 6.7–9).

God-kings were old hat in the Eastern or Near Eastern half of ancient world, and that various Romans were venerated as gods was nothing at all new with the Caesars (e.g. Romulus, Liv., 1.16, and Flaminius, Plut., *Flam.* 16.3–4). It was an old custom in the Near East and Greece to venerate god-kings: pharaohs were exhibit A, but there were also semi-divine kings in Persia, in Babylonia (Gilgamesh), and even in Greece: early, legendary Attic kings, such as Cecrops, were gods and demi-gods. Some Greek rulers had no problems adopting divinity, Alexander, for example (Plut., *Alex.* 28.1–6), and then the Ptolemys who ruled in Egypt. The Romans weren't keen on kings, and certainly not priest-kings or divine-kings as seen in the Near East, but some Republican Roman generals and avatars of Roma were worshipped by grateful people in the East in gratitude after wars. For example, the earliest worship of Roma, the personification of the Roman state, sprang up spontaneously in Greece and Asia Minor after 197 BCE when Roman leadership (under Flamininus) supplanted Hellenistic leaders. Other Romans so honoured included Sulla at Athens (Plut., *Sull.* 34.2), Pompey (see Cole, 2013:59–60). It was all part of allowing local custom to flourish, and some Romans embraced the idea to shore up their political position. Caesar allowed a statue of himself to be erected bearing the inscription *Deo Invicto* ('to the unconquered god') in the Temple of Quirinus in 45 BCE (Cass. Dio, 43.45.3) and started work on the massive temple to Venus Genetrix, the founder of his *gens* (App., *BC* 2.68–69, 102; Cass. Dio, 43.22.2). Then Caesar himself was proclaimed a god after his death by the Romans themselves, thanks to a bit of quick thinking by Mark Antony (Suet., *Iul.* 88).

The imperial cult was folded into the official state cults, beginning with the reign of Augustus. Caesar's divinity and divine associations were exploited by Julius Caesar's heir Octavian (cf. Cic., *Att.* 16.15.3), who needed every bit of leverage for public support that he could get in the face of Antony's experience, sizeable army, and money (not to mention his sugar-momma Cleopatra in Egypt). Octavian cashed in on being the son of the divine Caesar (see Zanker, 1988: 53–57, on the rivalry between Octavian and Sextus Pompey as the sons of gods), and after the civil war he was rewarded with a religious moniker by the Senate when they named him Augustus in 27 BCE. Consequently Octavian/Augustus was known as the son of a god from the get-go.

Religion and the revival of old religious tradition was a big part of Augustus's programme for Rome. He rebuilt many temples to, and encouraged continued worship of, gods such as Concord, Fortune, Peace, and Mercury (god of wealth) (Suet., *Aug.* 1–5, 30.2, 59.1; Cass. Dio, 53.1.3, Aug., *RG* 19). By doing so, he linked his name to these gods and cults – Fortuna Augusta, Pax Augusta, Mercurius Augustus – thus surrounding his person, and his family name, with the cloak of the divine. All told, he repaired or restored at least 82 temples (Aug., *RG* 20), including the Temples of Jupiter Capitolinus, of Quirinus, and of the Magna Mater (Cass. Dio, 54.4.3; Aug., *RG* 19). This practice and the commission of works such as the *Aeneid* reinforced the divine associations of his own and his family's name. That also explains the winged baby hanging out with the Augustus as part of the Prima Porta statue: the baby is Cupid, the son of Venus, progenitor of the Julian clan, and thus a sibling to Augustus – the Roman version of Our Kid. So, in his religious devotion, Augustus was dutiful to the gods as a good descendant of Aeneas ought to be, and as *pater patriae* he served as a role model for Romans who likewise ought to show their devotion to the state.

The imperial cult was meant to be viewed as an extension of the *mos maiorum* or worship of one's ancestors. It wasn't the emperor (or, in the days of the Republic, the military commander) who was worshipped, however, but rather his *genius*, that is, the embodiment of his divine favour. As a restorer of peace in the troubled Roman world, Augustus became associated with divinity in the East (Cass. Dio, 51.20.6–8). He felt that worship of his own *person* was a little oddball, but, again, he recognised that it was Eastern custom to show gratitude to generals who restored peace or won major battles for the Greeks. Augustus allowed worship of his good self, or, rather, the office of emperor, first in the East, then in the less urbanised West (in Rome itself it was not allowed). He also allowed the cult *Roma et Augusta* to flourish in the East (Cass. Dio, 51.20.6–8). You weren't meant to be praying to the emperor to cure your boils or to make your crops grow; these local cults were instead meant to enhance the mystique of imperial power. By 29 BCE, the earliest temples dedicated to Roma and Augustus were built in Pergamum and Nicomedia (in Bithynia) (51.20.6–8) and a quinquenniel festival called Romania Sebasta was founded in Naples (Strab., 5.6.7) ('Sebastus' was Augustus's name in Greek). By the time of Augustus's death, there was at least one altar dedicated to him in each of the Eastern provinces, that is, to Rome and the *princeps*. By 12 BCE in the West there was an altar (Sanctuary of the Three Gauls) to Roma and Augustus at Lyon by Drusus (Cass. Dio, 54.32.1; see Fishwick, 2002, vol. 3.1.12), This was where where the Rhone and Saone came together, the administrative centre of Transalpine Gaul where the Gauls showed an outward manifestation of their loyalty to Roman rule. A similar altar was erected by either Tiberius or Drusus in Cologne, in the land of the Ubii, between 9 BCE and 9 CE (Tac., *Ann.* 1.58.2).

9 A paterfamilias making a sacrifice with his family to the gods

MOS MAIORUM

The *mos maiorum* reflected reverence for ancestors and for traditional customs and practices of Roman civic religion. It generally referred to respect for one's ancestors and elders and was practised in Rome from the humblest individual household up to and including the major institutions of the Roman state. Augustus claimed that *pater patriae*, father of the country, was his favourite of all of the titles and honours that he was given (Aug., *RG* 35; Suet., *Aug.* 58), and he saw himself as the *paterfamilias* over Rome as his 'household'. He believed that one way to re-establish peace and prosperity after decades of civil war was the moral regeneration of the Roman people. He supported and encouraged revival of the old rites and customs (Aug., *RG* 8), which had fallen away because of the influx of Hellenistic influence, new cults from the east, scepticism, and disorder from all of the civil strife. In promoting the old customs and ideas about morality, he promoted legislation (from c. 18 BCE) against celibacy and adultery and rewarded those who married and had children. See, for example, the *lex Julia* laws against adultery (see L&R, 1, no. 204, pp. 602–604), penalties against which his own beloved daughter was not immune (Cass. Dio, 56.32.4), or the *lex Poppaea* which rewarded women who had borne more than three children) (54.16.1). The *univira*, or one-man woman (i.e. widow), was a respected status, but women were encouraged to remarry after widowhood on the chance of having more children. The famous Turia (*ILS*, 8393, in L&F, no. 191: 165–169) could not bear children (section 31 of her inscription), and she urged her husband to leave her for someone who could. He did not (sections 40, 44), and noted that Turia instead helped to raise her sister's children and thus still played the role of a good mother. The ultimate model of *mos maiorum* is Aeneas, who carried his elderly father Anchises out of Troy and then relied on him for advice (even after Anchises had died), and protected his young son, Ascanius or Iulus, who was destined to found the Roman line. Milnor's study (2005) focuses on how Augustus took the rituals and customs associated with the *domus* such as the *mos maiorum* and made his family *the* model family of the Roman state.

AUGUSTUS, HIS SUCCESSORS, AND THE IMPERIAL CULT

Back home in Italy Augustus remained only the son of a god until Tiberius and the Senate had him deified (Cass. Dio, 56.46; see L&R: 1, no. 207, p. 627). During his lifetime, he was seen as a divine deliverer from war and strife, and someone who provided peace and prosperity in a new world. He became the *pontifex maximus* in 2 BCE after Lepidus died (Aug., *RG* 9). In his role as *pontifex maximus* Augustus took on religious duties in the same way as a *paterfamilias* would with his individual household. Much iconography was created to show Augustus in these roles: check out how the imperial family is portrayed walking in procession towards the personification of Roma of the *Ara Pacis*. The *Ara Pacis* is an altar dedicated to Rome and Peace that was commissioned by the Senate in 13 BCE and consecrated in 9 BCE near what was the Campus Martius (in the twentieth century it was moved to its current location in central Rome). This monument showcases Augustan propaganda: the emperor and his family are shown at the centre of civic worship, and the imagery reinforced Augustus's connections to protection, stability, and the state cult.

Whilst there was no official imperial cult in Italy, there were some unofficial practices of Augustan devotion. Horace, for example, referred to Augustus as the new Mercury (*Carm.* 1.2); some of the some towns and people in southern Italy worshipped him (keeping in mind these were centuries-old, former Greek colonies). Augustus re-established other priestly colleges that were dedicated to particular gods and particular rites. Since priests were traditionally drawn from upper-class, or patrician, families, Augustus elevated families to this status so that more could join in the practice. There was created a college of priests, mainly made up of freedmen, called *Augustales* (Tac., *Ann.* 1.54) who probably had something to do with maintaining the cult of the emperor (the *genius augustus*) or perhaps a connection with some other divinity. There were also clubs revived in Italy and around Rome meant to awaken an interest in in religion, to maintain a martial spirit, and to enhance the atmosphere of religious mystique surrounding the personality of Augustus. Augustus allowed, fostered, and even directed the development of this cult. It wasn't because he was vainglorious, but because he understood the political value in such a type of reverence and devotion. There is plenty of evidence that Augustus himself was conservative and deeply religious, so it wasn't just cynical manipulation on his part.

The progress of the imperial cult after Augustus's death and deification ran hot and cold by turns (see, for example, Tac., *Ann.* 3.63, 4.37–38, 55–56), but it was inextricable that the imperial person was going to be associated thereafter with the state and its well-being, dependent on the favour of the gods and the sacrifice and devotion of the population. Some of the emperors gave the practice only pragmatic support: Tiberius allowed one temple to be created to worship himelf in Smyrna (Tac., *Ann.* 4.55–56) and one in Pergamum (Tac., *Ann.* 4.37), but would not be pressured to allow others (Suet., *Tib.* 26; Tac., *Ann.* 4.38). Claudius allowed a temple in Colchester (Tac., *Ann.* 14.31), the original capital of Britain, where he was worshipped as a god. He, too, became a god after his death as his stepson Nero played the dutiful child and had him deified (Suet., *Ner.* 9). Nero later abolished the cult in a fit of pique to annoy his mother. Claudius was restored to his divinity by Vespasian (Suet., *Claud.* 45). The process (*apotheosis*) of Claudius's transformation was mocked in the satire *Apocolocyntosis divi Claudii* (allegedly written by Seneca), which showed Augustus amongst the true gods (e.g., Sen., *Apoc.* 9–10, along with Livia) and his objection at having an old gambler and absent-minded fool as Claudius amongst their number. Vespasian and his older son Titus were deified after their deaths (Suet., *Dom.* 2); Vespasian saw the humour in the inevitable, allegedly remarking on his deathbed that he felt he was becoming a god (Suet., *Vesp.* 2.3). For a description of an imperial apotheosis, see Herodian (*History*, 4.2).

The other first-century emperors exploited deification to the extremes more familiar to cinema-goers and game players. Gaius Caligula insisted on being called a living god and deified his sister Drusilla (Suet., *Gai.* 24). He allegedly built a bridge between the Capitoline and Palatine hills so he could communicate directly not with Jupiter, whom he felt a poor Roman copy, but with the Greek god Zeus himself. He demanded that sacrifices be offered to himself and commended the Greeks for doing so (*IG*, 7.271.21–43) and adopted the Ptolemaic practice of marrying his sister. He also attempted to have people address him as *dominus*, 'lord', which had religious connotations. Check out Suetonius, Philo's *Legatio ad Gaium*, and Josephus for further tales of Gaius Caligula's divine shenanigans. Nero, for all of his other flaws, didn't hammer on much about his divine qualities so we can give him a pass here and move on to Domitian, who wasn't mad as Gaius Caligula was, but none the less a bitter, spoiled bully. Domitian threw off any semblance of pretending that Rome was still a Republic and ruled as an open autocrat. He took the title *Lord and God* (*dominus*) which was used unofficially but publicly by officers of the royal household, contemporary writers, and Domitian himself (Suet., *Dom.* 13.2; Cass. Dio, 67.4–7). He also insisted that he was a living divine – not the avatar of another god, but innately himself divine. He made an oath to the *genius* of the *princeps* obligatory in certain public declarations, and he also created a college of priests whose sole duty it was to maintain worship to his father and brother's cults. His legislation was coloured by his severe, old-fashioned morality; his punishments for immorality shocked the public (cf. Suet., *Dom.* 8).

During the period of the Antonine or the so-called 'Five Good Emperors' (98–196), the height of the *Pax Romana*, the emperors remained fairly tolerant of local religious practice. Read Pliny's exchange with Trajan about the Christians in Bithynia (Pliny, *Epist.* 10.96 and 97): if they aren't bothering anyone, said the emperor, leave them be. Several of the Antonines were keen on Hellenic culture and especially its philosophical practices. Antonius Pius – so called because one of his first acts was to deify his stepfather Hadrian (*HA, Ant. Pius* 5.2) – demonstrated his piety by completing Hadrian's tomb and establishing a temple for worship of the divine Hadrian. He and Marcus Aurelius were devoted to Greek philosophy, especially Stoicism. Aurelius was an intellectual and scholar from childhood (*HA, Marc.* 2.1–7, 3.1–8) as seen in his letters to his mentor Fronto and in his own work *Meditationes.*

Four of these five emperors were deified as premier acts of their successors; following them, after a brief period of civil war, came the Severan dynasty. It's at the far edge of our period, but note that Septimius Severus married a Syrian woman, and aspects of Near Eastern mystery and remoteness were added to the emperor's person – the full transformation to the emperor as a mystical and unapproachable divine being can be found in McCormick's study (1990). Meanwhile for our period, significant issues with the imperial cult came during Marcus Aurelius's reign: faced with plague, famine, and the inability to stop the barbarians from spilling over into Roman territory along the Rhine and Danube, Aurelius came to the conclusion that the problem must surely be a lack of devotion to the imperial cult and sacrifices to the state (Eus., *Hist. Ecc.* 5.1; cf. Justin Martyr, *Ap.* 68). By this point in time, the middle of the second century, Christianity had quietly grown and had a reputation enough for Aurelius to attempt the first organised (albeit localised) persecution of members of the sect as a danger to the state in a desperate bid to root out the cause of the gods' anger. (Yes, Nero blamed the Christians for the fire in CE 64 and tortured a group of them to death, but this was a case of looking for a group obscure enough to frame for the disaster, rather than recognising Christians as a cause of Empire-wide strife or treason.)

In theory, then, state cults and civic worship were viewed as a means for all the different people in the Empire to have an overall focal point of loyalty and devotion, and sacrifices were made to the emperor's health, and eventually to the emperor himself. As some emperors were deified after death, they would be part of that pantheon of gods who protected the state. Hence not to worship the emperor or, later in in our period, to make sacrifice to him, was tantamount to treason (*maiestas*) because the act of an individual could have an effect on the entire state. From the second century onwards you could pay someone else to make state sacrifices for you; all the imperial administrators needed to see was the receipt (*libellus*) (see Decius's legislation on the *libellus* in CE 249–251, Michigan Papyrus, no. 158 [250] in L&R, 2: no. 172, pp. 566–567). This is frequently how the Jews met their obligation to sacrifice to the Empire: Yahweh is one of many gods, but the Jews are in a contract to worship only him. Christians, on the other hand, believe that there are *no* other gods, and to pay someone else to make a sacrifice to false gods is blasphemy. Their refusal even to hire someone to sacrifice for them led to their persecution as the cause of misfortunes to the state.

DIVINATION

The Romans were keen on astrology, horoscopes (haruspices), and signs (augury), which included tracing the flights of birds – something you can still observe in the mass flocks of starlings that wheel overhead in Rome. Neither a reliance on oracles nor interpretation of signs was a practice original to the Romans. Prophecy was an old practice in the Near East, and the Etruscans probably imported it along with economic contacts with the Phoenicians.

The Egyptians practised divination, and evidence of training manuals for examining the entrails of sheep and goats is found amongst Babylonian artefacts as well as Etruscan (namely, the famous Piacenza Liver, a bucchero-ware (black clay pottery) model of a sheep's liver, marked up as a student guide to ovine guts). The Romans rarely did anything without consulting the omens – a practice left over from the days when the Etruscans did not have individual names or characteristics for their gods, but instead believed that the world of the gods and spirits was so interlinked with the human world that everything, alive or not, was inhabited by some sort of spirit (on the ubiquity of spirits and sprites, see, for example, Sen., *Epist.* 41.3). The augurs were powerful men, because they were the ones who pointed out the warnings and signs from the gods. Compare the fate that awaits T. Sempronius

Gracchus for ignoring the signs of the haruspices in 212 BCE (Liv., 25.16.1–5) and the punishment that awaits haruspices who provide false information (Aul. Gell., *NA* 4.5). On the perils of ignoring the signs given by sacred chickens on board a Roman warship, see Cic., *Div.* 1.77.

MYSTERY CULTS

In addition to showing proper duty towards the state gods, many people worshipped the gods who made up any number of so-called 'mystery cults'. These cults originated in the Near East, and their origins and earliest rituals predate written history. The majority of their rites were unknown because their adherents did not codify them either through instructive texts as the Jews and Christians did, or in myth and epic, as the Greeks and Romans did. Our descriptions of their practices are limited to those times when outside observers – many of whom did not approve of them – describe them. Rarely does one find any remotely sympathetic description of mystery rites; an excellent exception would be Apuleius's *Golden Ass* (*Metamorphoses*). The main character, Lucius, becomes a devotee of the goddess Isis; Apuleius may have belonged to the cult himself, hence the details about Lucius's conversion and rituals. Bowden's recent study (2010) on the mystery cults is an essential read because, as he notes, whilst the majority of people in our period prob- ably belonged to one of these cults, they wrote nothing about them for several reasons. In the first place, the majority of practitioners were not amongst the upper, literate classes. Second, if you were in one of the cults, there was no need to discuss it amongst others who already knew the rituals. Finally, if you belonged to one of the cults, you didn't discuss it with others who *weren't*, because, lacking the experience, they simply would not understand the ritual or meaning. Bowden makes as his par- allel study modern-day snake-handling cults in the American south and anthropological studies of modern tribal ritual in African and South American as a way to understand the social and emotional impact of the ancient cults.

Unlike state religions, in which everyone was expected to make a public show of participation, mystery religions were exclusive. There were different levels of initiation and access to the rites from the most basic (and most visible to outsiders) ritual through to intensive levels of devotion and secret practices. These cults tended to have syncretistic natures; that is, they combined rites and beliefs across the years and miles that the cult might travel on its way from East to West. Many of the mystery cults originated in the Near East (and almost always, once they got to Rome, had been Hellenised). Many of them remained obscure until the Romans got hold of them. For example, the cult of the god Mithras was popular amongst soldiers in the Roman West from the first century CE onwards, but the Roman version of Mithras had acquired a different character from his original, centuries-old Persian incarnation by the time he'd arrived; it's not entirely possible to pinpoint when or how these changes actually occur.

Mystery cult gods and practices tended to be detached from family and state; they were more individualised in terms of the gods anyone chose to worship. Both their inclusiveness and their versatility made them popular especially amongst the lower classes and the poor, slaves, women, and soldiers (the latter of whom were generally the means of transmission from the East back to the West). The mysteries appealed to many but had no general, unified organisation. Adherents of cults would form associations, sometimes headed by professional priests; the cult you joined might have rather detailed religious precepts and beliefs; there were frequently a number of levels of initiation. Each was a mix of gods and beliefs; despite some common ritualistic practice, the cults were not necessarily proprietary and made no demands for any special way of life unless you wanted to become a fully devoted initiate. There were sacred symbols and rites with magical efficacy, purification, asceticism, baptism and sacraments associated with these cults, and, because of the various levels of initiation, the adherents might be divided into two or more classes within the cult.

Mystery cults provided a sense of belonging and comfort that the impersonal state cults did not. For example, Isis appeals to poor Lucius in *The Golden Ass* because he's been transformed into a donkey, and she promises to rescue him, love him, and protect him. All he has to do is worship her and devote himself to her for the rest of his life (cf. Apul., *Met.* 11.25; 11.22–24 covers his initiation). Many people thus performed all of the state cult ritual, which was a public display and demonstrated civic pride and loyalty, but they also belonged to some form of cult that satisfied their individual needs for security and spiritual well-being. Cult rituals could be noisy and frenzied; women's cults especially allowed the chance for women to let their hair down and break free of the rigid social customs that dictated their lives. This is why women's cults, such as the many associated with Dionysius (the god traditionally associated with wine festivals and fertility cults, also known by the name Bacchus) or the Bona Dea (or the 'Good Goddess', an important cult exclusive to women at the time), were so secretive and forbidden for men to see. Keep in mind just how much trouble Clodius got into for spying on the activities of worshippers of Bona Dea, including Julius Caesar's wife. As a result of Clodius's actions, Caesar had to divorce his wife to maintain his own public reputation (Suet., *Iul.* 6.2; Plut., *Caes.* 9–10; Cass. Dio, 37.45.1–2).

Whilst there are a number of smaller cults and variations, major cults included the Eleusinian mysteries from Greece, the cult of Cybele, worship of Isis, and the followers of Mithras. All four of these predate the Roman Republic and Empire, and ultimately come from the Near East. The versions we know about transformed over the centuries as they moved west through the Egyptian world, then the Classical Greek (499–323 BCE) and Hellenistic (323–31 BCE) world, and finally down into the Empire.

ORACLES

The Romans borrowed religious practice from the Greeks (oracles) and the Etruscans (divination, including augury and haruspices, the study of divining the future from watching the flights of birds or reading the entrails of animals) as their own state religion came together. From the eighth century BCE, small sanctuaries dedicated to the gods were founded across the Greek world; these were originally intimate places of worship, unlike temples, which were large, public buildings. Shrines were often located in neutral territory amidst the otherwise quarrelling city-states. The Romans shared a number of these sacred places with the Greeks; the most famous was the shrine dedicated to Apollo at Delphi in Greece. Here lived an oracle called the Pythia, and she breathed in all day strange gases coming up from a fissure in a rock; her priests carefully interpreted her responses to questions posed to her – usually enigmatically enough to avoid any debate after the prophecy had been fulfilled one way or another. The Pythia was at the centre of Delphi's importance; she was consulted for weddings, colonisation, or when to go to war. In addition to providing divine sanction for endeavours, Delphi was the heart of big business in the Classical world: oracle seekers brought wealth as gifts in hopes of good answers to their queries; victors and satisfied customers bestowed treasure on the shrine. There were also regular athletic games, drama, and music competitions held here, which brought in business and tourists. The Pythia was not the only proph-etess in the Classical world; the Romans inherited another Greek oracle at Cumae, an old Greek colony to the south of Rome (more or less the border between Greek and Etruscan territory.) Here in the caves lived the Sibyl, and, in keeping with Roman practicality, her priests wrote down her prophecies in a series of books that the Romans then consulted (on the origins of the Sybil and her sacred books, see Cic., *ND* 3.5; Dion. Hal., *Rom. Ant.* 4.62.1–5; on divina-tion, see Cic., *Div.* 1.12, 24–25).

ROME AND JUDAEA

The history of the Hebrews or Jews, and their relationship with the Romans, is covered by a rich and vast field of scholarship, so only a sketch of their history is provided here. Politically, the Hebrew state flourished independently only briefly in the Near East, filling a power vacuum around the eleventh and tenth centuries BCE. Once that state was invaded and subsumed into the Assyrian empire, the Israelites were dispersed by the invaders. This event complemented the Hebrew tradition of a search for a homeland; when the Persians conquered the Assyrians, they allowed the Hebrews to resettle their own lands, the region that became known as Judaea (Ezra 1:1–8, possibly corroborated on the Cyrus Cylinder). The Hebrews, later known as the Jews, differed from the other Near Eastern religious practitioners in antiquity in that they equated cultural heritage with religious practice. They were monotheists, which means they believed in only one god; whilst this was an unusual practice, it wasn't unprecedented in antiquity. The Jews acknowledged that there *were* other gods, but they themselves worshipped only one: they were the Chosen People of a single god, and their relationship was one of protection from this god.

The Jews were keen to codify their moral and social practices: like the Romans, they had a contractual relationship with their god, but it wasn't the businesslike, patron–client arrangement that the Romans had with their state gods. Unlike other ancient gods, there was a personal relationship with the god of the Hebrews (although the Hebrews did borrow from practices of other desert nomads): this made them distinct amongst the rest of the people in the world, because they had a protective god who took an interest in them as a people. When the Greeks and the Romans interacted with the Judaeans, they sometimes weren't sure what to do with them; there were, especially for the Greeks, political practices that clashed with the Jews' cultural practices and identity. Some Jewish practices, for example, were frowned upon, even outlawed by the Seleucids, the Hellenistic dynasty who ruled over Jewish territory from the late fourth through to the mid-first century BCE. At this period, this ruling people took over the part of Alexander the Great's empire that encompassed the old lands of Judaea. In 167 BCE, Antiochus IV caused a crisis by outlawing circumcision as a barbaric practice (Joseph., *AJ* 12.5.4; 2 Macc. 6:1–12). This not only led to war – the Maccabean Revolt – but also led to an alliance between Judaea and Rome. The Romans were in that part of the world because of their own involvement in conflict amongst

Macedonia, old Alexandrian states, and federations of Greek city-states. Rome supported Judaea against Antiochus, and Judaea became a client-state of Rome and got on fairly well with the Romans. The Romans found Jewish laws and customs eccentric (they were baffled by the existence of so many rules to govern how one could eat, or hours of the day to keep work, or when to say prayers, for example). Romans, however, respected old ways and customs; the Hebrew or Jewish faith was far older than the Roman state, so Romans gave Jews some grudging respect. Ultimately the Romans established a working relationship with the Jews and the kingdom of Judaea.

JOSEPHUS

Aside from the Hebrews' and Jews' own writing, the best source for picking through the conflicts between the Romans and the Judaeans is the work of Josephus (37–c. 100). Josephus was a Romanised Jew who became a court reporter and historian during the era of the Flavians. He wrote two major works: *The Jewish War* (*Bellum Judaicum*) and the *Antiquities of the Jews* (*Antiquitates Judaicae*). Initially a Jewish Pharisee and diplomat who was pulled into the Jewish revolt in 66 CE, Josephus wrote about the event with pro-Roman sympathies. He was captured but ended up becoming an adviser to Titus (whence adopting Flavius as his *gens* name). *Antiquities* covers the history of the Jews to 65 CE. Josephus's language is sometimes flowery and steeped in rhetorical flourish, but he provides a source on how the Romans maintained their relationship with one of the more complex cultures within their empire.

The Jews and the Romans had a fairly unusual relationship. The quarrels between them were more the result of cultural clash than ideology, although sometimes they were resolved by compromise. In the imperial period, for example, whilst the Jews wouldn't sacrifice to the emperor, they were willing to get someone else to do it on their behalf – which satisfied the Romans. Due to internal strife, however, they came into conflict with the Romans several times between the second century BCE and the second century CE. Most of the problems were due to political issues and factional rebellions against Roman rule. Resolution of these conflicts would take Judaea from being an ally of the Romans to being a client-kingdom (63 BCE), to being a province (CE 44), to being completely subsumed into the Roman Empire and losing its special status (CE 135) after a series of conflicts between 66 and 135 – not to reappear as an independent sovereign state until 1948.

ROME AND THE CHRISTIANS

HollyRome loves pitting Christians against the Romans – and no wonder, as heroic defiance against the evil pagan Romans has its antecedents in Christian stories, plays, and histories dating back nearly two thousand years. Christianity adds an exciting element and nuance to any story taking place in the *Pax Romana*, but you must be aware of your contemporary sources. Remember their original audience, and read them critically to help shape your characters' behaviour, practice, and outlook. There are plenty of films and historical novels out there to help you decide if you're going to dip into that well-visited well, add a token nod to Christianity to your story, or perhaps simply colour the scene with a more nuanced acknowledgement of a cult that was pretty small potatoes in our time period, affected by our hindsight on its eventual significance and impact.

During the *Pax Romana*, the Christians appeared to most Romans as just another mystery cult since, superficially, they had some common features. For example, Christianity and the mystery cults originated in Near East, they were secretive, they had a ritual meal, they had a strong female character as part of their religion, and they had a baptism ceremony; their sacraments were akin to the various levels of initiation and practice seen publicly amongst the mystery cults. But Roman intellectuals were well aware that Christianity was *not* a mystery cult;

it was an offshoot sect of Judaism. That itself was nothing unusual; neither was their monotheism, as the Jews practiced a monotheistic religion, too. The Romans were aware that there were different flavours of Judaism, some practices of which, like Christianity, were criticised by the Jews themselves. Christians followed the teachings of the same Scripture as the Jews (with the 'new' testament later added to it with Christ's life and work, and then his followers'); originally one had to become circumcised to become a Christian – that is, become a Jew first. This all changed with the conversion of Saul of Tarsus (Acts 9:1–22). Saul, who became Paul, marks the beginning of explaining (or acting as an *apologist*) for the religion, in a series of letters that form part of the New Testament. Paul helped to introduce the religion to Greek philosophers, elevating it beyond a cult or ritual practised by the marginals in society. The Acts of the Apostles also provide context about how the religion was spread in the early days, and also for ideas about Roman interaction in the provinces. What baffled pagan critics of Christianity was Christians' rejection of Judaism and deliberate separation from that religion.

The Christians followed simple rules, knowing that that a faithful Christian would be rewarded with eternal life after death, and that a sinner would be condemned to eternal punishment. For those in the Empire who weren't aristocratic Roman men – women, slaves, the poor, Greek intellectuals (who enjoyed approaching some of the more difficult aspects of Christianity as logic puzzles) – the religion was extremely appealing. Jesus's teaching was simple and straightforward: love one another; love God the Father as the only God with all one's heart, soul, and mind; treat humans justly; and live in peace (Mt 22: 35–40; Mk 12:28–33). Christianity offered hope and community, especially at a time when state institutions did not. The idea of *caritas*, that is, charity and giving for its own sake, with no demands for payback or reciprocity, appealed to the poor and marginalised. Not everyone could go out and preach the Gospel as the apostles did, but one could live an exemplary life: slaves could convert their masters, women their husbands. Long-suffering Christian wives who had to deal with cruel pagan Roman fathers, husbands, and sons are a staple of early martyrologies.

The first adherents to Christianity were the urban, poor classes, and women of all classes. Christianity complemented extant burial clubs and societies which not only helped to pay for funeral rites and burials but also acted as social clubs for meals and get-togethers. These meetings were a chance for a break and relief from the everyday grind, and a place to give ordinary people a sense of worth and comradery. For similar reasons, Christianity appealed to soldiers, and they were the ones who helped the sect to spread quickly throughout the Empire's urban centres and military camps.

CHRISTIANS AND PAGANS

Frequently the last groups to be converted were those living in the countryside, where people tended to be the most conservative and reluctant to latch on to new ideas. *Paganus* means someone who lives in the countryside.

If the appeal of inclusion and companionship wasn't enough, Christianity attracted with displays of power: stories of miracles attracted converts. Yes, there are some showstoppers in the Gospels such as raising the dead, but look at how many miracles involve curing chronic illnesses or providing food. Christianity also had its own heroes: the martyrs who were willing to die for their faith demonstrated that greatness and commemoration could come even to the most humble. As a consequence of these appealing aspects of the sect, by the early fourth century there were perhaps as many as five million Christians across the Roman Empire.

Despite its own press (much of which was written by Christian intellectuals in response to arguments against by pagan intellectuals, or advice given on ritual and practice), there is little mention of the Christians and Christianity in Roman sources. The best known include

Pliny's exchange with Trajan (Pliny, *Epist.* 10.96 and 97): Pliny famously asked Trajan what to do about the Christians in his constituency when their neighbours complained. Trajan, cosmopolitan emperor that he was, advised Pliny not to waste time or money actively chasing up the Christians. If Christians *did* happen to come to court (Pliny was a lawyer as well as local governor) for another reason, then he could ask them about their beliefs and follow up as appropriate. They would be given a chance to recant and renounce their faith before being arrested or punished. If Pliny were to execute any of them, noted Trajan, it should not be because they were Christian, but because they were defying the magistrate and consequently Roman law and practice. Others mentioning Christians in the historical record include Tacitus, who notes them with disdain in the *Annales* with no real interest in their religion at all (cf. his brief discussion of Judiasm, *Hist.* 5.4–5). He notes that Christians were being executed for 'antisocial behaviour'. He tells us that they originated with someone called Christ who'd been executed in Tiberius's reign, that they practised *superstitio* ('magic' or 'witchcraft' – both illegal in the Roman Empire), they were a problem in Judaea, and their cult had spread to Rome (Tac., *Ann.* 15.44). He criticises Nero for executing them in response to the fire, but it is more a criticism of Nero's sadism than a defence of the Christians themselves. Suetonius also mentions them only in passing when he notes that Claudius expelled the Jews from Rome as they were being stirred up by a certain 'Crestus' (Suet., *Claud.* 25.4), and in his own criticism of Nero's cruelty at torturing a group of Christians as scapegoats of the fire of 64 CE (*Ner.* 16.2). Josephus, more interested in codifying the history between the Romans and the Jews, also briefly mentions the sect (*AJ* 18.3.3) and describes the condemnation and crucifixion of Jesus by Roman authorities and mentions James, the brother of Jesus (20.9.1). This latter passage is the topic of much scholarly debate and one that has fostered a number of websites devoted to discussion about how this so-called *Testimonius Flaviarum* is proof that the Jews secretly believe that Jesus is the Messiah.

More intriguing sources from the Roman point of view come from intellectuals such as Celsus (fl. c. 175–177 CE) and Porphyry of Tyre

(c. 234–c. 305 CE). These authors clarify how the Christians were perceived as a civil threat to Roman order and authority. Their work does
not survive in its entirety; both were considered dangerous by Christian
authorities as these authors are thoughtful and logical in their analysis
of the flaws of Christian belief and practice. Hence, Christian authorities
considered their works dangerously persuasive in the hands of the vulnerable. Celsus, for example, had no problem with the idea that Jesus
attained a godly status, but he took exception to the myth of Jesus as
the son of God, the 'apostasy' of the Christians as a Jewish sect, and the
Christians' negligence of civic duties. Celsus was also critical of Jesus's
divinity and was baffled why anyone would believe that an omniscient
god would need to come to live on earth as a mortal amongst mortals
(Or., *C. Cels.* 1.6, 4.2, 4.14, and elsewhere). He had no problem with Jesus
becoming a god, as it happened in the Roman world (cf. Plut., *De Def. Or.*
415c). What stuck in his craw was that Jesus had become *the* god and for
no demonstrable reason as far as he or any other pagan was concerned
(cf. Or., *C. Cels.* 8.14). The Neo-Platonist Porphyry also found Jesus's
code of conduct and suggestions of good behaviour reasonable and
found him to be a worthwhile philosopher (cf. Augustine's discussion
of Porphyry in *Civ. Dei* 19.23). Porphyry still contended, however, that
Christianity was logically unfounded. It wasn't Christ's basic philosophy
that Porphyry objected to, but that his disciples and followers equated
Jesus himself with God. Porphyry's objections are noted by Eusebius
(*Praep. Evang.* 1.3.1).

Celsus also rejected Christianity's practices and beliefs as *superstitio*,
more or less translated as 'magic'. He was bothered in particular about
the Christians' stubborn adherence to accepting beliefs strictly on faith,
which he saw as childish (citing 1 Cor. 1:25–26 in Or., *C. Cels.* 1.9; cf. 19)
and that there was no witness outside of Christian writings to support
any of the tenets of the religion. He felt that many Christians, being
uneducated, were thus vulnerable and taken advantage of by those
who would perform these miracles and tricks. To believe against your
will, or because you were afraid not to believe, struck the Romans as
irrational. *Superstitio* included those practices and beliefs that came

into Rome from the outside, e.g. from the Celts, Germans, people of the Near East, Egyptians, and so forth. Anything was *superstitio* that deviated from Roman ritual (rejection of all gods but their own), had no physical evidence (such as entrails or the flights of birds), and was supported by faith rather than practical result (hope of rewards in the afterlife instead of material reward or prosperity in this one). In this way, Christianity's beliefs were akin to the rituals of the mystery cults (3.17, 4.10). In this aspect of Jesus's career, Celsus is especially critical: he calls Jesus a magician (1.6, 6.40) and considered Jesus's miracles to be witchcraft (1.6; cf. Apuleius's trial in his *Apologia*; Paul., *Sent.* 5.23.14–19 in Warrior, 2002, no. 12.2:140). Miracles were tricks, and clever, but they were magic: they were not part of a contract as in the patron–client relationship. Look at it this way, consider Gospel accounts of Jesus's miracles, which include curing the blind (Jn 9), stilling storms (Mk 4:35), becoming invisible (Jn 8:59), driving out demons from those possessed (Mk 1:23), and so forth. No wonder Simon Magus begged the apostles to sell to him the secret of Jesus's 'tricks' (Acts 8:18) – from the outside looking in, tales of the miracles *would* have looked like an impressive magic act.

Celsus wrote around the time of the reign of Marcus Aurelius (reigned 160–180 CE), the emperor who organised the first persecution against the Christians as dangerous to the well-being of the state. The emperor, devoted not only to Stoic philosophy but also to the civic duties necessary to maintain good fortune and benevolence of the gods, sought an explanation for increasing crises in the Empire: famine, poor economy, endemic wars on the frontiers which the barbarians kept winning. In seeking answers, Aurelius became aware of the Christians, and how they refused to make sacrifices to the state gods (M. Aur., *Med.* 11.3), although scholars argue whether he really means the Christians here, or if he was using them as a simile for poor religious practice in general). Celsus also pointed out in his works that the Christians were disrupting the order of the Roman state because of their beliefs: they would not fight, which was a neglect of their duty to protect the empire physically (Or., *C. Cels.* 8.73); they would not sacrifice (7.62, 8.75), and thus neglected their civic duties (cf. Min. Fel., *Oct.* 12). They held, Celsus argued, the ancient traditions of Rome in contempt; this disregard for tradition would lead to social anarchy. Members of the new upstart sect ignored proper reverence for the past and tradition; they desired to make society private, neglect public duties, and undermine the authority of the emperor and Empire (cf. Or., *C. Cels.* 8.63). The end result would be chaos and barbarism (8.68).

So it wasn't that the Romans disliked Christianity as a religion; the Empire tolerated many local cults and practices. What worried them about Christianity was its adherence to blind faith and its discussion of a second coming, a new kingdom, and worldly redemption. As things got difficult for Marcus Aurelius (and after his reign into the third and early fourth centuries, when persecutions continued in earnest), Christians challenged state authority. Their refusal to show their *pietas* to the state cults posed a real threat to long-held social institutions and consequently the stability of the Empire. Others saw them as fanatics, self-righteous, and arrogant outsiders, especially because they tended to shun any involvement in politics and lay low. Nevertheless, after our period, they acquired an imperial champion in Constantine (reigned 306–337 CE). Christianity became the official religion of the Empire during the reign of Theodosius II (reigned 402–450 CE), with Christian emperors turning around and persecuting non-Christians, pagans, and people who practised the wrong *kind* of Christianity with aplomb – another theme explored in fiction and film (see 2010's *Agora*, about the persecution of the pagan scientist Hypatia by Clement, the bishop of Alexandria, while the pagan governor was too ineffectual to maintain order).

PRIMAL ROMAN GODS

Some primal Roman gods had no Greek or other foreign antecedents. These include a number of household and family gods, as in the following examples.

Janus
God of doorways, associated with Quirinus, which was an old name for Romulus (cf. Liv., 1.32.6–14).

Lares
Old deities protecting the house and represented as tiny statues (cf. Plaut., *Aul.* 1–27).

Penates
Patron gods of the storeroom, then later the whole house. Also represented by tiny statues usually paired with a *lars* (cf. Plaut., *Mer.* 830–837).

Genius
In this context the 'life force' or 'life spirit'. Probably originally related to the fertility of the *paterfamilias*. Another god represented by a small statue of an individual human-like being (see Ov., *Fast.* 2.533–570).

Quirinus
A war god adapted from the Sabines who was also merged as an avatar of the deified Romulus. He was associated with horses and considered the oldest and chief executive of the Roman pantheon – but so was Jupiter: sometimes they get merged, sometimes they don't (cf. Liv., 8.9.1–11).

MYSTERY CULTS

Eleusinian mysteries
Focused on Demeter and Persephone. Possibly date back to the sixteenth century BCE and the Myceneans. Under Athenian state control from the sixth century BCE. There is a Homeric hymn composed around 600 BCE that tells us some of the ritual, mostly just the highest rites (which involve a procession and ritual bathing) (*Homeric Hymn to Demeter* 2.90–94; see Foley, 1994). The hymn tells the story

of Demeter and Persephone, and Persephone's descent into the underworld; it ends by promising the initiates that they will have wealth and a happy life there. The cult had an enormous following as anyone could be in it; there was no blood-spilling as in a number of other Eastern cults – and it wasn't considered a barbarian practice amongst the Greeks because you had to speak Greek to be a participant. Festival time: mid-September.

Cybele (Mater Magna): the Great Mother

Cybele was a Lydian earth mother goddess originating in Anatolia (Hdt., 5.102) in Neolithic times. She is usually represented as enthroned in a *naiskos* (a type of small temple), wearing a crown, carrying a small dish used to pour offerings (*patera*) and a drum (*tympanum*), and flanked by lions or holding a lion on her lap. She is associated with a consort called Attis, and part of her ritual involves mourning his death (he himself was not worshipped until Roman times, when he took on the status of a sun god; Catullus wrote a poem about Attis). Her cult became Hellenised before it showed up in Rome by 264 BCE, although it wasn't officially allowed till about 205 BCE (and worship of her was associated with the Punic Wars – see Liv., 29.10.4–11 on the adoption of her cult. Cf. Ovid's account of the arrival of the cult into Rome, *Fast.* 4.247–273). In Rome she was known as the Magna Mater. Originally her cult was grudgingly allowed publicly by limited public games in her honour and a small temple on the Palatine; Claudius, normally conservative when it came to oriental cults, gave permission for Roman citizens to worship her. She also shows up in the *Aeneid* as the one who gives her sacred trees (her consort is associated with pine) to Aeneas so that he and his men c build ships to escape Troy (Verg., *Aen.* 9.99–109, 143–147). The cult was very popular in Gaul and North Africa; those who castrated themselves were given women's clothes and assumed female identities. It was more popular in the municipalities in the provinces as it was an agricultural cult, and it was very popular with women due to Cybele's role as a powerful mother. Festival time: mid- to late March.

Isis (from Persia then Egypt by way of Greece)

This cult was popular with both sexes and all classes, but especially women. Back in Egypt, Isis was wife and sister to Osiris, and the ideal mother-wife. Evidence of her worship goes back to the fifth millennium BCE, and she was usually worshipped in conjunction with Osiris and Horus, as a sort of national deity in Egypt. The cult spread throughout the Near East and Roman Empire as far north as Britain. She was a versatile and adaptable goddess, as, by the time the Romans got hold of her, she had assimilated the character of Hellenic and Semitic goddesses including Demeter and Aphrodite. Isis on her own was very popular in the West from the middle Republic but especially from the imperial period onwards; her best-preserved temple is found at Pompeii. Many of her followers considered her another avatar of Cybele. Despite allowing local religions to continue after Roman occupation, neither Augustus nor Tiberius (Joseph., *AJ* 18.66–80; Cass. Dio, 53.2.4) thought much of her cult (in Rome, where temples dedicated to her were prohibited in 28 BCE). Gaius Caligula may have revived her worship in Rome (he tolerated Eastern cults in general); Claudius remained ambivalent. Under the Flavians, Vespasian and Domitian constructed the Iseum. The cult continued to flourish during the *Pax Romana* (see Apuleius, as noted above; another detailed source on her cult is Plutarch's *Isis and Osiris*, which is a work in the *Moralia*); Hadrian decorated his villa with scenes from her myths. The cult's popularity is indicated by the number of temples and iconography on jewellery, tombs, statues, and monuments found throughout the Empire. When her last temple was finally shut at Philae in 529 CE by Justinian, the historical period of Egyptian religion came to an end. Festival time: around 5 March.

Mithras (originally from Persia)

Mithras was originally an ally and agent of the Zoroastrian good guy god Ahura Mazda (according to the ancient source, which is called the *Avesta*). Mithras helped Ahura in his fight against evil and darkness, and, after he killed a bull, the cult and its practices. The bull was the first living creature; from the bull's blood came all people. Mithras thus acted as an intermediary and protector between the gods and men. When he finished his tasks against evil, he was taken into heaven in the sun's chariot. The Persian Mithras and the one worshipped later in Rome are one and the same, but he gets new attributes once he gets to Rome. How this transformation occurs is obscure; the Roman cult ignores most of his Zoroastrian adventures, but keeps some of his main characteristics. For example, in Roman art, he wears his Persian clothes, trousers, and Phrygian cap. He also maintains his association with bulls; *tauroctony* is the term for those statues that show him cutting the bull's throat. Statius says that Mithras killed a bull beneath a Persian cave (Stat., *Theb.* 1.719–720; cf. Cass. Dio, 63.5.2), and followers of Mithras entered into a small grotto to be drenched in bull's blood as part of their initiation. There are seven levels of initiation into his cult; not everyone completed all seven, but this doesn't seem to have been required to be a follower. Very popular with soldiers, he is sometimes merged with Sol Invictus and known as the god of battles. His earliest appearance in the West was among a band of pirates near Anatolia (67 BCE according to Plutarch, *Pomp.* 24); his followers were almost exclusively male. His cult was probably spread by the army and merchant seamen; there are surviving dedications that show that he was worshipped by soldiers and by well-to-do businessmen. He also appealed to marginal people in society (i.e. anyone not a male aristocrat) because his worship seemed to promise something better in the next life or indeed hopes of individual immortality. Most of his press comes from Christian writers speaking out against the cult and its practices. Born, hatched, and created in mid-to-late December.

8

RESOURCES AND SUGGESTIONS FOR FURTHER READING

This book is only a survey when it comes to the amount of material that can be consulted when creating a fictional Roman world, and this final chapter provides some additional suggestions to complement reading and resources suggested throughout Chapters 1–7. It is by no means comprehensive, and new publications, online resources, and transcriptions of contemporary sources aimed at both a general audience and the scholar appear regularly.

TEXTBOOKS AND REFERENCE WORKS

Sometimes you just need a basic textbook to lay out chronology, facts, and events. Two *Very Short Introductions* include David M. Gwynn's *The Roman Republic* (Oxford: Oxford University Press, 2012) and Christopher Kelly's *The Roman Empire* (Oxford: Oxford University Press, 2006). More substantial textbooks include Allen Ward et al.'s *A History of the Roman People*, sixth edition (London: Routledge, 2013) or M.T. Boatwright et al.'s *The Romans: From Village to Empire: A History of Rome from Earliest Times to the End of the Roman Empire*, second edition (Oxford: Oxford University Press, 2012). Older textbooks include Chester G. Starr, *A History of the Ancient World*, fourth edition (Oxford: Oxford University Press, 1991), a general work but still a good starting place; do bear in mind, however, that it has not been updated in nearly thirty years. Another older, but detailed, textbook is Arthur E.R. Boak's

A History of Rome to 565 A.D., reprinted in 2018 by Forgotten Books; Boak published originally in the mid-twentieth century. The work was revised by William S. Sinnegan, if you pick up the sixth edition published by Macmillan in 1977. This was a standard, substantial textbook for students of Classical history (including the author) for years.

The Oxford Classical Dictionary is a key reference work for the Classical historian, and it is available in a print and electronic version (the latter through either a university library or larger public libraries). Another good reference is *The Encyclopedia of Ancient History* (Oxford: Wiley-Blackwell). Like the *OCD*, it is available online. Longer, scholarly essays can be found in *The Cambridge Ancient History*, a multi-volume work that covers the Classical world from the Greek period through to the late Western Roman Empire (CE 600). The *CAH* is fourteen volumes in all; for our period between 200 BCE and 200 CE, you want volumes 7–12. The most recent edition contains a mix of political, economic, and social essays by leading scholars in those fields; the earlier editions, published before 1960 are more focused on war, politics and the economy – topics reflective of the prewar and immediately postwar era in which the *CAH* was originally compiled. The more recent editions cast their net more widely to consider social and cultural issues widely overlooked in the early twentieth century but now a robust part of Classical historiography. Finally, whilst not peer-reviewed, Barbara McManus's *VRoma* or *Livius.org* website can provide a quickly sketched overview for context and foundation on many topics of Roman political, economic, and social history; there are many illustrations on the site, as well.

There are many useful 'handbooks' and 'companions' to the Roman world published by Oxford, Cambridge, and Wiley-Blackwell. Edited again by current scholars in the field, these volumes are themed collections of essays that not only provide foundation for subject areas but also exemplify the state of current scholarship. Oxford's companions on Classical Studies (www.oxfordhandbooks.com/page/classics) include volumes on topics such as Roman law, comedy, and childhood, and Classical education. Cambridge's collections (www.cambridge.org/

core/series/cambridge-companions-to-the-ancient-world/6DD2A5A03
B17CF5D8ED48D98EA4097D8) include the Roman Republic, the age
of Augustus, the age of Nero, and numerous other specialised topics
in social, political, and cultural history. Wiley-Backwell's range, found
at http://eu.wiley.com/WileyCDA/Section/id-324320.html, includes a
growing collection of volumes on for example, the Roman Republic, the
Roman Empire, childhood, food and drink, sex, the army, and specific
eras, such as the age of Nero or the Flavian emperors.

PRIMARY SOURCES (IN TRANSLATION)

Rather than suggest specific editions of texts and collections, I've
attempted to include those contemporary works readily available in
print or online in English translation. Many Penguin paperback translations of Classical are available new and second-hand; Oxford and
Cambridge translations are also invariably excellent, annotated editions.
The Loeb series, published by Harvard University Press, includes a growing collection of texts translated with the original Greek or Latin on the
facing page to the English. If you can afford a subscription (as of 2019,
around $150 a year – actually quite a bargain, considering that individual
volumes cost around £15 to £25 each, and the online version allows for
you to search, save, and collect references), the Loeb Classical Library is
available online (www.loebclassics.com/) – if not, you might be able to
access it through a local research or university library.

If you prefer to have a sift online for ancient sources, the Perseus
Digital Library (hosted by Tufts, www.perseus.tufts.edu/hopper/) is
an ongoing project to provide free, accessible translations of Classical
texts. Beware that some texts are from much older translations (often
from Loeb volumes that have been superseded by newer editions), and
some are downright arcane: for ages, the only easily available translation
of Apuleius's *Metamorphoses* (*The Golden Ass*) was a transcription of
Dryden's seventeenth-century translation (Apuleius's work, including
Apologia, is now available in Loeb translations). University-hosted databases include Perseus, MIT's *Internet Classics Archive* (http://classics.

mit.edu/) and Fordham's *Internet Ancient History Sourcebook* (https://sourcebooks.fordham.edu/ancient/asbook.asp).

Sometimes you might want not a specific author but rather a themed collection of sources – on women, on law, on the army, and so forth. There are many sourcebooks of this type that divide up diverse sources by theme or category; they include key Classical authors and translations of selections from papyri, inscriptions, laws, and other non-literary forms of writing. Sourcebooks noted throughout this book include N. Lewis and M. Reinhold's two-volume collection *Roman Civilisation: Selected Readings*, third edition (New York: Columbia University Press, 1990). Published originally in 1955, it's still a hard set of volumes to beat, with Volume 1 covering the Republic through to the Augustan Age and Volume 2 covering the Empire. M. Dillon and L. Garland's *Ancient Rome: Social and Historical Documents from the Early Republic to the Death of Augustus* (London: Routledge, 2015) is a solid complementary text, although it stops in the first century CE and the age of Augustus. Many sourcebooks are available on specialist topics in Roman history as well, too numerous to list here, but keywords plugged into library and book databases online such as the British Library catalogue, Worldcat, and even Amazon will bring up specific primary source collections and selections on, for example, women (Rowlandson, 2009; Grubbs, 2002; Kraemer, 2004; Gardner, 1987; Lefkowitz and Fant, 2016), daily life (Harvey, 2004; Shelton, 1997; Parkin and Pomeroy, 2007), animals (Newmyer, 2010), death (Hope, 2007), slavery (Wiedemann, 1980), sex (Johnson, 2004), the army (Sage, 2008; Campbell, 1994), sports (Futrell, 2006; Mahoney, 2001), religion (Warrior, 2002; MacMullen and Lane, 1992; Lee, 2015; Cotter, 1999), and so forth.

CHAPTER 1: ROMAN PEOPLE

The subject of Roman identity and Roman social relations covers the family and household, social relations, and scholarship on identity and character. You might start with Michael Peachin, *The Oxford Handbook of Roman Social Relations* (Oxford: Oxford University Press, 2014). This

10 The second-century CE library at Apollonia(Albania) © 2016
Carole Raddato

collection kicks off with two essays on historiography and historical context. Subsequent essays include the foundation and source of character and behaviour in Roman society (with essays on family, education, and law), communication (such as literature, inscription, and symbolism on coins), communal contexts (public speaking, representation, and entertainment), modes of interpersonal relations (friendship, hospitality, meals), non-familial societies in the Roman world (*collegia*, the army, cults and sects), and marginalised groups (slaves, women and children, criminals, disabled people). A complementary collection is T. Parkin and A. Pomeroy's *Roman Social History: A Sourcebook* (London: Routledge, 2007), which ranges from the late Republic to the end of the *Pax Romana*; it focuses on social and cultural history, especially the social classes and Roman social relations. Included are actuary tables (life expectancy), social hierarchy tables, and useful information about weights and measures.

Any one of the chapters in Peachin's collection will provide you with additional bibliography on Roman social and interpersonal relations. Other works to consider on the Roman family and household relations include a pair from Suzanne Dixon, *The Roman Mother* (London: Croom Helm, 1988) and *The Roman Family* (Baltimore: Johns Hopkins Press, 1992), and Keith Bradley, *Discovering the Roman Family: Studies in Roman Social History* (Oxford: Oxford University Press, 1991). Beryl Rawson, another scholar of family and social relations, edited *A Companion to Families in the Greek and Roman World* (Oxford: Blackwell, 2010). A different perspective on motherhood, that is, the idealisation of motherhood found in poetry and drama, comes from Mairéad McAuley, *Reproducing Rome: Motherhood in Virgil, Ovid, Seneca, and Statius* (Oxford: Oxford University Press, 2015). The study of youth and education in the Classical and Roman world is also formative for understanding the development of and attitudes towards character and value systems. Other starting places include Martin Bloomer, *A Companion to Ancient Education* (Oxford: Blackwell, 2015) and Judith Evans Grubbs and Tim G. Parkin, *The Oxford Handbook of Childhood and Education in the Classical World* (Oxford: Oxford University Press, 2014). A complementary sourcebook on education is M. Joyal, *Greek and Roman Education: A Sourcebook* (London: Routledge, 2009). On Roman childhood and youth, there is Christian Laes, *Children in the Empire: Outsiders Within* (Cambridge: Cambridge University Press, 2011), Beryl Rawson, *Children and Childhood in Roman Italy* (Oxford: Oxford University Press, 2005), and Lauren E. Caldwell, *Roman Girlhood and the Fashioning of Femininity* (Cambridge: Cambridge University Press, 2015). Emotion – love and affection – can be difficult to trace from contemporary sources; Ruth Rothaus Caston, ed. *Hope, Joy, and Affection in the Classical World* (Oxford: Oxford University Press, 2016) provides recent insights on what the sources might tell us.

Studies of family and collectives in Roman society provide guidance on those characteristics that were admired and how particular aspects of social conduct were codified. The majority of the surviving voices that we have from the past are those of aristocratic men, and much of the written evidence on correct social behaviour comes down in the form of rhetoric, moral writings, letters, histories – all with a purpose of exonerating the lives of the great (usually, but not always) men and reinforcing these social codes: respect one's elders, maintain allegiance to authority, show dignity and nobility in the face of adversity, remain loyal to the group. These notions drive letters, speeches, biographies, and history. You'll find them throughout Plutarch's *Moralia* and his *Parallel Lives*, Suetonius's and Cornelius Nepos's biographies, Sallust's and Tacitus's histories, Pliny's letters, Cicero's letters and speeches, Julius Caesar's commentaries. Women and children are presented as reflections of or foils to these great men; if the writings aren't praising the great men (and some women) for their actions, then they become examples of the dire effects of the inversion of social norms.

A critical reading of contemporary sources is essential for understanding how and why these authors present their subjects as either exempla or figures of shame. If you want sensational anecdotes, you can take the tales of excess as found in the biographies of Suetonius or the *Historia Augusta* literally – that's often the case with authors of popular media, and it is why some of the crazier stories about Caligula or Nero have persisted over the centuries. For a more critical reading, consider the rhetoric and intended audience for these sources. Recent scholarship on antiquity has taken a multidisciplinary approach to interpreting the depiction of a number of famous figures. Over the past forty or so years, scholars have re-examined the contemporary sources' take on, for example, the audience for public images, the role and influence of imperial women, or notions of gender and sexuality in the Classical world. Scholars in these just these three areas continue to renegotiate previous understanding of contemporary literary sources, and many of them practise multidisciplinary methodology, combining, for example, historiography with archaeological studies, art history, sociology, or linguistic study. Examples of scholarship that considers the language of rhetoric and the depiction of women includes Judith Ginsburg, *Representing Agrippina: Constructions of Female Power in the Early Roman Empire* (Oxford: Oxford University Press, 2006), and F. Santoro L'Hoir, *The Rhetoric of Gender Terms 'Man', 'Woman', and the Portrayal of Character in Latin Prose* (Leiden: Brill, 1992). Studies which complement study of literature with public images include Josiah Osgood, *Claudius Caesar: Image and Power* (Cambridge: Cambridge University

Press, 2010), and Susan Wood, *Imperial Women: A Study in Public Images 40 B.C.–A.D. 68* (Leiden: Brill, 2000). Another growing area of study considers gender roles, sexuality, and social expectations in Classical Rome; start with Marilyn Skinner, *Sexuality in Greek and Roman Culture* (Oxford: Blackwell, 2005), and complement it with a sourcebook edited by Laura K. McClure, *Sexuality and Gender in the Classical World: Readings and Sources* (Oxford: Blackwell, 2002); a recent collection that looks at the role of homosexuality in Roman culture and the long-reaching effects and characterisation into modern culture is Jennifer Ingleheart, ed., *Ancient Rome and the Construction of Modern Homosexual Identities* (Oxford: Oxford University Press, 2015). Audience expectations in the face of literature and drama can be indicative of social expectations; T.P. Wiseman *The Roman Audience: Classical Literature as Social History* (Oxford: Oxford University Press, 2015), unpacks the significance of social behaviour in Roman literature and entertainment. Harriet I. Flower, *The Art of Forgetting: Disgrace and Oblivion in Roman Political Culture* (Chapel Hill: University of North Carolina Press, 2011), and Rhiannon Ash et al., eds, *Fame and Infamy: Essays on Characterization in Greek and Roman Biography and Historiography* (Oxford: Oxford University Press, 2015), have studied how and why people were commemorated – or not – in the Roman world.

The concept of 'Roman people' also considers social standing, hierarchy, and snobbery. The Romans started to think about their own identity only when they came up against outsiders and when they began to write their own histories from the third century BCE. The Romans were not only snobby within the indigenous community (aristocrats look down on equestrians look down on freedmen look down the urban mob ...) but against outsiders – provincial upstarts and the 'barbarians' who included the Carthaginians, Egyptians, Germans, Goths, and Greeks. Contemporary sources here include Livy's history of the Punic wars, Plutarch's lives of Fabius, Cato, and Antony, any of the propaganda against Cleopatra (Cicero's *Philippics*, for example, Horace, Appian's account of the civil wars, or Plutarch's life of Antony), Caesar's commentary on Gaul, or Ovid's lament from exile in his *Tristia* or *Ex Ponto*.

Comedy inverts social norms and the constraints of conservative behaviour by showing the worst excesses of Roman society through the behaviour of foreigners. Plautus's characters were Greek, Persian, or Punic; they commit horrible faux pas and verbal gaffes, but were, in fact, frequently mocking strait-laced Roman conventions. Tacitus's *Germania* or *Agricola* might seem no-brainers when it comes to discussion of Germanic and Celtic barbarians. Again, of course, remember he's a rhetorician and critic of his own class; many of his diatribes against the barbarians are criticisms of the aristocratic classes. In addition to the essays in Peachin's *Handbook of Roman Social Relations*, look at R. MacMullen, *Roman Social Relations, 50 B.C.–A.D. 284* (New Haven: Yale University Press, 1981), an older, but still good introduction to Roman social relations and to social snobbery, and Judith Perkins, *Roman Imperial Identities in the Early Christian Era* (London: Routledge, 2010), especially pp. 17–44 on 'Cosmopolitan Identities', 62–89 on 'Constructing a Patriarchal Elite', and 127–143 on 'Trimalchio: Transformation and Possibilities'. Further complementary studies on how the Romans grappled with the double-edged sword of local assimilation yet locating a distinct 'Roman character' are from Louise Revell: *Roman Imperialism and Local Identities* (Cambridge: Cambridge University Press, 2010) and *Ways of Being Roman: Discourses of Identity in the Roman West* (Barnsley: Oxbow Books, 2015). Similarly, David J. Mattingly examines the Roman presence and interaction with local cultures in *Imperialism, Power, and Identity: Experiencing the Roman Empire* (Princeton: Princeton University Press, 2013). On the Romans and barbarians, there are E. Adler, *Valorizing the Barbarians* (Austin: University of Texas Press, 2001), and Thomas S. Burn's survey, *Rome and the Barbarians, 100 B.C.–A.D. 400* (Baltimore: Johns Hopkins University Press, 2009). Finally, there are specialised studies of Roman interaction, socialisation, and assimilation in the provinces. Greg Woolf's *Becoming Roman: The Origins of Provincial Civilization in Gaul* (Cambridge: Cambridge University Press, 2000) is one example; other recommended recent works include Laurens Ernst Tacoma, *Moving Romans: Migration to Rome in the Principate* (Oxford: Oxford University Press, 2016), John Weisweiler, ed., *Cosmopolitanism and Empire: Universal Rulers, Local Elites, and Cultural Integration in the Ancient Near East and Mediterranean* (Oxford: Oxford University Press, 2016), and C. Whittaker, *Rome and Its Frontiers* (London: Routledge, 2008). Two case studies in the provinces include Leonard A. Churchin, 'Social Relations in Central Spain: Patrons, Freedmen and Slaves in the Life of a Roman Provincial Hinterland' (*Ancient Society* 18 (1987): 75–89), and Peter M. Brennen, 'The Last of the Romans: Roman Identity and the Roman Army in the Late Roman Near East' (*Mediterranean Archaeology* 11 (1998): 191–203).

CHAPTER 2: THE BASIC NECESSITIES

There are many studies on food and the Romans' relationship with repasts, including social customs, importation of food, and cultural imagery associated with dining – and of course recipes. Starting places include John Wilkins and Robin Nadeau, ed., *A Companion to Food in the Ancient World* (Oxford: Blackwell, 2015), Joan P. Alcock's *Food in the Ancient World* (Westport: CT, Greenwood Press, 2000) and *Food in Roman Britain* (Stroud: Tempus, 2001), and Patrick Faas, *Around the Roman Table: Food and Feasting in Ancient Rome* (Chicago: Chicago University Press, 2009). K.M.D. Dunbabin's *The Roman Banquet: Images of Conviviality* (Cambridge: Cambridge University Press, 2003) covers dining practice in the Greek as well as the Roman world; she draws her information from both pictorial and literary sources. Pedar W. Foss, 'Kitchens and Dining Rooms at Pompeii: The Spatial and Social Relationship of Cooking to Eating in the Roman Household', a 1994 PhD thesis currently (July 2018) available as a Web document, is a study on who cooked and who served in the Classical world based on age, gender, rank, and status. Foss includes resources on scholarship on eating and drinking, especially the use of mealtimes as opportunities for conviviality, the association between meals and family relationships and household duties, and the function of food and eating in the early Roman Empire. Other studies include Andrew Dalby's works, *Food in the Ancient World from A to Z* (London: Routledge, 2013) and *Empire of Pleasures:*

Luxury and Indulgence in the Roman World (London: Routledge, 2000), Matthew Roller, *Dining Posture in Ancient Rome: Bodies, Values, and Status* (Princeton: Princeton University Press, 2006), and Dennis Smith and Hal Taussig, *Meals in the Early Christian World: Social Formation, Experimentation, and Conflict at the Table* (New York: Palgrave, 2012).

Contemporary sources that mention food and dining frequently focus on the unusual, remarkable, or excessive in culinary matters. Historians, biographers, and satirists often criticised the extravagant and praised the frugal as they discussed mealtimes, food, and the entertainment provided by the host. A small selection of sources for descriptions of the wealthy at table include Juvenal's fourth *Satire* on banquets, Horace's *Satire* 2.4 in which Catius waxes lyrical about fine foods and wines and *Satire* 2.8 on a dinner party gone wrong. Suetonius describes the excesses of the emperors (Gaius Caligula and Nero are usual go-tos here, but see also the shenanigans at Tiberius's dinner parties in Capri, or tales of Vitellius's gluttony); the *Historia Augusta* details the excesses of Elagabulus's banquets; the later author Sidonius Apollonarius's letters are useful for descriptions of the parties and hospitality he enjoyed. As always, rhetoricians praise simplicity; they describe excess in detail because it's meant to shock and to be an aberration whether practised by the decadent elite or by social-climbing freedmen aping their betters. The stars of Petronius's *Satyricon* include the vulgar freedman Trimalchio and his tacky wife Fortunata, who are prime examples of this sort of satire. For more sources of contemporary inspiration, see J.F. Donahue's *Food and Drink in Antiquity: A Sourcebook* (London: Bloomsbury, 2014). Finally, if the recipes in Chapter 2 intrigued you, Apicius's cookbook (*De Re Coquinaria*), beloved by high-school Latin teachers everywhere, remains readily available in various translations and editions. Some fans of the gourmand prefer Elisabeth Rosenbaum and Barbara Flower's 1958 translation, reprinted in 2012 (Mansfield Centre, CT: Martino Fine Books). Apicius is also included amongst the volumes in the Loeb series, with Latin and English texts facing. For a scholarly commentary, Christopher Grocock (a Classical scholar) and Sally Grainger (a professional cook) joined forces to publish an annotated edition of the work with Latin and

English on the facing pages, *Apicius: A Critical Edition* (Totnes: Prospect, 2006). One bonus with this edition is their inclusion of Vinidarius's contemporary document on tips for the Roman kitchen.

Clothing is mentioned in passing in contemporary sources, and, as with food and drink, is used to remark on social status and character, ranging from indications of the wearer's modesty through to his or her vulgar extravagance. One of the few sources sympathetic towards women's attire, cosmetics, and beauty regimen is Ovid and his *Medicamina Faciei Femineae*. In these didactic elegies, Ovid happily details his preferences in women's make-up and hairstyles, discusses current fashions, and offers advice and caveats. It's written with humorous flair and includes recipes and information on cosmetic ingredients. It's in the Loeb series, but Marguerite Johnson has also recently translated and annotated the text (*Ovid on Cosmetics: Medicamina Faciei Femineae and Related Texts*, London: Bloomsbury, 2016). She includes a contextual introduction as well as a detailed annotation and explication of some of the technical words and phrases. Pliny's *Natural History* also contains fairly objective descriptions of minerals and plants used for medicinal and cosmetic purposes. Juvenal mocks the lady's toilette (*Satire* 6), and Ovid details the excesses of a woman (and man) primping themselves in *Ars Amatoria*, Book 3.

For modern interpretation of clothing and accessories, you're spoiled for choice as sources range from academic studies to practical handbooks and advice written by and for re-enactors. Whilst not necessarily peer-reviewed or academic works, books on clothing and costuming by published by Osprey and Oxbow are useful for illustrations and ideas from dressing your Romans. There are also a number of websites for reference images, ranging from wikicommons to McManus's *VRoma* site (www.vroma.org/~bmcmanus/clothing2.html) and, for detailed types of male and female clothing, Scott Robinson's homepage at Central Washington University, www.cwu.edu/~robinsos/ppages/resources/Costume_History/roman.htm (he also has links back to *VRoma*). Don't overlook re-enactor sites, as many of these enthusiasts take great pains with their clothing and footwear, and compete against one another at festivals and shows. The Legio XX, a group of dedicated re-enactors established in 1991 and based in Washington, DC, maintain a site with information about (mainly) military clothing and accessories, but they do include links to civilian clothing and clothing references (www.larp. com/legioxx/). Likewise are the Ermine Street Guard, established in the UK in 1972; they are scrupulous in the detail of their military garb, accessories, and civilian accoutrements (www.erminestreetguard.co.uk/). The Guard perform re-enactments throughout Britain and Europe, give talks and consultations at schools and universities, and are sometimes recruited for film and television performances.

Scholarly studies and essay collections on clothing and attire include, for example, A. Croom's *Roman Clothing and Fashion* (Stroud: Amberley, 2010), which surveys briefly clothing from the first to the sixth century, both its manufacture and use in status; this work is used by re-enactors and theatre professionals. K. Olson's longer academic study, *Dress and the Roman Woman: Self-Presentation and Society* (London: Routledge, 2008), examines the dichotomy of women's dress, cosmetics, and accessories. She considers how male moralists and writers used attire and accoutrements as examples of excess, how women took seriously the language of adornment, and how their appearance signposted their status. Olson similarly looks at how clothing and appearance signify masculinity in her *Masculinity and Dress in Roman Antiquity* (London: Routledge, 2017). This significant study complements not only the many sources available on Roman military dress but also current scholarship that takes civilian men's fashion and adornment as case studies on Roman notions of masculinity and gender roles. Eve D'Ambra provides an introduction to cosmetics and jewellery (especially as part of the regimen of the *cultus*) in her *Roman Women* (Cambridge: Cambridge University Press, 2007, pp. 111–128), as does Susan Stewart's *Cosmetics and Perfumes in the Roman World* (Stroud: Tempus, 2007). Stewart has also written a summative overview of cosmetics, 'How Vain Were the Romans?', which can be found at /www.historytoday.com/susan-stewart/how-vain-were-romans. Both D'Ambra and Stewart provide the basics in terms of popular looks and ideas for accoutrements needed for the dressing table and supply the reader with additional primary and secondary sources for further reference. Other academic authors include Judith Lynn Sebesta, *The World of Roman Costume* (Madison: University of Wisconsin Press, 2006), Carole Gillis and Marie-Louise Nosch, *Ancient Textiles: Production, Crafts and Society*, reprinted edition (Oxford: Oxbow, 2014), and Mary Harlow and Marie-Louise Nosch, *Greek and Roman Textiles and Dress* (Oxford: Oxbow, 2015).

For visual sources of clothing and accessories, there are many images and material remains for reference – statues, paintings, frescos, mosaics, casket covers – all readily accessible via Google image search, wikicommons, Pinterest, McManus's *VRoma*, and other social media sites. Such visuals are most indicative of the styles of the aristocratic classes and the tombs and portraits of freed people proud of their successful rise in status. Tomb portraits reflect the various clothing styles, accessories, and hairstyles of the merchant and lower classes in all of their (funeral) finery. Many examples survive from Fayum (Egypt) and Pompeii. Useful sites for Fayum images include museum and art gallery websites, especially larger collections as housed in the Ashmolean Museum in Oxford, the British Museum in London, and the Metropolitan Museum of Art, New York. Consider following media-sharing sites, as well, such as Pinterest, Instagram, Flickr, Twitter, and Facebook, which have been used effectively by interest groups to collect images on Classical themes and topics. The main caveat here is that sometimes images lack any information about provenance, and you may recognise errors in the (mis)identification of particular images.

CHAPTER 3: LOCATION, LOCATION, LOCATION

Sources on housing and homes frequently not only inform about buildings, furnishing, and décor but also consider how homes and locations reflect Roman attitudes towards city and country life. Again most of the contemporary literary sources are written from the aristocratic male point of view, and they lay emphasis on moral character or social status associated with living in the country or in the city. You'll also find contemplation of the joys of gentleman farming, as discussed in Chapter 3. Cato the Elder's, Columella's, and Varro's texts on estate management are partly guides to the ideal estate and partly intellectual exercises that reflect the Roman aristocratic love of order. Check out, for example, Grant A. Nelsestuen, *Varro the Agronomist: Political Philosophy, Satire, and Agriculture in the late Republic* (Columbus: Ohio State University, 2015). Similarly, the love of the land and the tranquillity it brings as a gentleman's pursuit can be found in Vergil's gentle bucolic *Georgics*. More mundane are Pliny the Younger's experiences as a landlord and land buyer, scattered throughout his *Letters*; even more practical still are two surviving inscriptions that cover real-life estate management. These are the *Veleai Romana* and the *Ligures Baebiani*, discussed in Chapter 3 in connection to the dichotomy between idealised country living and its actuality.

For scholarship on urban planning, enter 'Roman cities' in the Worldcat, JSTOR, or even Amazon. You'll spoiled for choice if you want to focus on a specific city (a quick click just on Amazon produced academic and general books on London, Wroxeter, and St Albans right on the front page) or city life in general. Suggested reading includes Ray Laurence, Simon Esmonde Cleary, and Gareth Sears's *The City in the Roman West* (Cambridge: Cambridge University Press, 2011); this study provides a general survey to introduce you to urban character, civic connections between the centre and provinces, and the social, economic, and political importance of cities in the West. P. Goodman's *The Roman City and Its Periphery* (London: Routledge, 2012) examines the suburbs and area surrounding a Roman city. On the topography of Rome itself, see Andrea Carandini, *The Atlas of Ancient Rome: Biography and Portraits of the City* (Princeton: Princeton University Press, 2017). An older, but extensive survey of the City that gives you the gist of the buildings and streets is *A Topographical Dictionary of Ancient Rome* (S.B. Platner, revised by T. Ashby, 1929) found at penelope.uchicago.edu/Thayer/E/Gazetteer/Places/Europe/Italy/Lazio/Roma/Rome/_Texts/PLATOP*/home.html. This source describes monuments, houses, and baths found in fourth-century CE Rome, but this is still useful for our period. Another older overview of traffic issues in the Roman city is Kenneth D. Matthews, Jr, 'The Embattled Driver in Ancient Rome' (*Expedition Magazine* 2.3 (May 1960): n. pag., www.penn.museum/sites/expedition/?p=135). There are many works on cities in the provinces, and much is on offer simply with keywords including 'city', 'town', 'construction', and so forth plus the province in question. Far too many are available to list here comprehensively.

Moving inside the house and considering domestic space, an essential contemporary source for housing construction and room design is Vitruvius, *On Architecture*. Book 3 covers the placement and sizes of the rooms of the average house, Book 6 is especially useful for designing private houses, and Book 7 covers wall paintings and other household décor. *VRoma* provides a description of the typical plans for a basic Roman house: www.vroma.org/~bmcmanus/house.html. Check out, too, *The Guardian*'s article on the restoration of Augustus's palace (www.theguardian.com/world/gallery/2007/dec/11/world.archaeology); it is a general read rather than an academic one, but it includes useful photographs of the interior of the palace rooms. A modern work to help you construct your city is Tony Rook, *Roman Building Techniques* (Stroud: Amberley Publishing, 2013), written by an archaeologist and engineer and full of useful illustrations. Studies on other opulent digs include a number of Romano-British villas, such as Steven Willis and Peter Carne's collection on the houses at Barwick, *A Roman Villa at the Edge of Empire: The Excavations at Ingleby Barwick* (Durham: Council for British Archaeology, 2013), B. Cunliffe on the *Roman Villa at Brading, Isle of Wight* (Oxford: Oxford University School of Archaeology, 2013), or M. Russell and D. Rudling on *Bignor Roman Villa* (Stroud: The History Press, 2015). For furniture and other furnishings, check out A.T. Croom, *Roman Furniture* (Stroud: The History Press 2007) and *Running the Roman Home* (Stroud: The History Press, 2011). She covers how to supply the house with basic goods, maintaining the house, and disposing of waste.

For public, shared civic structures and decoration, see M.L. Laird, *Civic Monuments and the Augustales in Roman Italy* (Cambridge:

Cambridge University Press, 2015). Part three of this work discusses the use of monuments and statues to create public personae and to advertise social status in a Roman town and includes many inscriptions as examples. Studies on art and architecture on shape and design include M. Wheeler, *Roman Art and Architecture* (London: Thames and Hudson, 1964). B. Ward-Perkins, *Roman Imperial Architecture* (New Haven: Yale University Press, 1992) discusses changes in the City of Rome due to the invention and ubiquitous use of concrete; he also presents a comparison of the architecture of Rome and how Roman and local styles merged into some unique provincial construction. M. Wilson-Jones, *Principles of Roman Architecture* (New Haven: Yale University Press, 2003), looks at how Roman architects approached deign and considers how they combined design and practicality – like Ward Perkins, Wilson-Jones draws on an archaeological background. Entire studies have been dedicated to aqueducts, baths, and latrines; on baths and bathing, see F. Yegul, *Bathing in the Roman World* (Cambridge: Cambridge University Press, 2009), and G.G. Fagan, *Bathing in Public in the Roman World* (Ann Arbor: University of Michigan Press, 2002). Both are useful on not only the designs of the public baths but also the social culture surrounding them. Contemporary discussion on water supply into the city is found in Vitruvius and also Frontinus's survey *De Aquis* ('On the Water Supply in Rome') where he talks about the history and construction of aqueducts as well as the roads going in and out of the city. A transcription of the older Loeb text can be found at http://penelope.uchicago.edu/Thayer/E/ Roman/Texts/Frontinus/De_Aquis/home.html; Deane R. Blackman has an edited collection of essays on Frontinus, *Frontinus's Legacy: Essays on Frontinus' De aquis Urbis Romae* (Ann Arbor: University of Michigan Press, 2001).

On the relationship between living space and status and identity, see John R. Clarke, *The Houses of Roman Italy, 100 B.C.–A.D. 250: Ritual, Space, and Decoration* (Berkeley: University of California Press, 1992), Alexander G. McKay, *Houses, Villas, and Palaces in the Roman World* (Baltimore: Johns Hopkins University Press, 1998), and Andrew Wallace-Hadrill, *Houses and Society in Pompeii and Herculaneum*

(Princeton: Princeton University Press, 1996). H. Parkins, *Roman Urbanism: Beyond the Consumer City* (London: Routledge, 2011), is a collection of essays ranging from the connection between the ideology of city living and elite status, mobility and social change in Italian towns, and Roman households from an archaeological perspective. S.T. Roselaar, ed., *Processes of Integration and Identity Formation in the Roman Republic* (Leiden: Brill, 2012) is a collection of essays on not only Roman identification (what makes us Roman, but these other people outsiders) but also discussion of how trade and travel networks worked, integration between town and city, and Romanisation and locals in the provinces (especially as a result of military garrisons in the West). These collections would complement reading on integration and identity between the Romans and 'others' during the Republic through various means, including such social interaction as trade, religion practice, and the shaping of settlements. Another collection of essays on the relationship between country and city in both Classical Greece and Rome is edited by R.M. Rosen and I. Sluiter, *City, Countryside, and the Spatial Organization of Value in Classical Antiquity* (Leiden: Brill, 2006). These essays address living space by looking at archaeology and material remains on the one hand, and literary and philosophical or rhetorical works by contemporaries on the other. Here is discussion on what the ancient rhetoricians would have argued were strict opposites (that is country versus city living and character), but in fact the sources reveal that the Romans understood the subtle if not complex distinction between the character and inhabitants of both districts.

On the gendered use of space in the Roman house, two scholars are Katherine Milnor, *Gender, Domesticity, and the Age of Augustus: Inventing Private Life* (Oxford: Oxford University Press, 2005), and Penelope Allison's work, *The Archaeology of Household Activities: Dwelling in the Past* (London: Routledge, 1999) and *Pompeian Household: An Analysis of the Material Culture* (Berkeley: University of California, 2004). Allison focuses on the connection between the space of the household and gendered roles and behaviour within the domestic setting. Her other work includes Vol. 15, 'Building Communities: House, Settlement and Society in the Aegean and Beyond', *The British School at Athens Studies* (2007): 343–350, and 'Using the Material and Written Sources: Turn of the Millennium Approaches to Roman Domestic Space', *American Journal of Archaeology*, 105.2 (April 2001): 181–208.

Finally, collections of contemporary sources on town and country, buildings and houses include J.F. Gardener, *The Roman Household: A Sourcebook* (London: Routledge, 1991), A.E. Cooley and M.G.L. Cooley, *Pompeii: A Sourcebook* (London: Routledge, 2004), and F. Dolansky and S. Raucii, *Rome: A Sourcebook on the Ancient City* (London: Bloomsbury, 2018). On engineering, there is John Peter Oleson, *The Oxford Handbook of Engineering and Technology in the Classical World* (Oxford: Oxford University Press, 2009), and John W. Humphrey, John P. Oleson, and Andrew N. Sherwood's *Greek and Roman Technology: A Sourcebook* (London: Routledge, 1997).

CHAPTER 4: THE SENATE AND THE PEOPLE OF ROME

When it comes to contemporary sources on law, administration, authority figures, and the army, the Romans *loved* writing about their political and military leaders. They hit their stride in the first centuries BCE and CE especially as many contemplated why the Republic fell, how Augustus restored it, and why and how subsequent leaders did or didn't fulfil Augustus's legacy.

For contemporary sources on law there is what survives of the original fourth-century BCE Roman law code, the *Twelve Tables*; at the other end of the scale is Justinian's sixth-century CE *Codex*, an enormous compendium of Roman law in five parts, assembled by a team of jurists to untangle a thousand years of contradictory, superseded, and obscure laws. The centuries in between include jurists who wrote about and commented on the law and legal procedure. Surviving texts by lawyers and legal experts include those by Cicero (many of his famous court cases are readily available in translation) and Sallust (who, like Cicero, wrote about Cataline's court case). Pliny the Younger's letters provide reflection from a down-to-earth lawyer who balances hearing cases in Bithynia with being a loving husband, a patron to his clients, a landlord, and a governor who kept in close touch with the emperor on administrative matters. On how to declaim, see Quintilian, whose handbooks on education are lessons in speech and deportment and include sample and practice court cases for the young man studying for public life. Many imperial legal writers were concerned about procedure and application of the law, such as Gaius (*Institutes*), Ulpian (*Regulae*) (a prolific jurist who wrote commentaries on civil law, commentary on the *Praetor's Edicts*, and collections of legal opinion, legal rules, and the functions of the magistrates), Paulus (*Sententiae*), and pseudo-Ulpian (*Regulae*). Collections of primary sources pertaining to laws and court cases include Judith Evans Grubbs, ed., *Women and the Law in the Roman Empire: A Sourcebook* (London: Routledge, 2002), or Barbara Levick, *The Government of the Roman Empire*, second edition (London: Routledge, 2000). N. Lewis and M. Reinhold *Roman Civilization: Selected Readings, Volume II: The Empire*, third edition (New York: Columbia University Press, 1990), pp. 498–513, provide sources that cover the definitions of civil and criminal law, and the rules of evidence from the earliest period of Rome through to Justinian's codification. For a look at the Roman presence in the provinces in terms of law and administration, see, for example, the Acts of the Apostles, Philo's *Embassy to Gaius*, or, for a satirical look at provincial trials and administration, Apuleius's *Metamorphoses* and his *Apologia* – the latter featuring the author's recollection of his defence at a trial in which he is accused of witchcraft and murder, and how he wins the initially hostile locals over to his side at the expense of the prosecution's dignity. A good companion for forays into the labyrinthine world of Roman law is Paul Plessis, ed., *The Oxford Handbook of Roman Law and Society* (Oxford: Oxford University Press, 2016).

For contemporary sources on administration and authority, there is often overlap with military issues. Sources include, for example, Livy's *History* which covers the foundation of the city of Rome and development of the magisterial offices and the so-called Conflict of the Orders (the civil struggle for power between the patricians and the plebeians which lasted from the fifth to the third century BCE), the Punic wars, and the wars in the Greek East. Polybius's *History*, Book 6, details the formation of the army (as well as the organisation of the Roman government), but he, too, covers the Punic Wars and Macedonian Wars. On the period of Marius, the New Roman Army, and the Jugurthine War, see Plutarch's lives of Marius and of Sulla, and Sallust's account of the Jugurthine War. For the civil wars and the armies of the Triumvirs, selected sources include Plutarch's lives of Pompey, Crassus, Sertorius, and Julius Caesar, Suetonius's life of Caesar and of Augustus, Appian's *Civil Wars*, Lucan on the civil wars, and Caesar's commentaries on the wars in Gaul and on the civil wars. In the imperial period through to the end of the second century, there's Suetonius on the lives of the Caesars through to Domitian, Tacitus's *Annals* on the reigns of Tiberius through to Nero (the books on Gaius Caligula and the beginning of Claudius's reign have not been recovered yet) and his *Histories* on the civil war of 69, and Josephus's *Jewish Wars*. For the lives of the Antonine and Severan emperors the *Historia Augusta*, Cassius Dio, and Herodian's epitomes are essential literary sources. Ammianus Marcellinus is after our period, but you might find his descriptions of warfare and administrative actitivies in the fourth century CE of use. The Vindolanda Tablets provide a glimpse into the daily running of a frontier military fort on Hadrian's Wall in the late first and early second centuries CE; see Bowman, 1998; the Tablets themselves are transcribed and translated online.

On warfare, strategy, and engineering the army itself, see Frontinus (second century CE) on strategies and tactics for the military commander, Vitruvius's *De Architectura* (Book 10 on siege machines), and Vegetius (late fourth century) and his *De Re Militari* on military organisation. Greek works that you might find of use include Aeneas Tacitus (around the fourth century BCE) on defending against a siege and the philosopher Onasander's first-century CE handbook for generals, *Strategikos* (which is more about the ideal personality of a commander). For other, shorter excerpts and collections which include contemporary sources on the military, see the general collections of primary sources noted in the first section of this chapter. Specialised collections on military matters include J.B. Campbell, *The Roman Army, 31 B.C.–A.D. 337: A Sourcebook* (London: Routledge, 1994), C.B. Champion, *Roman Imperialism: Readings and Sources* (Oxford: Oxford University Press, 2003), M.M. Sage, *The Republic Roman Army: A Sourcebook* (London: Routledge, 2008) and (for maps of hotspots) Christopher Scarre, *The Penguin Historical Atlas of Ancient Rome* (London: Penguin Books, 1995). Finally, as you read these accounts beware as always that the purpose of history and biography for the Romans was to contemplate and reward the deeds of great men, whilst pointing out the weaknesses of poor leaders. There is an agenda of moral rhetoric involved as you peruse Plutarch's *Lives* and the sources above as they speak about the individuals who came to power from the era of the Gracchi (mid-second century BCE) to the reigns of the Antonine emperors (that is, from Antonius Pius through to Septimius Severus).

Starting places for topics such as the Roman constitution and political authority include Harriet I. Flower, *The Cambridge Companion to the Roman Republic* (Cambridge: University of Cambridge, 2014), and A. Barchiesi, *The Oxford Handbook of Roman Studies* (Oxford: Oxford University Press, 2010). Other overviews of Roman administration include D. Braund, *The Administration of the Roman Empire: 241 B.C.– A.D. 193* (Exeter: University of Exeter, 1988), and L.A. Burckhardt, 'The Political Elite of the Roman Republic: Comments on Recent Discussion of the Concepts "Nobilitas and Homo Novus"', *Historia: Zeitschrift für Alte Geschichte*, 39.1 (1990): 77–99). A recent study that covers that period of the late Republic to the imperial age is Benjamin Straumann, *Crisis and Constitutionalism: Roman Political Thought from the Fall of the Republic to the Age of Revolution* (Oxford: Oxford University Press, 2016). On how the Romans reflected on the role of magistrates and the impact of civil war on Roman authority, there's A.H. Lushkov, *Magistracy and the Historiography of the Roman Republic: Politics in Prose* (Cambridge: Cambridge University Press, 2015). On the political campaign trail, there is T.R.S. Broughton, 'Candidates Defeated in Roman Elections: Some Ancient Roman "Also-Rans"', *Transactions of the American Philosophical Society*, 81.4 (1991): i–vi, 1–64; A. Lintott,

'Electoral Bribery in the Roman Republic', *The Journal of Roman Studies*, 80 (1990): 1–16, or Jeffery Beneker, *The Passionate Statesman: Erōs and Politics in Plutarch's Lives* (Oxford: Oxford University Press, 2012). For law, order, and crime, see David Johnson, ed., *The Cambridge Companion to Roman Law* (Cambridge: University of Cambridge Press, 2015), and Andrew M. Riggsby, *Roman Law and the Legal World of the Romans* (Cambridge: Cambridge University Press, 2010); for discussion and resources of Roman legal presence in the provinces, see Benjamin Kelly, *Petitions, Litigation, and Social Control in Roman Egypt* (Oxford: Oxford University Press, 2011). On imperial influence in jurisprudence, see Kaius Tuori, *The Emperor of Law: The Emergence of Roman Imperial Adjudication* (Oxford: Oxford University Press, 2016). For the intersection of marginalised people and the law in Roman society, see Jane F. Gardner, *Women in Roman Law and Society* (London: Routledge, 1987), and K.R. Bradley, *Slaves and Masters in the Roman Empire: A Study in Social Control* (Oxford: Oxford University Press, 1987). On the *lack* of law and order, and an overview of the brutality and violence that coloured the Roman world, see Garrett G. Fagan, *The Topography of Violence in the Greco-Roman World* (Ann Arbor: University of Michigan Press, 2016).

On patronage and public munificence, see Kathryn Lomas and Timothy Cornell, *'Bread and Circuses': Euergetism and Municipal Patronage in Roman Italy* (London: Routledge, 2013), which explores how patronage and public benevolence gained politicians votes during the time of the Republic, and then reinforced authority, status, and goodwill during the Principate. Other studies on patronage include E. Hemelrijk, *Hidden Lives, Public Personae: Women and Civic Life in the Roman West* (Oxford: Oxford University Press, 2015); E. Deniaux, 'Patronage', in Nathan Stewart Rosenstein and Robert Morstein-Marx, eds, *A Companion to the Roman Republic* (Oxford: Blackwell, 2010), pp. 401–420; S. Dixon, 'A Family Business: Women's Role in Patronage and Politics at Rome 80–44 B.C.', *Classica et Mediaevalia* 34 (1983): 91–112, and A. Wallace Hadrill, ed., *Patronage in Ancient Society* (London: Routledge, 1989).

On the army, there's P. Erdkamp, *A Companion to the Roman Army* (Oxford: Blackwell, 2007) and L.J.F. Keppie *The Making of the Roman Army: From Republic to Empire* (Norman: University of Oklahoma Press, 1987), L. Tritle *The Oxford Handbook of Warfare in the Classical World* (Oxford: Oxford University Press, 2013); J.B. Campbell, *War and Society in Imperial Rome, 31 B.C.–A.D. 284* (London: Routledge, 2002); David J. Breeze, *The Roman Army* (London: Bloomsbury, 2016); and Rikke D. Giles, *Roman Soldiers and the Roman Army: A Study of Military Life from Archaeological Remains* (Oxford: Oxford University Press, 2012). Whilst the legalisation of Christianity is after our period, you might look at John F. Shean, *Soldiering for God: Christianity and the Roman Army* (Leiden: Brill, 2010). On the composition of the legions, their 'lifespan', and where they were stationed, see S. Dando-Collins's *Legions of Rome: The Definitive History of Every Imperial Legion* (New York: Thomas Dunne, 2010). For life in the camps and on the frontier (and the interaction between the Romans and the barbarians), see Thomas S. Burns's survey, *Rome and the Barbarians, 100 B.C.–A.D. 400* (Baltimore: Johns Hopkins University Press, 2009). E. Adler, *Valorizing the Barbarians* (Austin: University of Texas Press, 2001) considers the use of rhetoric used to distinguish – or to criticise – Roman behaviour, or see any of the works on Vindolanda and the forts on Hadrian's Wall by the Birley dynasty of archaeologists and scholars. Check out, too, C. Whittaker, *Rome and Its Frontiers* (London: Routledge, 2008) and 'Supplying the Army: Evidence from Vindolanda', in P. Erdkamp, ed., *The Roman Army and the Economy* (Amsterdam: J.C. Gieben, 2002: 204–234). On what happens *after* battle and conquest, see E.P. Moloney and Michael Stuart Williams, eds, *Peace and Reconciliation in the Classical World* (London: Routledge, 2017), and, on Rome specifically, Hannah Cornwell, *Pax and the Politics of Peace: Republic to Principate* (Oxford: Oxford University Press, 2017). On how warfare and military *gloria* were folded into the public psyche through display and entertainment, see Anastasia Bakogianni and Valerie Hope, eds, *War as Spectacle: Ancient and Modern Perspectives on the Display of Armed Conflict* (London: Bloomsbury, 2015).

Finally, do have a look at non-academic sources on the Roman military, including children's books on the army, the Osprey, Usborne, or Pen & Sword military books, and books written with the popular audience in mind. These works are aimed at the enthusiast and cover frequently the details that meet with the expectations of the general audience of pop-culture Rome. Recommended on this score, and written by an academic, is P. Matyszak, *Legionary: The Roman Solder's Manual* (London: Thames and Hudson, 2009); it's written as a 'handbook for the new recruit' around the year 100 CE with loads of information drawn from the same contemporary sources noted above (and far more).

CHAPTER 5: *VENI, VIDI, VISA*

A bricolage of documents related to the Roman economy can be found in, for example, L&R, 1: 156–222, which includes documents on economic resources around the empire, management of large estates, leasing lands and tenants, operation and administration of mines, a labour contract, internal trade and agents, speed of travel, transporting grain from Egypt to Rome, foreign trade (luxury goods such as amber and silk), financial crises, real estate transactions, advertisements for rentals, loans and mortgages, slave sales. Dillon and Garland (2015) include examples of sources that focus on conspicuous consumption; Parkin and Pomeroy (2007: 244–291) include texts on the general economy, including agriculture and farming, local markets, estates, being a landlord, transporting goods, taxes and goods liable to taxation, grain supply for Rome, feeding the provinces (supply and famine), alimentary schemes, vineyards as an investment, mining, management of trades, and the occupations of freedmen. Another source for contemporary material are the *Selected Papyri* volumes in the Loeb Classical Library – receipts, wills, transactions, contracts; it's a forensics chartered accountant's paradise.

The scholarship of the Roman economy covers vast and multifaceted areas, and it brings together archaeologists, economic historians, and researchers on demographics. These diverse methodologies will help to shape your understanding of Rome's agrarian society and the Roman love of and idealisation of land ownership and protection. Two places with which to begin are W. Schiedel, ed., *The Cambridge Companion to the Roman Economy* (Cambridge: University of Cambridge, 2012), and A. Bowman, *Quantifying the Roman Empire: Methods and Problems* (Oxford: University of Oxford, 2013). A. Bowman, ed., T*he Roman Agricultural Economy: Organization, Investment, and Production* (Oxford: Oxford University Press, 2013), covers the effects of the huge cash flow into Rome after the second Punic War and into the first century BCE; his study provides a good foundation for understanding the effects of wealth on the state administration and the long-term effects it had on the *Pax Romana*. Peter Temin, *The Roman Market Economy* (Princeton: Princeton University Press, 2012), uses modern measures of the economy to show the importance of trade, markets, and how the period of administrative peace in the first two centuries of the Principate allowed for a quality of life for ordinary people not achieved again until the Industrial Revolution. In terms of the effects of the influx of money and wealth on Republican politics, see Hames Tan, *Power and Public Finance at Rome, 264–49 BCE* (Oxford: Oxford University Press, 2017), and Neil Coffee, *Gift and Gain: How Money Transformed Ancient Rome* (Oxford: Oxford University Press, 2017). For the importance of land and its resources in the agrarian economy, see Paul Erdkamp et al., eds, *Ownership and Exploitation of Land and Natural Resources in the Roman World* (Oxford: Oxford University Press, 2015). Other names to keep an eye out for include Peter Garnsey and Richard Saller, *Trade in the Ancient Economy* (Cambridge: Cambridge University Press, 1980), and Peter Garnsey, Richard Saller, et al., eds, *The Roman Empire: Economy, Society, and Culture* (Oakland: University of California Press, 2015), Kevin Greene (*Archaeology of the Roman Economy*, reprinted edition (Berkeley: University of California, 1992)), and André Tchernia, *The Romans and Trade* (Oxford: Oxford University Press, 2016), provides a recent look at Roman trade within and without the Empire in general; Scott Meikle ('Modernism, Economics, and the Ancient Economy', pp. 233–250) and Richard Saller ('Framing the Debate over Growth in the Ancient World', pp. 251–269), both in W. Schiedel and S. von Reiden's

The Ancient Economy (London: Routledge, 2002), are good for under-standing in perspective and context the nature of the Roman economy against modern paradigms. James Tan's *Power and Public Finance at Rome, 264–49 B.C.E.* (Oxford: Oxford University Press, 2017), fills a gap in economic studies as he considers how aristocratic attitudes towards land ownership and snobbery towards business and industry hobbled potential for Rome's economic development. A more complex consid-eration of the methodology of studying the Roman economy comes from A. Bowman, *Quantifying the Roman Economy: Methods and Problems* (Oxford: Oxford University Press, 2013).

General studies on trade include Andrew Wilson, ed., *Trade, Commerce and the State in the Roman World* (Oxford: Oxford University Press, 2017); studies of Roman trade networks with specialised areas include Steven Sidebotham, *Berenike and the Ancient Maritime Spice Route* (Berkeley: University of California Press, 2011); Grant Parker, *The Making of Roman India* (Cambridge: Cambridge University Press, 2011); and Raoul McLaughlin, *Rome and the Distant East: Trade Routes to the Ancient Lands of Arabia, India, and China* (London: Bloomsbury, 2010). In addition to Holleran's work on shopping and consumerism in the Roman world (see Chapter 5), another recent look at Roman consumer-ism is Steven J.R. Ellis, *The Roman Retail Revolution: The Socio-economic World of the Tabernae* (Oxford: Oxford University Press, 2018) – also useful in the study of food and drink; Ellis uses both written and archae-ological sources for his study. Trade and commerce also invite questions about travel (see below) and communication across the Roman Empire; see F.S. Naiden and Richard J.A. Talbert, *Mercury's Wings: Exploring Modes of Communication in the Classical World* (Oxford: Oxford University Press, 2017).

Slaves made up a substantial portion of the labour force of our period. Collections of contemporary sources on Roman slaves include Thomas Wiedemann, *Greek and Roman Slavery, A Sourcebook* (Baltimore: Johns Hopkins University Press, 1980); Matthew Dillon and Lynda Garland, *Ancient Rome: Social and Historical Documents from the Early Republic to the Death of Augustus*, second edition (London: Routledge, 2015), pp. 257–297; T. Parkin and A. Pomeroy, *Roman Social History: A Sourcebook* (London: Routledge, 2007), pp. 154–243; and are found throughout both volumes of Lewis and Reinhold's *Roman Civilization* sourcebooks. Several key historians have shaped the modern study of Roman slavery over the past thirty or so years, including M.I. Finley (2003), Keith Hopkins (2010), Keith R. Bradley (1998), and Sandra Joshel (2010, 2014). They have studied slave demographics (Bradley), domestic and family studies (Saller), and the material lives of Roman slaves (Joshel). For studies comparing aspects of Classical slavery and modern ideology and debate, see Finley's *Ancient Slavery and Modern Ideology* (Princeton: Markus Wiener Publishers, 1998), a series of essays and lectures edited by Brent D. Shaw. A similar study with a focus on slavery from a religious point of view is Ilaria Ramelli's *Social Justice and the Legitimacy of Slavery: The Role of Philosophical Asceticism from Ancient Judaism to Late Antiquity* (Oxford: Oxford University Press, 2016).

On manumission and the social impact of freed slaves on Roman society (economically and culturally) there is H. Mouritsen's *The Freedman in the Roman World* (Cambridge: Cambridge University Press, 2015), and M. Perry, *Gender, Manumission, and the Roman Freedwoman* (Cambridge: Cambridge University Press, 2016). Other works include Ulrike Roth, ed., *By the Sweat of Your Brow: Roman Slavery in Its Socio-economic Setting* (London: Institute of Classical Studies, 2010), a collection of conference papers, and Alan Watson, *Roman Slave Law* (Baltimore: Johns Hopkins University Press, 1987). A number of scholars have studied the role of the slave in Roman comedy; for example, Kathleen McCarthy looks at contemporary audience response to authority and inversion in *Slaves, Masters, and the Art of Authority in Plautine Comedy* (Princeton: Princeton University Press, 2004), and Roberta Stewart studies slavery in the context of Plautus's plays, *Plautus and Slavery* (Oxford: Wiley-Blackwell, 2012). For another perspective of the depiction of slaves in contemporary Roman literature, see William Fitzgerald, *Slavery and the Roman Literary Imagination* (Cambridge: Cambridge University Press, 2010) – it's not about the comedy depiction of slaves but rather slaves as characters in intellectual exercise on the idea of humanity and freedom. Finally, labour and work weren't exclusive to servile workers; see, for example, Peter Garnsey, ed., *Non-slave Labour in the Greco-Roman World* (Cambridge: Cambridge Philological Society, 1980), Teresa Ramsby, ed., *Free at Last!: The Impact of Freed Slaves on the Roman Empire* (London: Bloomsbury, 2013), and Andrew Wilson and Miko Flohr, eds., *Urban Craftsmen and Traders in the Roman World* (Oxford: Oxford University Press, 2016).

On coinage and taxation see William E. Metcalf, *The Oxford Handbook of Greek and Roman Coinage* (Oxford: Oxford University Press, 2016), M. Grant, *Roman History from Coins* (Cambridge: Cambridge University Press, 1958), chapter 4 of Kenneth W. Harl's *Coinage in the Roman Economy 300 B.C. to A.D. 700* (Baltimore: Johns Hopkins Press, 1996). Christopher Howgego et al., *Coinage and Identity in the Roman Provinces* (Oxford: Oxford University Press, 2008), is a collection of essays that examines coinage as a means of communicating local and Roman identity through imagery on coins. On taxation, see Ramsey MacMullen, 'Tax-pressure in the Roman Empire', *Latomus* 46 (1987): 737–754, and P.A. Brunt, 'The Revenues of Rome', *JRS* 71 (1981): 161–172. On poverty, see M. Atkins and R. Osborne, *Poverty in the Roman World* (Cambridge: Cambridge University Press, 2006). On relief for the poor, and the *alimenta* schemes, there's Greg Woolf, 'Food, Poverty and Patronage: The Significance of the Epigraphy of the Roman Alimentary Schemes in Early Imperial Italy', *Papers of the British School at Rome* 58 (1990): 197–228. Other essays on the subject of *alimenta* and social relief schemes include R. Duncan-Jones, 'The Purpose and Organisation of the *Alimenta*', *Papers of the British School at Rome* 32 (1964): 123–146, and Peter Garnsey, 'Trajan's *Alimenta*: Some Problems', *Historia: Zeitschrift für Alte Geschichte* 17.3 (July 1968): 367–381.

CHAPTER 6: ROMANS JUST WANT TO HAVE FUN

Spectacle and sport are well supported both in current scholarship and amongst media aimed at general audiences. Useful sourcebooks include A. Mahoney, *Roman Sports and Spectacles: A Sourcebook* (Newburyport,

MA: Hackett, 2001), A. Futrell, *The Roman Games* (Oxford: Blackwell, 2006), and D. Matz, *Greek and Roman Sport: A Dictionary of Athletes and Events from the Eighth Century B.C. to the Third Century A.D.* (Jefferson, NC: McFarland, 1991). See also D.G. Kyle, ed., *A Companion to Sport and Spectacle in Greek and Roman Antiquity* (Chichester: Wiley-Blackwell, 2014). For the Roman attitude towards athletics and the games, see Garrett G. Fagan, *The Lure of the Arena: Social Psychology and the Crowd at the Roman Games* (Cambridge: Cambridge University Press, 2011), especially the opening essay, which discusses the viability of applying social psychology to the study of Roman crowd mentality. Two other essays in Kyle's volume which examine the current trends in scholarship in studying the social aspects of Roman spectacle are by Roger Dunkle, 'Review of Roman Spectacle', pp. 381–395, and Jerry Toner, 'Trends in the Study of Roman Spectacle and Sport', pp. 451–464. Because animals are frequently involved in Roman entertainment, see Jo-Ann Shelton, 'Beastly Spectacles in the Ancient Mediterranean World', in Linda Kalof, ed., *A Cultural History of Animals in Antiquity* (Oxford: Berg, 2011: 97–126), and Alastair Harden, *Animals in the Classical World: Ethical Perspectives from Greek and Roman Texts* (Boston: Palgrave Macmillan, 2013). Aside from beast hunts, *the* sport featuring animals was chariot racing, but you won't find as much scholarship on the horses as you will on gladiators. Kyle (2007), Futrell (2006), and Mahoney (2001) all include chapters on chariot racing; the main monograph at the moment is Fik Meijer and Liz Waters, *Chariot Racing in the Roman Empire* (Baltimore: Johns Hopkins Press, 2010); beware, however, that this book has been criticised for flaws and inaccuracies in places. H.A Harris's venerable *Sport in Greece and Rome* (1894; London: Thames and Hudson, 1972) remains a good reference not only for chariot racing from the Greek, through to Roman, through to Byzantine eras but also for other activities such as ball games and swimming.

Studies on gladiators also usually include beast hunts, triumphs, and other public displays. In addition to giving you a good foundation on the atmosphere of the arena, these works address issues of social stratification, cultural or audience expectations, and the use of spectacle to reinforce codes of behaviour, authority, and imperial imagery (that is, the strength and stability of empire, how the Empire protects its citizens against the chaos of nature). Recommended are Donald Kyle, *Spectacles of Death in Ancient Rome* (London: Routledge, 2007), T. Wiedemann, *Emperors and Gladiators* (London: Routledge, 1992), and Donald Kagan, *Sport and Spectacle in the Ancient World* (Oxford: Wiley-Blackwell, 2014). For studies on the use of sport and entertainment as means of shaping social norms and values, see A. Bell, *Spectacular Power in the Greek and Roman City* (Oxford: Oxford University Press, 2004), A. Futrell, *Blood in the Arena: The Spectacle of Roman Power* (Austin: University of Texas, 1997), H.I. Flower, *The Art of Forgetting: Disgrace and Oblivion in Roman Political Culture* (Chapel Hill: University of North Carolina Press, 2011).

For complementary visual and online sources on the gladiators and other arena games, explore B. McManus's *VRoma* website and *Historius: Mapping History* (www.historvius.com/amphitheatres-roman-amphitheatre-list/fr256). The latter is a somewhat cluttered site, but has an interactive map of the major amphitheatres in the Roman Empire. Other useful sites include *LacusCurtius*'s *Roman Amphitheatres* (http://penelope.uchicago.edu/Thayer/E/Gazetteer/Periods/Roman/Topics/Architecture/Structures/amphitheatres/home.html) and the Metropolitan Museum of Art's *Theater and Amphitheater in the Roman World* (www.metmuseum.org/toah/hd/tham/hd_tham.htm). You'll find a number of websites dedicated to individual amphitheatres; for example Chester (www.english-heritage.org.uk/daysout/properties/chester-roman-amphitheatre/), El Djem (http://whc.unesco.org/en/list/38), and of course the Colosseum (www.the-colosseum.net/idx-en.htm is one of many). The University of Oxford's *Web Sources for Classics* page includes a section on searchable databases on art, archaeology, and pictures which can be mined for images of the theatre, entertainment, and spectacles discussed in Chapter 6 (www.classics.ox.ac.uk/web.html). For an idea of modern popular engagement with the world of the gladiator, you might also look at the BBC's interactive *Dressed to Kill* game, wherein the user can kit out a gladiator, arm him, and send him off to combat in the arena (www.bbc.co.uk/history/interactive/ games/gladiator/index_embed.shtml); considering the game is aimed at children it is revelatory about the view of slaughter for entertainment – both contemporary and modern. Another website aimed at young children called *You Wouldn't Want to Be a Roman Gladiator!* (www. salariya.com/web_books/gladiator/). While its descriptions of spectacle are simplified, they are accurate. This site provides a fascinating look at the disconnect between modern consumers of Roman culture and the contemporary audience for spectacle; both of these websites are again most useful for an appreciation of audience expectation and reception of the ancient world in the modern era. Along these lines, see also Kathleen Coleman, '"The Contagion of the Throng": Absorbing Violence in the Roman World' (*Hermathena* 164 (1998): 65–88).

On the history of the Roman theatre, performance, and the plays themselves see M. McDonald and M. Walton's *The Cambridge Companion to Greek and Roman Theatre* (Cambridge: Cambridge University Press, 2007), which covers the various aspects of ancient theatre buildings, plays, and performance issues. On the general history, timeline, key events, developments, and performers and writers of Roman comedy and drama, M. Bieber's *History of the Greek and Roman Theatre* (reissue, Princeton: Princeton University Press, 1981) is still considered an excellent introduction and overview despite its age (it was originally published in 1961). Bieber's well-illustrated work provides details on how Roman theatre buildings were constructed, their principal parts, and the experience of attending the theatre. Other surveys include R.G. Chase, who has compiled a collection of surviving Greek and Roman entertainment buildings, including theatres, in *Ancient Hellenistic and Roman Amphitheatres, Stadiums, and Theatres: The Way They Look Now* (Portsmouth, NH: P.E. Randall, 2003); and M. Erasmo, *Roman Tragedy: Theatre to Theatricality* (Austin: University of Texas Press, 2010). On forms of theatrical performance, surveys include B. Gentili, *Theatrical Performances in the Ancient World: Hellenistic and Early Roman Theatre* (Amsterdam: Gieben, 1979), C.W. Marshall, *The Stagecraft and Performance of Roman Comedy* (Cambridge: Cambridge University

Press, 2009); E. Hall and Rosie Wyles's *New Directions in Ancient Pantomime* (Oxford: Oxford University Press, 2008); and Martin T. Dinter, *The Cambridge Companion to Roman Comedy* (Cambridge: Cambridge University Press, 2019). Web resources for Roman theatre include the University of Maryland's *Guide to Greek & Roman Theatre* (http://lib.guides.umd.edu/content.php?pid=258533&sid=2133694) and *VRoma*'s page on *Representations of Roman Theatre in Visual Art* by Sarah Elmore (http://vroma.org/~plautus/artelmore.html). Another online source is *The Ancient Theatre Archive*, which offers a 'virtual reality tour of Greek and Roman Theatre Architecture' across the Empire (www. whitman.edu/theatre/theatretour/home.htm). As with spectacle, games, sport and so forth, the theatre was another means to reinforce public codes of behaviour as well as display public munificence – see Holt N. Parker, 'The Observed of All Observers: Spectacle, Applause, and Cultural Poetics in the Roman Theater Audience', *Studies in the History of Art* 56 (1999): 162–179, and Nicholas Horsfall, 'The Cultural Horizons of the "Plebs Romana"', *Memoirs of the American Academy in Rome* (1996): 101–119, for examples of scholarship along these lines. An older survey of audience is Richard Beacham, *The Roman Theatre and Its Audience* (Cambridge, MA: Harvard University Press, 1996); he ties together the strands of the history of the theatre, performance, staging, and audience through his experience as an academic and performer.

On the baths, swimming, and exercise, scholarship focuses on the social and cultural aspects of the Roman baths which includes attitudes towards hygiene, exercise, and social activities. For contemporary sources, see Vitruvius's work on architecture and his discussion of plumbing and aqueducts, and Frontinus, a civil engineer who detailed the means to keep the city of Rome watered. Pliny the Elder covers the subject of water and its uses in *Natural History* (Book 31), Plutarch includes bathing in his essay 'Advice about Keeping Well' in the *Moralia*, and Lucian composed an entire piece called *Hippias, or The Bath*. For the historiography of public baths, see Garrett G. Fagan, 'The Genesis of the Roman Public Bath: Recent Approaches and Future Directions',

American Journal of Archaeology 105.3 (2001): 403–426. Relevant mono-graphs include Garret G. Fagan, *Bathing in Public in the Roman World* (Ann Arbor: University of Michigan Press, 2002), I. Nielsen, *Thermae et blanea: The Architecture and Cultural History of Roman Public Baths* (Aarhus: Aarhus University Press, 1990), and F. Yegul, *Bathing in the Roman World* (Cambridge: Cambridge University Press, 2009).

For additional readings and contemporary sources on sex and gender roles, see, for example, Laura McClure, *Sexuality and Gender in the Classical World: Readings and Sources* (Oxford: Blackwell, 2002), Marguerite Johnson, *Sexuality in Greek and Roman Literature and Society* (London: Routledge, 2004), and Mary R. Lefkowitz and Maureen B. Fant, *Women's Life in Greece and Rome*, fourth edition (London: Bloomsbury, 2016). See also Thomas K. Hubbard's *A Companion to Greek and Roman Sexualities* (Oxford: Blackwell, 2014), and Craig A. Williams, *Roman Homosexuality: Ideologies of Masculinity in Classical Antiquity* (Oxford: Oxford University Press, 1999). For prostitution, cur-rent scholars are Thomas McGinn, *Prostitution, Sexuality and the Law in Ancient Rome* (Oxford: Oxford University Press, 1998), and Anise K. Strong, *Prostitutes and Matrons in the Roman World* (Cambridge: Cambridge University Press, 2016). There is no shortage online of illus-trations (mosaics, frescos, material goods and decorations) of Classical and Roman depictions of sex and erotica; *caveant videres* who hit up Google Image with 'safe search' turned off.

CHAPTER 7: OH DEAR, I'M BECOMING A GOD

Religion in the Roman world is a multifaceted field of study: there are plenty of specialised studies available; the focus here is on those studies that reflect the intersection of religion and Roman social and political life (rather than specifically mythology). Two general resources by J. Rupke are *A Companion to Roman Religion* (Oxford: Blackwell, 2011) and *From Jupiter to Christ: On the History of Religion in the Roman Imperial Period* (Oxford: Oxford University Press, 2014). Other general introductions include R. Turcan, *The Gods of Ancient Rome: Religion in Everyday Life from Archaic to Imperial Time* (Edinburgh: Edinburgh University Press, 2000); C. Ando, *The Matter of the Gods: Religion and the Roman Empire* (Berkeley: University of California, 2008); E.M. Orlin, *Temples, Religion, and Politics in the Roman Republic* (Leiden: Brill, 2003); and Valerie M. Warrior, *Roman Religion* (Cambridge: Cambridge University Press, 2006).

For sourcebooks of contemporary evidence (which includes history, biography, poetry, plays, inscriptions, artwork, and coinage), see both volumes of L&R, and Valerie Warrior, *Roman Religion: A Sourcebook* (Newburyport, MA: Focus, 2002). For women and religion, see Ross S. Kraemer, *Women's Religions in the Greco-Roman World: A Sourcebook* (Oxford: Oxford University Press, 2004). For the more personal and social aspect of cult and religion, there's Richard S. Ascough, et al., eds, *Associations in the Greco-Roman World* (Waco: Baylor University Press, 2012) which includes an annotated bibliography. For the Roman public calendar (the *fasti*) and sources of festivals and sacred dates, contemporary sources include Ovid for the first six months (*Fasti*), and Macrobius on the Saturnalia (sixth century, but Macrobius covers practices from our period). The volumes in Cambridge's *Documents Illustrating the Reigns of* ... (e.g. Augustus and Tiberius, Claudius and Nero, Nerva, Trajan, and Hadrian) are useful as they include (in Latin) selections from the Arval Brothers, a priesthood that kept track of public holidays and sacrifices associated with them. The University of Chicago's *Penelope Project* on the Roman Calendar (http://penelope.uchicago.edu/~grout/encyclopaedia_romana/calendar/romancalendar.html) includes many useful reference works and contemporary sources that can be sifted through for calendar references.

Seneca allegedly mocked the deification of Claudius in a satire called *Apocolocyntosis* (see Chapter 7); for modern scholarship on the state and imperial cult, see I. Gradell, *Emperor Worship and Roman Religion* (Oxford: Oxford University Press, 2002); P. Zanker, *The Power of Images in the Age of Augustus* (Ann Arbor: University of Michigan Press, 1988); B. Levick, *Augustus: Image and Substance* (London: Routledge, 2010); and Oliver Hekster, *Emperors and Ancestors: Roman Rulers and the Constraints of Tradition* (Oxford: Oxford University Press, 2015). Specialist studies include, for example, J.B. Rives, 'Imperial Cult and Native Tradition in Roman North Africa', *The Classical Journal* 96.4 (2001): 425–436, Larry Kreitzer, 'Apotheosis of the Roman Emperor', *The Biblical Archaeologist* 53.4 (1990): 211–217, and Andrew Erskine, 'Rhodes and Augustus', *Zeitschrift für Papyrologie und Epigraphik* 88 (1991): 271–275. Case studies on imperial worship in the provinces include Fernando Lozano, 'Divi Augusti and Theoi Sebastoi: Roman Initiatives and Greek Answers', *The Classical Quarterly* 57.1 (2007): 139–152, and Giles Standing, 'The Claudian Invasion of Britain and the Cult of Victoria Britannica', *Britannia* 34 (2003): 281–288. Several authors have studied cults dedicated to the Julio-Claudians and Flavians in the Greek east, including R.R.R. Smith, 'The Imperial Reliefs from the Sebasteion at Aphrodisias', *The Journal of Roman Studies* 77 (1987): 88–138, on the Julio-Claudians, and Giancarlo Biguzzi, 'Ephesus, Its Artemision, Its Temple to the Flavian Emperors, and Idolatry in Revelation', *Novum Testamentum* 40.3 (1998): 276–290. On women's participation in state cults and priesthoods, see A. Staples, *From Good Goddess to Vestal Virgins: Sex and Category in Roman Religion* (London: Routledge, 1998); Molly Lindner, 'The Woman from Frosinone: Honorific Portrait Statues of Roman Imperial Women', *Memoirs of the American Academy in Rome* 51/52 (2006): 43–85; and Emily A. Hemelrijk, 'Local Empresses: Priestesses of the Imperial Cult in the Cities of the Latin West', *Phoenix* 61.3/4 (2007): 318–349.

On the assimilation of local religious practice into Roman religious life, see I.P. Haynes, 'The Romanisation of Religion in the "*auxilia*" of the Roman Imperial Army from Augustus to Septimus Severus', *Britannia* 24 (1993): 141–157, and E.M. Orlin, *Foreign Cults in Rome: Creating a Roman Empire* (Oxford: Oxford University Press, 2010). As noted in Chapter 7, the foreign cults called 'mystery cults' coexisted with the state religion. In addition to Bowden's recent work on the study of mystery cults, see R. Beck, *The Religion of the Mithras Cult in the Roman Empire: Mysteries of the Unconquered Sun* (Oxford: Oxford University Press, 2007). Older studies of the mystery cults include M. Beard and J.A.

North, *Pagan Priests: Religion and Power in the Ancient World* (Ithaca: Cornell University Press, 1990), and R. Turcan, *Cults of the Roman Empire* (Oxford: Wiley-Blackwell, 1992).

Entire fields are based on the study of Judaism and Christianity during the Roman imperial period; suggested here are only the tips of two enormous icebergs. On Roman–Jewish relations in general, for example, see Seth Schwartz, 'Ancient Jewish Social Relations', in M. Peachin, ed., *The Oxford Handbook of Social Relations in the Roman World* (Oxford: Oxford University Press, 2011): 548–566; M. Goodman, *Rome and Jerusalem: The Clash of Ancient Civilisations* (New York: Knopf, 2007); M. Goodman, *The Ruling Class of Judaea: The Origins of the Jewish Revolt against Rome, A.D. 66-70* (Cambridge: Cambridge University Press, 1987); and D.R. Edwards, *Religion and Society in Roman Palestine: Old Questions, New Approaches* (London: Routledge, 2004). On the political and cultural clash with the Jews from the Roman aspect, see, for example, W. Eck, 'The Bar Kokhba Revolt: The Roman Point of View', *Journal of Roman Studies* 89 (1999): 76–89, and J.J. Bloom, *The Jewish Revolts Against Rome, A.D. 66- 135: A Military Analysis* (Jefferson, NC: McFarland, 2010). On the vibrant mélange of religious-based culture, conflict, and compromise, see D.R. Edwards, *Religion and Power: Pagans, Jews, and Christians in the Greek East* (Oxford: Oxford University Press, 1996), and a collection of essays put together by J. Lieu, J.A. North, and T. Rajak, eds, *The Jews among the Pagans and the Christians in the Roman Empire* (London: Routledge, 1994). For a sourcebook, see Margaret Williams, *The Jews among the Greeks and Romans* (Baltimore: Johns Hopkins University Press, 1998).

Magic and *superstitio* as threats to authority were taken seriously by the Romans: for an introduction, see C. Fuhrmann, *Policing the Roman Empire: Soldiers, Administration, and Public Order* (Oxford: Oxford University Press, 2012), and D. Ogden, *Magic, Witchcraft and Ghosts in the Greek and Roman Worlds* (Oxford: Oxford University Press, 2002). The arguments by Celsus against the Christians (Chapter 7) are summarised by Robert S. Wilken, *The Christians as the Romans Saw Them* (New Haven: Yale Universty Press, 203); similar arguments by Porphyry are unpacked by M.B. Simmons, *Universal Salvation in Late Antiquity: Porphyry of Tyre and the Pagan–Christian Debate* (Oxford: Oxford University Press, 2015).

You may find overwhelming the amount of scholarship and resources on the relationship between the Romans and the Christians. Sourcebooks for a selection of the vast contemporary remains on Christianity and the Roman world include A.D. Lee, *Pagans and Christians in Late Antiquity* (London: Routledge, 2015), and David M. Gwynn, *Christianity in the Latin Roman Empire* (London: Bloomsbury, 2014). For an overview of the Christians in Roman society, see A.H. Becker, 'Christian Society', in M. Peachin, ed., *The Oxford Handbook of Social Relations in the Roman World* (Oxford: Oxford University Press, 2011): 567–588, and S. Heid, 'The Romanness of Roman Christianity', in J. Rupke, ed., *A Companion to Roman Religion* (Oxford: Oxford University Press, 2007): 406–26. Another study on the pagan perception of Christianity is Bart Wagemakers, 'Incest, Infanticide, and Cannibalism: Anti-Christian Imputations in the Roman Empire', *Greece & Rome*, second series 57.2 (2010): 337–54. If, however, you read only one study on the relationship between the immoveable object of Rome and irresistible force of Christianity, make it Wilken's study, *The Christians as the Romans Saw Them*. Wilken's work on early Christian thought, *Spirit of Early Christian Thought* (New Haven: Yale University Press, 2008), and *The Myth of Christian Beginnings* (Eugene, OR: Wipf and Stock, 2009) are excellent complementary studies.

Finally, on how Christianised was the Empire, a point of departure for religious studies not just in antiquity but through to the central Middle Ages, see Peter Brown, *Authority and the Sacred: Aspects of the Christianization of the Roman World* (Cambridge: Cambridge University Press, 1995) and Ramsey MacMullen, 'Christian Ancestor Worship in Rome', *Journal of Biblical Literature* 129.3 (2010): 597–613. On the role of marginalised people and the appeal and spread of Christianity, see, for example, D. Sawyer, *Women and Religion in the First Christian Centuries* (London: Routledge, 1996); Andrea Sterk, 'Mission from Below: Captive Women and Conversion on the East Roman Frontiers', *Church History*

79.1 (2010): 1–39; and Guy G. Stroumsa, 'Sacrifice and Martyrdom in the Roman Empire', *Archivio Di Filosofia* 76.1/2 (2008): 145–154.

CONCLUSION

Have I left stuff out? Probably! Sadly, there simply isn't enough space to cram everything into this little volume, and of course new works, collections, and discoveries are published in print and online every day. The recommendations in this and the other chapters are the ones I happened to have at hand at this place and time – tomorrow they might have been something else. My plan with this chapter, and indeed the book as a whole, is for you to take away some information, make some inquiries, and enjoy some inspiration as you create your fictional Rome.

APPENDIX 1:
KEY WARS, BATTLES,
AND HOTSPOTS,
c. 280 BCE–180 CE

Battle/war	Opponents	Outcome/significance
Pyrrhic War (280–275 BCE). Battles: Asculum; Beneventum.	Pyrrhus of Epirus (c. 319–272 BCE) and his elephants versus the Romans.	Result of tangled alliances amongst the Greeks (Epirus, Macedonia, Magna Graeca) and the Romans (and their allies at this time, the Carthaginians). Enormous loss of Roman troops at Asculum, but even in defeat they reduced severely Pyrrhus's ranks. He found victory too costly and returned to the mainland after losing to the Romans at Beneventum. The wars brought Rome to the attention of the civilisations of the East for the first time. Main sources: Plutarch, Livy, Polybius, Cassius Dio.
First Punic War (264–241 BCE). Battles: Agrigentum; Mylae; Ecnomus.	Carthage (Hamilcar Barca) versus Rome (Regulus).	Rome built a fleet and engaged in naval warfare for the first time; victory resulted in the first provinces (Sicily, Sardinia, and Corsica). An important military device invented during this war was the *corvus* ('crow' or 'raven'), a boarding device that allowed the Romans to drive a platform through the deck of an enemy ship, hooking it with the metal 'beak' at one end of the platform, and to then board by cross the plank from one ship to the next. Main sources include Livy, Polybius, Cassius Dio.

Battle/war	Opponents	Outcome/significance
Second Punic War (218–201 BCE). Battles: Ticinus River; Trebia River; Lake Trasimene; Cannae; Sicily; Zama.	Carthage (Hannibal) versus Rome (Fabius Maximus; Paullus and Varro; Scipio Africanus).	Rome's 'darkest hour'. Defeat of Carthage broke their domination of the western Mediterranean. Main sources include Livy, Polybius, and Plutarch.
Macedonian Wars (214–148 BCE).	Macedonia versus (variously) Greek Leagues (Aetolian and Athenian), Pergamum, Rhodes, and Rome.	Rome eventually defeated Macedonia and added to its growing empire numerous Eastern territories including Macedonia, Greece, and Pergamum (the latter by inheritance rather than by war), and Asia Minor. Influx of wealth and cultural influence from the East had a profound and lasting effect on internal Roman politics and culture. Main sources include Livy and Polybius.
Jugurthian War (112–106 BCE).	Jugurthan of Numidia versus Rome.	Former ally of the Romans during the Punic Wars, Numidia became a client state, then later a province of Rome. War came as the result of Jugurtha's rebellion; military action lent opportunities to Marius and Sulla to advance politically. Main sources include Sallust, Livy, and Plutarch (lives of Marius and Sulla).
Gallic Wars (58–50 BCE). Battles: Alesia (52).	Julius Caesar versus the Gauls.	Roman victory meant political power for Julius Caesar, Roman subjugation of Gaul as a province, and the sphere of influence of Roman culture shifted beyond the Mediterranean and into northern Europe. Main sources include Caesar's own account, Plutarch, Suetonius.
Social War (91–88 BCE).	Rome's Italian allies (*socii*) versus Rome.	Rome's allies rebelled in 91 BCE, planning for independence completely from Roman domination, irritated that they were contributing human resources to Rome's many wars without seeing

Battle/war	Opponents	Outcome/significance
		much return (especially in terms of citizenship and issues with economic disparity). Rome defeated then made concessions to the allies. The wars were also means to political power for Sulla. Main sources include Plutarch's life of Sulla.
Civil War(s) (Republic) (variously from 133 BCE through to 30 BCE).	Multiple, most frequently the result of strong men seizing power (Gracchi, Pompey, Julius Caesar, Antony versus Octavian, etc.), and various rebellions by the Italian allies or aristocratic-led conspiracies between supporters of the *Populares* and the *Optimates*.	Unrest and domestic warfare and violence became commonplace after the Gracchi's support of *populares* politics in the late second century BCE. By the mid- to late first century BCE, the main conflicts were struggles for supremacy between a pair of ambitious men for control of Rome – Pompey and Caesar or Antony and Octavian – with various conspiracies and uprisings scattered about in between. Through propaganda, ruthlessness, support from an excellent general and the military, and sheer luck, Octavian stood alone without competitors after the Battle of Alexandria in 30 BCE. He returned to Rome, whereas the Senate handed over to him myriad executive powers. Through canny policies and his own *auctoritas*, Octavian restructured the political framework of the Republic and initiated the *Principate*, effectively a one-man rule with the façade of Republicanism, which lasted through to the reign of Diocletian (284–301). Main sources include Plutarch's *Lives* of the Gracchi, Marius, and Sulla, Pompey, Crassus, Caesar, and Antony; Cicero, Suetonius, Appian, Lucian, Julius Caesar, and Augustus (*Res Gestae*).
Conquest of Britain (52–50 BCE; 43 CE).	Julius Caesar, then Vespasian and Suetonius	Claudius rode an elephant in triumph through Colchester to demonstrate Roman conquest of Britain, but the

Battle/war	Opponents	Outcome/significance
	Paullus on behalf of Claudius.	groundwork was laid by Caesar on his recce in the 50s BCE, and Gaius Caligula's supplying of an army before his death in 41 CE. Rome would struggle to subdue and maintain control over Britain for the next four centuries, investing more money, time, and human resources in the province than any other (proportionate to its size). Main sources include Caesar on the Gallic wars, Suetonius (Caesar and Claudius in particular), Tacitus, *Agricola*; Cassius Dio.
Jewish Wars (several phases, 66–73; 115–117; 132–136 CE (Bar Kochba Revolt)).	The province of Judaea versus Rome.	Rebellion of the province of Judaea against Roman rule; much tension existed between the Roman state and Jewish culture on a number of complex issues. Jewish defeats resulted in loss of local autonomy in Judaea. The conflicts, especially the failed Bar Kochba Revolt, had long-term effects on the development of Jewish philosophy. Main sources include Josephus, Cassius Dio, *Historia Augusta* (*Life of Hadrian*).
Civil War (69 CE).	'The Year of Four Emperors' as Galba, Otho, Vitellius, and Vespasian, and their supporting legions, battled for control of the Roman Empire.	The Julio-Claudian dynasty gave way to other rulers and subsequent dynasties; the shift of Roman cultural dynamics moved into the provinces. Vespasian proved a capable ruler and restored peace and stability, but the role of the army in support of the emperor and the idea of emperor as 'first citizen' eroded, a trend that would continue through to the end of the *Pax Romana*. That this civil war lasted only a year demonstrates the force of the peace and stability established by Augustus. Main sources: Suetonius's lives of Nero, Galba, Otho, Vitellius, and Vespasian; Cassius Dio, Tacitus's *Histories*.

Battle/war	Opponents	Outcome/significance
Trajan's campaigns (98–117 CE).	Various: Rome versus Dacia, Nabataea, Parthia.	Trajan was an imperialist who expanded the Empire to its greatest extent – most of his aims were economic, and Rome reached the heights of its wealth and prosperity as a result of his conquests. Long-term results included the effects of new provinces replacing previous buffer states and client kingdoms, reduction of the Empire leading to economic crisis (a couple of generations later). Main sources include Cassius Dio (in epitome form). There is also Pliny the Younger's *Panegyricus* and Dio Chrysostom's orations (*Discourses*). Only fragments of specific accounts of the wars against Partha (*Parthika* by Arrian; Lepper's (1948) edition is a careful study of the literary sources but does not consider archaeological evidence) and a single sentence of Trajan's own account survives. For a visual record of the wars in Dacia, there is Trajan's column in Rome (and a plaster model in the Victoria & Albert Museum, London, bought by the museum in good faith in the nineteenth century as it thought it was getting the original).
Marcomannic Wars (166–180 CE).	Marcus Aurelius versus the Marcomanni (and others).	For the first time, the Romans were faced with Germanic invasions that they could not easily quell or subjugate. Because of the loss of the buffer states between such tribes and the northern frontiers along the Danube (after Trajan's conquests), the Marcomanni became the first of numerous tribes to invade the Empire successfully; subsequent Gothic tribes were pushed into the Empire ahead of other invaders in a quest to find safety. Main sources include the *Historia Augusta*, Cassius Dio, Herodian; for a visual record, there is Aurelius's column in Rome.

Battle/war	Opponents	Outcome/significance
Civil War (including the 'Year of Five Emperors', 192–194 CE).	Pertinax, Didius Julianus, Pescennius Niger, Clodius Albinus, Septimius Severus.	Unrest followed the murder of the Emperor Commodus, with the Praetorian Guard unhappy with the succeeding emperor, Pertinax. Severus claimed power in 193, but there was folderol as Julianus bought the *imperium* at auction (only to be assassinated by the Senate a few weeks later), and Niger's and Albinus's soldiers tangled with Severus's for supremacy of their candidate. When the smoke cleared, Severus was emperor, ushering in peace (via harsh martial law) and the so-called 'African' or Severan dynasty that included Caracalla, Elagabulus, and Severus Alexander (d. 235). Main sources: the lives of key players in the *Historia Augusta*, Cassius Dio, and Herodian.

APPENDIX 2:
POLITICAL AND MILITARY MOVERS AND SHAKERS, c. 250 BCE–235 CE

Mover or shaker	Known for	Primary source(s) (select)
Hannibal (247–c. 181 BCE).	Commanding general of the Carthaginians, invaded Italy during the Second Punic War (218–202).	Livy (21–22); Polybius (9.3–7.10; 10.1–20, 32–40; 11.1–3, 20–33; 14.1–10; 15.1–19); Plutarch, *Life of Fabius Maximus*; Cornelius Nepos, *Life of Hannibal*.
Fabius Maximus (c. 280–203 BCE).	Politician and general made dictator to cope with Hannibal's invading army. His study of Hannibal's tactics and his delaying response irritated the Romans, who removed him from office, replaced him with two consuls, and promptly had their backsides handed to them at Cannae, one of the worst losses in Roman history.	Plutarch, *Life of Fabius Maximus*; Livy (Book 22).
Scipio Africanus (236–183 BCE).	One of the heroes of the Second Punic War, the army under his command defeated Hannibal at Zama in 202. His grandson by adoption, Scipio Aemilianus, another general, was successful in the Eastern Wars and set standards in Rome for	Livy (26, 28–9). Orosius, *Against the Pagans*, Book 4.

Mover or shaker	Known for	Primary source(s) (select)
	aristocrats to embrace Greek culture. His daughter Cornelia, mother of the Gracchi, was regarded as the epitome of the virtuous Roman wife and mother.	
Tiberius (c. 169–133 BCE) and Gaius Gracchus (154–121 BCE).	Sons of Cornelia, daughter of Scipio Africanus, best known as tribunes of the plebeians; *Populares* politicians whose defiance of convention led to the introduction of violence in political proceedings.	Plutarch, *Life of Tiberius Gracchus*; *Life of Gaius Gracchus*.
Marius (157–86 BCE).	'New Man' who rose to power through military service rather than through patronage of a patrician; major overhaul of the army led to client armies. Clashed with Sulla. Defied conventions of the *cursus honorum*. Related to Julius Caesar by marriage.	Plutarch, *Life of Marius*. Sallust, *The Jugurthine War*.
Sulla (139–78 BCE).	*Optimate*, conservative politician, patrician. Fought in the Social Wars. Rival to Marius. Became dictator of Rome to undo Marius's radical legislation. Supporters continued to clash with Marian supporters.	Plutarch, *Life of Sulla*.
Pompey (106–48 BCE).	Rose to prominence through client armies and sheer ruthlessness; colleague of and rival to Julius Caesar, part of the First Triumvirate. His clashes with Julius Caesar exacerbated civil war in Rome.	Plutarch, *Life of Pompey*. Julius Caesar, *Civil Wars*. Cassius Dio, 3.

Mover or shaker	Known for	Primary source(s) (select)
Cicero (106–43 BCE).	Lawyer and orator *par excellence*; legacy of letters, court cases, and other writings capture the ambitions and chaos of the late Republic and exemplify the power of speech in politics and rise to political power.	Plutarch, *Life of Cicero*. Cicero, *Letters*. His essays and court cases are also worth a look, especially his speech against Cataline and his *Philippics* against Mark Antony.
Julius Caesar (100–44 BCE).	Member of the First Triumvirate and rival to Pompey; dictator of Rome set on reforming the state. Came to power through military career, self-promotion, and charismatic charm over the mob, freedmen, and *equites* (disliked by the senatorial aristocracy). Assassinated by fellow senators who feared he would make himself king.	Suetonius, *Life of Julius Caesar*. Plutarch, *Life of Julius Caesar*. *Life of Mark Antony*. Julius Caesar, *Civil Wars*. *Gallic Wars*. Appian, *Civil War*, Book 13. Cassius Dio, 37–44.
Mark Antony (83–30 BCE).	Caesar's general; came to power after Caesar's death; rival to Octavian, joined with him to lead the Second Triumvirate. Controlled the eastern part of the empire, assisted by Cleopatra of Egypt. Defeated at Actium by Octavian.	Appian, *Civil War* 1–5. Julius Caesar, *Civil War*. Plutarch, *Life of Mark Antony*. *Life of Pompey*. Josephus, *The Jewish War*. You can also work out his responses to Cicero's speeches against him by reading *The Philippics*.
Cleopatra (69–30 BCE).	Ptolemaic ruler of Egypt. Allied with the Romans as a client first with Caesar then Mark Antony; defeated by Octavian. Her death concludes the pharaonic era of Egyptian history when the territory was annexed by Rome.	Plutarch, *Life of Antony*. *Life of Julius Caesar*. Appian, *Civil War*. Suetonius, *Life of Julius Caesar*. *Life of Augustus*. Horace, *Odes* 1.37. Lucan, *Civil War* 9.909–911, 10. Macrobius, *Saturnalia* 3.17.14–18. Suetonius, *Life of Julius Caesar*.

Mover or shaker	Known for	Primary source(s) (select)
Octavian/ Augustus (63 BCE–14 CE).	Julius Caesar's sickly nephew and teenaged successor; overcame the odds to defeat rival Antony through a programme of propaganda and *auctoritas* – brought about peace and stability after generations of civil war, and reshaped the Republic into a principate: rule by the 'first citizen' (*princeps Senatum*).	Suetonius, *Life of Augustus*. Augustus, *Res Gestae*. Cassius Dio, 45–56. Nicolaus of Damascus, *Life of Augustus* (which may be cribbed from Augustus's lost autobiography).
Tiberius (42 BCE–37 CE).	Second emperor of Rome, excellent general and competent administrator known for 'retiring' from political life to Capri and alleged paranoia and depravity in his later years.	Suetonius, *Life of Tiberius*. Tacitus, *Annals*. Cassius Dio, 57–58. Josephus, *Jewish Antiquities*, Book 18. Velleius Paterculus, *Roman History*, Book 2.
Gaius (Caligula) (12–41 CE).	First 'Julio-Claudian' emperor of Rome; infamous for mad behaviour and humiliation of his Senators. Murdered by the Praetorian Guard.	Suetonius, *Life of Gaius (Caligula)*. Philo, *Embassy to Rome*. Cassius Dio, Book 59. Josephus, *Jewish Antiquities* 18–19.
Claudius (10 BCE–54 CE).	Physically disabled Claudian emperor thought by his family to be mentally feeble. Named emperor by the Praetorian Guard. Competent rule, marred by reliance on advisers (his freedmen and wives, if the sources are to be believed).	Suetonius, *Life of Claudius*. Tacitus, *Annals*. Cassius Dio, 60–61. Seneca, *Apocolocyntosis*.
Nero (37–68 CE).	Last Julio-Claudian emperor and a Graecophile. Popularly accused of ordering his mother's assassination; Great Fire of 64 during his reign. Declared an outlaw by the	Suetonius, *Life of Nero*. Tacitus, *The Annals* 13–16. *The Histories* 1–4. Cassius Dio, 61–63. Josephus, *The Jewish War* 2–6; *Jewish Antiquities*,

Mover or shaker	Known for	Primary source(s) (select)
	Senate in 68, reign followed by year-long civil war, 'The Year of Four Emperors'.	Book 20. Plutarch *Life of Galba*. Check out the ageing Nero from the British Museum: http://bmmedia.blob.core.windows.net/media/nero_channel.mp4.
Boudicca (d. 60/61 CE).	Queen of the Iceni, led a rebellion against the Romans in Britain. Chosen to lead her people on the death of her husband; she attacked the Romans in response to being beaten and her daughters raped. She and her allies targeted several Roman cities including Colchester and London, defeating at one point the famed Legio IX. The Romans rallied and defeated her army; according to tradition she poisoned herself.	Tac., *Ag.*, Book 16; Cass. Dio, 57.1–12 (following and simplifying Tacitus). Gildas (sixth century CE) mentions her in his history of Britain (*De Excidio*, Book 6).
Vespasian (9–79 CE).	Won the civil war of 69; founded the Flavian dynasty. An *eques* and military man, pragmatic and down-to-earth. Maintained some of the Republican façade, but also made no attempt to hide that he'd created a dynasty by naming both sons his successors (for stability's sake). Colosseum begun in his reign.	Suetonius, *Life of Vespasian*. Tacitus, *The Histories*. Cassius Dio, 64–66. Josephus, *The Jewish War* 2–4.
Domitian (51–96 CE).	Second son of Vespasian and last of the Flavians. Ruled openly as an autocrat; expected oaths to his divinity. Murdered and succeeded by Nerva, the first of the 'Five Good Emperors'. Nerva had vague ties to Claudius and	Suetonius, *Life of Domitian*. Cassius Dio, Book 67. Tacitus, *Agricola*; *Histories*.

Mover or shaker	Known for	Primary source(s) (select)
	was seen as a means to restore the peace and stability of the Julio-Claudian/Augustan era.	
Trajan (53–117 CE).	Second of the 'Five Good Emperors', a military man and imperialist. Stretched the Empire to its greatest boundaries. Succeeded by his adopted son Hadrian.	Pliny the Younger, *Letters*, Book 10. Cassius Dio, Book 68.
Hadrian (76–138 CE).	Third of the 'Five Good Emperors', first emperor born in the provinces (but not in a military camp as Claudius was in Gaul), cosmopolitan Graecophile. The *Pax Romana* and prosperity were at their height during his reign. Succeeded by his adopted son Antonius Pius whose 27-year reign was peaceful and prosperous.	*Life of Hadrian* (*Historia Augusta, or The Lives of the Later Caesars*). Cassius Dio, Book 69. Aurelius Victor, *The Lives of the Caesars*, Book 14.
Marcus Aurelius (121–180 CE).	Last of the 'Five Good Emperors', a Graecophile, Stoic, and scholar, Aurelius was a military man and dutiful emperor. Named a co-ruler to cope with the increasing crises during his reign. Died of the plague on the Danube while campaigning against the Marcomanni – outsiders who, for the first time, could not be completely subdued by Roman forces.	*Life of Marcus Aurelius* (*Historia Augusta, or The Lives of the Later Caesars*). Marcus Aurelius, *Meditations*. Fronto, *Letters*. Cassius Dio, 71–72.
Commodus (161–192 CE).	Son of Marcus Aurelius and co-emperor until succeeding in 180, more interested in playing at being a gladiator and spectacles than ruling; neglect and abuse of power led to his assassination. Reign followed by civil war.	*Life of Commodus* (*Historia Augusta, or The Lives of the Later Caesars*). Cassius Dio, Book 73. Herodian, *History*.

Mover or shaker	Known for	Primary source(s) (select)
Septimius Severus (145–211 CE).	Founder of the brief Severan dynasty, a military man, Severus restored peace through martial law. His marriage to Julia Domna introduced Eastern ritual and ideas into the image of emperor. Names of Roman administrative offices and institutions remain from this period (into the Middle Ages), but implementation begins here sharply to change from the original Augustan settlement two hundred or so years earlier.	*Life of Septimius Severus* (*Historia Augusta, or The Lives of the Later Caesars*). Cassius Dio, 74–77. Herodian, *History*, Book 3.
Caracalla (188–217 CE).	Son of Severus, harsh and cruel emperor, assassinated during a personal moment on the side of the road whilst on campaign. Brief civil war and a series of short-term emperors follow. Murdered his co-ruler and brother Geta (211–212).	*Life of Caracalla* (*Historia Augusta, or The Lives of the Later Caesars*). Cassius Dio, 78–79.
Elagabulus (Bassianus) (c. 203–222 CE) and Severus Alexander (208–235 CE).	Alleged son of Caracalla, Elagabulus (not called that in his lifetime) was by all accounts a teenaged megalomaniac, his reign stage-managed by his mother, aunt, and grandmother. Assassinated and succeeded by his even less competent and more malleable cousin Alexander, who was assassinated. The ends of their reigns usher in the chaos of the so-called 'Barracks Emperors' and the political, social, and economic crises of the third century.	Both have lives in *Historia Augusta, or The Lives of the Later Caesars*. Cassius Dio, Book 79. Herodian, *History*, Book 5, covers Elagabulus. Severus Alexander is covered by Cassius Dio, Book 80; Herodian, *History*, Book 6.

Abbreviations

Caes., *BC*	Caesar, *Commentarii de Bello Civili* (*Commentaries on the Civil War*)
Caes., *BG*	Caesar, *Commentarii de Bello Gallo* (*Commentaries on the Gallic War*)
Cass., *Var.*	Cassiodorus, *Variae Epistolae* (*Miscellaneous Letters*)
Cass. Dio	Cassius Dio, *Historia Romana* (*Roman History*)
Catull.	Catullus, *Carmina* (*Poems*)
Cic. *Att.*	Cicero, *Ad Atticum* (*Letters to Atticus*)
Cic., *Brut.*	Cicero, *Epistulae ad Brutum* (*Brutus*)
Cic., *Cael.*	Cicero, *Pro Marco Caelio* (*For Marcus Caelius*)
Cic., *Cat.*	Cicero, *Orationes in Catilinam* (*Against Catiline*)
Cic., *De Or.*	Cicero, *De Oratore* (*On Oratory*)
Cic., *Div.*	Cicero, *De Divinatione* (*On Divination*)
Cic., *Dom.*	Cicero, *De Domo Sua* (*On His House*)
Cic., *Fam.*	Cicero, *Ad Familiares* (*Letters to His Friends*)
Cic., *Leg.*	Cicero, *De Legibus* (*On the Laws*)
Cic., *Lig.*	Cicero, *Pro Ligario* (*For Ligarius*)
Cic., *Mur.*	Cicero, *Pro Murena* (*For Lucius Murena*)
Cic., *ND*	Cicero, *De Natura Deorum* (*On the Nature of the Gods*)
Cic., *Off.*	Cicero, *De Officiis* (*On Duty*)
Cic., *Phil.*	Cicero, *Orationes Philippics* (*Philippics against Mark Antony*)
Cic., *Rep.*	Cicero, *De Republica* (*On the Republic*)
Cic., *Rosc. Am.*	Cicero, *Pro Sexto Roscio Amerino* (*For Sextus Roscius Amerinus*)
Cic., *Tusc.*	Cicero, *Tusculanae Disputationes* (*The Tuscan Disputations*)
Cic., *Ver.*	Cicero, *In Verrem* (*Against Verres*)
Cod. Just.	*Codex Justinianus* (*Law Code of Justinian*)

Cod. Theodos.	*Codex Theodosianus* (*Law Code of Theodosius*)
Digest	Justinian, *Digesta* (*The Digest of Justinian*)
Dio Chrysostom, *Or.*	*Orationes* (*Orations*)
Diod. Sic.	Diodorus, *Bibliotheca Historica* (*Historical Library*)
Dion. Hal., *Ant. Rom.*	Dionysius of Halicarnassus, *Antiquitates Romanae* (*Roman History*)
Ein., *VKM*	Einhard, *Vita Karoli* (*Life of Charlemagne*)
Enn., *Trag.*	Ennius, *Tragedies*
Eus., *Hist. Ecc.*	Eusebius, *Historia Ecclesiastica* (*Ecclesiastical History*)
Eus., *Praep. Evang.*	Eusebius, *Praeparatio Evangelica* (*Preparation for the Gospel*)
Eutr.	Eutropius, *Breviarium Historiae Romanae* (*Summary of Roman History*)
Front., *Aq.*	Frontinus, *De Aquae Ductu Urbis Romae* (*On the Aqueducts of the City of Rome*)
Front., *Princ. Hist.*	Fronto, *Principia Historiae* (*The Principles of History*)
Gai., *Instit.*	Gaius, *Institutiones* (*Institutions*)
Gildas, *De Excidio*	Gildas, *De Excidio et Conquestu Britanniae* (*On the Ruin and Conquest of Britain*)
GT, *HF*	Gregory of Tours, *Historia Francorum* (*The History of the Franks*)
HA	*Historia Augusta* (also *Scriptores Historiae Augustae*) (*The History of the Caesars*)
HA, Ant. Pius	*Historia Augusta, Antoninus Pius* (*The History of the Caesars, the Life of Antoninus Pius*)
HA, Comm.	*Historia Augusta, Commodus* (*The History of the Caesars, the Life of Commodus*)
HA, Did. Jul.	*Historia Augusta, Didius Iulianus* (*The History of the Caesars, the Life of Didius Julianus*)

HA, Hadr.   Historia Augusta, Hadrian (*The History of the Caesars, the Life of Hadrian*)

HA, Heliog.   Historia Augusta, Elagabulus (*The History of the Caesars, the Life of Elagabulus*)

HA, Marc.   Historia Augusta, Marcus Aurelius (*The History of the Caesars, the Life of Marcus Aurelius*)

HA, Pert.   Historia Augusta, Pertinax (*The History of the Caesars, the Life of Pertinax*)

HA, Prob.   Historia Augusta, Probus (*The History of the Caesars, the Life of Probus*)

HA, Sev.   Historia Augusta, Septimius Severus (*The History of the Caesars, the Life of Septimius Severus*)

HA, Sev. Alex.   Historia Augusta, Severus Alexander (*The History of the Caesars, the Life of Severus Alexander*)

HA, Tyr. Trig.   Historia Augusta, Tyranni Triginta (*The History of the Caesars, the Life the 30 Tyrants*)

HA, Ver.   Historia Augusta, Lucius Verus (*The History of the Caesars, the Life of Lucius Verus*)

Hdt.   Herodotus, *Historia (History of the Persian War)*

Hor., *Carm.*   Horace, *Carmen Saeculare (Odes)*

Hor., *Epod.*   Horace, *Epodi (Epodes)*

Hor., *Sat.*   Horace, *Satirae (Satires)*

Isid., *Etym.*   Isidore of Seville, *Etymologiae (Etymology)*

Jn   New Testament, Gospel of John

Jord., *Geth.*   Jordanes, *Gethica (History of the Goths)*

Joseph., *AJ*   Flavius Josephus, *Antiquitates Judaicae (Jewish Antiquities)*

Joseph., *BJ*   Josephus, *Bellum Judaicum (Jewish War)*

Just., *Dig.*   Justinian, *Digesta (The Digest of Justinian)*

Justin Martyr, *Ap.*   Justin Martyr, *Apologia*

Juv.   Juvenal, *Satires*

Lactant., *De mort. pers.*   Lactantius, *De mortibus persecutorum* (*On the Death of the Persecutors*)

Liv.   Livy, *Ab Urbis Condite* (*The History of Rome*)

Liv., *Epit*   Livy, *Epitomae* (*Fragments and remains of books of Ab Urbis Condite*)

Lucil.   Lucilius *Carminum Reliquiae* (*Satires*)

M. Aur., *Med.*   Marcus Aurelius, *Meditationes* (*Meditations*)

Marc., *Dig.*   Aelius Marcianus, *Pandects* (aka the *Digest* compiled by the Emperor Justinian)

Mart.   Martial, *Epigrams*

Mart., *Spect.*   Martial, *Spectacula* (*The Spectacles*)

Min. Fel., *Oct.*   Minucius Felix, *Octavius*

Mk   New Testament, Gospel of Mark

Mt   New Testament, Gospel of Matthew

Nic. Dam.   Nicolaus Damascenus, *Bios Kaisaros* (*Life of Augustus*)

Orig.   *Origines*, an alternative name for Isidore of Seville's *Etymologiae*

Or., *C. Cels.*   Orosius, *Contra Celsus* (*Against Celsus*)

Ov., *Am.*   Ovid, *Amores* (*Loves*)

Ov., *Ars.*   Ovid, *Ars Amatoria* (*Art of Love*)

Ov., *Fast.*   Ovid, *Fasti* (*Six Books of the Calendar*)

Ov., *Met.*   Ovid, *Metamorphoses*

Ov., *Nux*   Ovid, *Nux* (*The Nut-tree*)

Ov., *Trist.*   Ovid, *Tristia* (*Sorrows*)

Paul., *Sent.*   Paulus, *Sententiae* (*Opinions on the Law*)

Paus.   Pausanias, *Periegesis* (*Description of Greece*)

Petron., *Sat.*   Petronius, *Satyricon*

Philostratus, *VA*   Philostratus the Athenian, *Vita Apolloni* (*Life of Apollonius of Tyana*)

Plaut., *Aul.*   Plautus, *Aulularia* (*The Little Pot*)

Plaut., *Capt.*   Plautus, *Captivi* (*The Captives*)

Plaut., *Mer.*   Plautus, *Mercator* (*The Merchant*)

Plaut., *Poen.*   Plautus, *Poenulus* (*The Little Carthaginian*)

Plaut., *Pseud.*   Plautus, *Pseudolus* (*Pseudolus*)

Plaut., *Rud.*   Plautus, *Rudens* (*Rope*)

Pliny, *Epist.*   Pliny the Younger, *Epistulae* (*Letters*)

Pliny, *NH*   Pliny the Elder, *Naturalis Historia* (*The Natural History*)

Pliny, *Pan.*   Pliny the Younger, *Panegyricus* (*Panegyric to Trajan*)

Plut., *Alc.*   Plutarch, *Alcibiades* (*Life of Alcibiades*)

Plut., *Alex.*   Plutarch, *Alexander* (*Life of Alexander the Great*)

Plut., *Ant.*   Plutarch, *Antonius* (*Life of Mark Antony*)

Plut., *Caes.*   Plutarch, *Caesar* (*Life of Julius Caesar*)

Plut., *Cat. Ma.*   Plutarch, *Marcus Cato* (*Life of Cato the Elder*)

Plut., *Cic.*   Plutarch, *Cicero* (*Life of Cicero*)

Plut., *Comp. Aristid. Cat.*   Plutarch, *Comparison of Aristides with Marcus Cato*

Plut., *Cor.*   Plutarch, *Caius Marcius Coriolanus* (*Life of Coriolanus*)

Plut., *Crass.*   Plutarch, *Crassus* (*Life of Crassus*)

Plut., *De Def. Or.*   Plutarch, *De Defectu Oraculorum* (*On the Failure of Oracles*)

Plut., *De Lib.*   Plutarch, *De Liberis Educandis* (*On the Education of Children*)

Plut., *De Vit.*   Plutarch, *De Vitando Aere Alieno* (*That We Ought Not to Borrow*)

Plut., *Fab.*   Plutarch, *Fabius Maximus* (*Life of Fabius Maximus*)

Plut., *Flam.*   Plutarch, *Titus Flamininus* (*Life of Flamininus*)

Plut., *GG*   Plutarch, *Gaius Gracchus* (*Life of Gaius Gracchus*)

Plut., *Luc.*   Plutarch, *Lucullus* (*Life of Lucullus*)

Plut., *Mar.*	Plutarch, *Caius Marius* (*Life of Gaius Marius*)
Plut., *Mor.*	Plutarch, *Moralia*
Plut., *Nic.*	Plutarch, *Nicias* (*Life of Nicias*)
Plut., *Num.*	Plutarch, *Numa* (*Life of Numa*)
Plut., *Pomp.*	Plutarch, *Pompey* (*Life of Pompey the Great*)
Plut., *Rom.*	Plutarch, *Romulus* (*Life of Romulus*)
Plut., *Sull.*	Plutarch, *Sulla* (*Life of Sulla*)
Plut., *TG*	Plutarch, *Tiberius Gracchus* (*Life of Tiberius Gracchus*)
Plut., *Themist.*	Plutarch, *Themistocles* (*Life of Themistocles*)
Proc., *Arc.*	Procopius, *Historia Arcana (Anecdota)* (*The Secret History*)
Proc., *Goth.*	Procopius, *De Bellis* (*On the Wars*)
Ps.-Luc.	Pseudo-Lucian, *Aonkias e Onos* (*The Ass*)
Quint., *Inst.*	Quintilian, *Institutio Oratoria* (*The Education of an Orator*)
Sall., *Epist. ad Caes.*	Sallust, *Epistulae ad Caesarem Senem* (*Letters to the Old Caesar*)
Schol. ad Pers.	Persius Flaccus – *Scholia ad Persium* (*Commentary on Persia*)
Sen., *Apoc.*	Seneca, *Apocolocyntosis* (*The 'Pumpkinificiation' of the Emperor Claudius*)
Sen., *Brev. Vit.*	Seneca, *De Brevitate Vitae* (*On the Shortness of Life*)
Sen., *Con.*	Seneca the Elder, *Controversiae* (*Controversies*)
Sen., *Cons. Hel.*	Seneca, *De Consolatione ad Helviam* (*The Consolation for Helvia*)
Sen., *Epist.*	Seneca, *Epistulae* (*Letters*)
Sen., *Tranq.*	Seneca, *De Tranquilitate Animi* (*On the Tranquillity of the Mind*)
Serv., *A.*	Servius, *In Vergilii Aeneidem Commentarii* (*Commentary on the Aeneid of Vergil*)
Sid. Apoll., *Carm.*	Sidonius Apollinaris, *Carmina* (*Poems*)

Sid. Apoll., *Epist.*	Sidonius Apollinaris, *Epistulae* (*Letters*)
Sil. It., *Pun.*	Silius Italicus, *Punica* (*On the Punic War*)
Stat., *Silv.*	Statius, *Silvae* (*Forests*)
Stat., *Theb.*	Statius, *Thebias*
Strab.	Strabo, *Geographica* (*Geography*)
Suet., *Aug.*	Suetonius, *Divus Augustus* (*Life of the Divine Augustus*)
Suet., *Claud.*	Suetonius, *Divus Claudius* (*Life of the Divine Claudius*)
Suet., *Dom.*	Suetonius, *Domitianus* (*Life of Domitian*)
Suet., *Gai.*	Suetonius, *Gaius Caligula* (*Life of Gaius Caligula*)
Suet., *Iul.*	Suetonius, *Divus Julius* (*Life of the Divine Julius Caesar*)
Suet., *Ner.*	Suetonius, *Nero* (*Life of Nero*)
Suet., *Otho*	Suetonius, *Otho* (*Life of Otho*)
Suet., *Tib.*	Suetonius, *Tiberius* (*Life of Tiberius*)
Suet., *Tit.*	Suetonius, *Divus Titus* (*Life of the Divine Titus*)
Suet., *Verg.*	Suetonius, *Vergil* (*Life of Vergil*)
Suet., *Vesp.*	Suetonius, *Divus Vespasianus* (*Life of the Divine Vespasian*)
Suet., *Vit.*	Suetonius, *Vitellius* (*Life of Vitellius*)
Tac., *Agr.*	Tacitus, *Agricola*
Tac., *Ann.*	Tacitus, *Annales* (*Annals*)
Tac., *Dial.*	Tacitus, *Dialogus* (*Dialogue*)
Tac., *Hist.*	Tacitus, *Historiae* (*Histories*)
Ter., *Hecy.*	Terence, *Hecyra* (*The Mother-in-Law*)
Tert., *Apol.*	Tertullian, *Apologeticus* (*Apology*)
Tert., *De Spect.*	Tertullian, *De Spectaculis* (*On the Spectacles*)
Theod., *Eccl. Hist.*	Theodosius, *Historia Ecclesiatica* (*Ecclesiastical History*)
Thuc.	Thucydides, *Historiai* (*Histories*)
Ulp. *Reg.*	Ulpian, *Regulae* (*Rules*)

Val. Max.	Valerius Maximus, *Facta et Dicta Memorabilia* (*Memorable Deeds and Sayings*)
Var., *De Ling.*	Varro, *De Lingua Latina* (*On the Latin Language*)
Var., *Rust.*	Varro, *De Re Rustica* (*On the Countryside*)
Veg.	Vegetius, *De Re Militaria* (*On the Military*)
Vell. Pat.	Velleius Paterculus, *Historiae* (*History*)
Ver., *Aen.*	Vergil, *Aeneid*
Verg., *Ecl.*	Vergil, *Eclogues*
Verg., *Geor.*	Vergil, *Georgics*
Vit., *De Arch.*	Vitruvius, *De Architectura* (*On Architecture*)
Zon.	Zonaras, *Epitome Historiarum* (*Extracts of History*)

MODERN ANTHOLOGIES OF TEXTS

ADA	*Acta Divi Augusti pars prior, Regia Academia italic* (Rome, 1945)
AE	*L'Année épigraphique* (Paris, 1889–)
CAH	*Cambridge Ancient History*, 2nd edn (Cambridge, 1961–; 1st edn 1923–39)
CIL	*Corpus Inscriptionum Latinarum* (Berlin, 1863–1959)
D&G	Matthew Dillon and Lynda Garland, *Ancient Rome: Social and Historical Documents from the Early Republic to the Death of Augustus*, 2nd edn (London, 2015)
FIRA	S. Riccobono et al., *Fontes iuris Romani antique*, 7th edn (Florence, 1940–43)
IG	*Inscriptiones Graecae* (Berlin, 1873–)
ILS	H. Dessau, *Inscriptiones Latinae Selectae* (Berlin, 1892–1916)
L&F	Mary R. Lefkowitz and Maureen B. Fant,

*Women's Life in Greece and Rome: A
Sourcebook in Translation*, 4th edn (London,
2016)

L&R, 1 Naphtali Lewis and Meyer Reinhold, *Roman
Civilization: Selected Readings, Volume I:
Roman Republic and the Augustan Age*, 3rd
edn (New York, 1990)

L&R, 2 Naphtali Lewis and Meyer Reinhold, *Roman
Civilization: Selected Readings, Volume II:
The Empire.* 3rd edn (New York, 1990)

LTUR E.M. Steinby, ed., *Lexicon Topographicum
Urbis Romae* (Rome, 1993)

RFA *Annales Regni Francorum, Quellen zur
Karolingischen Reichsgeschichte, Erster Teil.*
ed. Reinhold Rau (Darmstadt, 1962)

RIB R.G. Collingwood and J.N.L. Myres, *Roman
Britain and the English Settlements*, 2nd edn
(Oxford (1937; repr. 1963)

ROL *Remains of Old Latin*, ed. E.H. Warmington
(London and Cambridge, MA, 1938)

SEG *Supplementum Epigraphicum Graecum*
(Leiden, 1923–)

Select Papryi A.S. Hunt and C.C. Edgar, *Select Papyri,
Volume II: Public Documents* (Cambridge,
MA, 1934)

References

Alcock, Joan P. (2001). *Food in Roman Britain*. Stroud: Tempus.

Arkenburg, Jerome (2000). *East Asian History Sourcebook: Chinese Accounts of Rome, Byzantium and the Middle East, c. 91 B.C.E.–1643 C.E.* Fordham University: The Ancient History Sourcebook. https://sourcebooks.fordham. edu/eastasia/romchin1.asp. Accessed 20 September 2019.

Atkins, E.M., and Robin Osbourne, eds (2006). *Poverty in the Roman World*. Cambridge: Cambridge University Press.

Austin, R.G. (1935). 'Roman Board Games II', *Greece and Rome* 4.11: 76–82.

Austin, R.G. (1934). 'Roman Board Games 1', *Greece and Rome* 4.10: 24–34.

Bagshawe, R.W. (2000). *Roman Roads*. Princes Risborough: Shire.

Bailey, D.M. (1972). *Greek and Roman Pottery Lamps*. London: British Museum Press.

Barrett, Anthony (2004). *Livia: First Lady of Imperial Rome*. New Haven: Yale University Press.

Barrett, Anthony (1996). *Agrippina: Mother of Nero*. London: B.T. Batsford.

BBC (1965). BBC Written Archive, 'The Romans' Episode 1 T5/1, 234/1 Dr Who TX 65.0.1.16 Series M).

Beard, Mary (2013). 'Banter about dildoes', *London Review of Books* 35.1: 27–28. www.lrb.co.uk/v35/no1/mary-beard/banter-about-dildoes, accessed 7 June 2018.

Beard, Mary (2012). 'Ex-slaves of Rome and historians' snobbery', *TLS online*, 29 February. www.the-tls.co.uk/tls/public/article879727.ece, accessed 21 September 2019.

Beard, Mary (2010). *The Parthenon*. Cambridge, MA: Harvard University Press.

Beard, Mary (2007). 'Were ancient statues painted?', *Times Literary Supplement*, 17 December. www.the-tls.co.uk/articles/public/ex-slaves-of-rome-and-historians-snobbery/, accessed 13 October 2019.

Beard, Mary, and Keith Hopkins (2011). *The Colosseum*. London: Profile Books.

Bowden, Hugh (2010). *Mystery Cults of the Ancient World.* Princeton: Princeton University Press.

Bowman, Alan (2011). *Life and Letters on the Roman Frontier: Vindolanda and Its People.* London: Routledge.

Bowman, Alan, Peter Garnsey, and Dominic Rathbone, eds (2000), *The Cambridge Ancient History: Volume 11, The High Empire, A.D. 70–192,* second edition. Cambridge: Cambridge University Press.

Bradley, Keith R. (1998). *Slavery and Rebellion in the Roman World, 140 B.C.–70 B.C.* Bloomington: Indiana University Press.

Bradley, Keith R. (1991). *Discovering the Roman Family: Studies in Roman Social History.* Oxford: Oxford University Press,.

Bradley, Keith R. (1987). *Slaves and Masters in the Roman Empire: A Study in Social Control.* Oxford: Oxford University Press.

Buckland, W.W. (2010). *Roman Law of Slavery: The Condition of the Slave in Private Law from Augustus to Justinian* (1908), reprint edition. Cambridge: Cambridge University Press.

Campbell, Brian (1994). *The Roman Army, 31 B.C.–A.D. 337: A Sourcebook.* London: Routledge.

Carandini, Andrea (2017). *The Atlas of Ancient Rome: Biography and Portraits of the City.* Princeton: Princeton University Press.

Casson, Lionel (1994). *Travel in the Ancient World.* Baltimore: Johns Hopkins Press.

Casson, Lionel (1991). *The Ancient Mariners: Seafarers and Sea Fighters of the Mediterranean in Ancient Times,* second edition. Princeton: Princeton University Press.

Chapman, Graham, John Cleese, et al. (2002). *Monty Python and the Holy Grail: Screenplay.* London: Methuen Publishing.

Cole, Spencer (2013). *Cicero and the Rise of Deification at Rome.* Cambridge: Cambridge University Press.

Cotter, Wendy (1999). *Miracles in Greco-Roman Antiquity: A Sourcebook for the Study of New Testament Miracle Stories.* London: Routledge.

Courture, Thomas, *The Romans in the Decadence of the Empire.* Quoted at 'Apicius', *Penelope.* http://penelope.uchicago.edu/~grout/encyclopaedia_romana/wine/apicius.html, accessed 13 June 2018.

Cunliffe, B. (2011). *Fishbourne Roman Palace.* Stroud: Tempus.

Cuomo, S. (2009). 'Ancient Written Sources for Engineering and Technology', in John P. Oleson, ed., *The Oxford Handbook of Engineering and Technology in the Classical World.* Oxford: Oxford University Press: 15–34.

Davies, H.M. (2008). *Roman Roads in Britain.* Stroud: Tempus.

Davis, William Stearns, ed. (1912–13). *Readings in Ancient History: Illustrative Extracts from the Sources,* 2 vols: Volume 2: *Rome and the West.* Boston: Allyn and Bacon.

De la Bedoyere, Guy (2010). *Cities of Roman Italy*. London: Bristol Classical Press.

Dillon, Matthew, and Lynda Garland (2015). *Ancient Rome: Social and Historical Documents from the Early Republic to the Death of Augustus*, second edition. London: Routledge.

Dixon, Suzanne (2001). *Reading Roman Women*. London: Duckworth.

Dixon, Suzanne (1992). *The Roman Family*. Baltimore: Johns Hopkins Press.

Eco, Umberto (1998). 'Dreaming of the Middle Ages', in *Faith in Fakes: Travels in Hyperreality*. London: Vintage.

Erdkamp, Paul (2009). *The Grain Market in the Roman Empire*. Cambridge: Cambridge University Press.

Eschebach, Liselotte, and Jürgen Müller-Trollius (1993). *Gebäudeverzeichnis und Stadtplan der antiken Stadt Pompeji*. Cologne: Böhlau.

Eveleth, Rose (2013). 'This woman is a hair-style archaeologist: like a superhero of the coiffe, Janet Stephens spends her days as a regular hair dresser and her nights recreating the hairstyles of ancient Rome', *Smithsonian.com*. 28 May. www.smithsonianmag.com/smart-news/this-woman-is-a-hair-style-archaeologist-82478448/, accessed 22 September 2019.

Fagan, Garrett G. (2002). *Bathing in Public in the Roman World*, reprint edition. Ann Arbor: University of Michigan Press.

Fagan, Garrett G. (2001), 'The Genesis of the Roman Public Bath: Recent Approaches and Future Directions', *American Journal of Archaeology* 105.3: 403–426.

Falka, Mike. *Coins for Education*. http://ancientcoinsforeducation.org/content/view/79/98/, accessed 20 June 2017.

Finley, M.I. (2003). *Classical Slavery*, reprinted edition. London: F. Cass.

Fishwick, Duncan (2002). *The Imperial Cult in the Latin West: Studies in the Ruler Cult of the Western Provinces of the Roman Empire*. Leiden: Brill.

Fishwick, Duncan (1972). 'The Temple of the Three Gauls', *The Journal of Roman Studies* 62: 46–52.

Fitzgerald, William (2010). *Slavery and the Roman Literary Imagination*. Cambridge: Cambridge University Press.

Flach, D. (1978). '*CIL* VIII Suppl. 4 25902', *Chiron* 8: 441–492. www.trismegistos.org/tm/detail.php?tm=200199, accessed 11 August 2018.

Flower, H.I. (2011). *The Art of Forgetting: Disgrace and Oblivion in Roman Political Culture*. Chapel Hill: University of North Carolina Press.

Foley, Helene (1994). *The Homeric Hymn to Demeter*. Princeton: Princeton University Press.

Fraser, George MacDonald (1988). *The Hollywood History of the World*. London: Michael Joseph.

Fraser, P.M., and E. Matthews (1987–2005). *A Lexicon of Greek Personal Names*, 4 vols. Oxford: Clarendon Press.

Frecer, R. (2015). *Gerulata: The Lamps: A Survey of Roman Lamps in Pannonia.* Chicago: University of Chicago Press.

Freudenburg, Kirk, ed. (2005). *The Cambridge Companion to Roman Satire.* Cambridge: Cambridge University Press.

Futrell, Alison (2006). *The Roman Games: Historical Sourcebooks in Translation.* Oxford: Blackwell.

Gardner, Jane F. (1987). *Women in Roman Law and Society.* London: Routledge.

Gaughan, Judy E. (2010). *Murder Was Not a Crime: Homicide and Power in the Roman Republic.* Austin: University of Texas Press.

Ginsburg, Judith (2006). *Representing Agrippina: Constructions of Female Power in the Early Roman Empire.* Oxford: Oxford University Press.

Goodman, Martin (2007). *Rome and Jerusalem: The Clash of Ancient Civilizations.* New York: Random House.

Goodman, Martin (1993). *The Ruling Class of Judaea: The Origins of the Jewish Revolt Against Rome, A.D. 66–70,* paperback reprint. Cambridge: Cambridge University Press.

Gorski, G.J., and J.E. Packer (2015). *The Roman Forum: A Reconstruction and Architectural Guide.* Cambridge: Cambridge University Press.

Grubbs, Judith Evans (2009). 'The Family', in D. Potter, ed., *Companion to the Roman Empire.* Oxford: Oxford University Press: 312–326.

Grubbs, Judith Evans (2002). *Women and the Law in the Roman Empire: A Sourcebook on Marriage, Divorce, and Widowhood.* London: Routledge.

Gurewitsch, Matthew (2008). 'True colors: archaeologist Vinzenz Brinkmann insists his eye-popping reproductions of ancient Greek sculptures are right on target', *Smithsonian Magazine,* July. www.smithsonianmag.com/arts-culture/true-colors-17888/, accessed 22 September 2019.

Hallett, Judith P. (1984). *Fathers and Daughters in Roman Society: Women and the Elite Family.* Princeton: Princeton University Press.

Hardwick, Lorna (2003). *Reception Studies: Greece and Rome,* New Surveys in the Classics, No. 33. Oxford: Oxford University Press.

Hardwick, Lorna, and Christopher Stray, eds (2008). *A Companion to Classical Receptions.* Oxford: Wiley-Blackwell.

Harlow, Mary, and Marie-Louise Nosch (2015). *Greek and Roman Textiles and Dress.* Oxford: Oxbow.

Harries, Jill (2011). *Law and Crime in the Roman World.* Cambridge: Cambridge University Press.

Hartley, L.P. (1953). *The Go-between.* London: Penguin.

Harvey, Brian (2004). *Roman Lives, Corrected Edition: Ancient Roman Life Illustrated by Latin Inscriptions.* London: Focus.

Hemelrijk, Emily (2015). *Hidden Lives, Public Personae: Women and Civic Life in the Roman West.* Oxford: Oxford University Press.

Hemelrijk, Emily A. (1999). *Matrona Docta: Educated Women in the Roman Elite from Cornelia to Julia Domna.* London: Routledge.

Hill, Walter M. (1936). *Apicius: De Re Coquinaria.* Cedar Rapids, IA: Torch Press, reprinted at *LacusCurtius: Penelope* Project. http://penelope.uchicago.edu/Thayer/e/roman/texts/apicius/home.html, accessed 7 June 2018.

Hirth, F. (1885). *China and the Roman Orient: Researches into Their Ancient and Medieval Relations as Represented in Old Chinese Records.* Leipzig and Munich: Georg Hirth: Shanghai and Hong Kong: 35–96. Edited and scanned by Jerome S. Arkenberg as 'East Asian History Sourcebook: Chinese Accounts of Rome, Byzantine, and the Middle East, c. 91 B.C.–1643 C.E.', Fordham University, 2000. https://sourcebooks.fordham.edu/halsall/eastasia/romchin1.asp, accessed 7 June 2018.

Hobden, Fiona. 'History Meets Fiction in *Doctor Who,* 'The Fires of Pompeii': A BBC Reception of Ancient Rome on Screen and Online,' *Greece and Rome,* Volume 56, Issue 02 (Oct. 2009): 147–63.

Hobson, Barry (2009). *Latrinae et Foricae: Toilets in the Roman World.* London: Bristol Classical Press.

Hodge, A. Trevor (2002). *Roman Aqueducts and Water Supply.* London: Bristol Classical Press.

Holleran, Claire (2012). *Shopping in Ancient Rome: The Retail Trade in the Late Republic and the Principate.* Oxford: Oxford University Press.

Holleran, Claire. 'A Handbook to Shopping in Ancient Rome', *HistoryExtra.* www.historyextra.com/article/romans/shopping-ancient-rome, accessed 7 June 2018.

Hope, Valerie (2007). *Death in Ancient Rome: A Sourcebook.* London: Routledge.

Hopkins, Keith (2010). *Conquerors and Slaves,* Sociological Studies in Roman History 1. Cambridge: Cambridge University Press.

Humphrey, J.W., John P. Oleson, and Andrew N. Sherwood (1997). *Greek and Roman Technology: A Sourcebook.* London: Routledge.

Hunt, Arthur S., and Colin H. Roberts (1911). *Catalogue of the Greek Papyri in the John Rylands Library at Manchester. Vol. 1: Literary Texts.* Manchester: Manchester University Press.

Hunt, Peter (2017). *Ancient Greek and Roman Slavery.* Oxford: Wiley-Blackwell.

Irby-Massie, G.L., and P.T. Keyser (2001). *Greek Science of the Hellenistic Era: A Sourcebook,* Routledge Sourcebooks for the Ancient World. London: Routledge.

Johnson, Marguerite (2004). *Sexuality in Greek and Roman Literature and Society.* London: Routledge.

Joshel, Sandra R., ed. (2014). *The Material Life of Roman Slaves.* Cambridge: Cambridge University Press.

Joshel, Sandra R. (2010). *Slavery in the Roman World.* Cambridge: Cambridge University Press.

Kagan, Donald (2014). *Sport and Spectacle in the Ancient World,* second edition. Oxford: Wiley-Blackwell.

Kampen, Natalie (1981). *Image and Status: Roman Working Women in Ostia.* Berlin: G. Mann Verlag.

Koloski-Ostrow, A.O. (2015). *The Archaeology of Sanitation in Roman Italy: Toilets, Sewers, and Water Systems*, Chapel Hill: University of North Carolina Press.

Konstan, David (1986). *Roman Comedy.* Ithaca: Cornell University Press.

Kropff, Antony. 'New English Translation of the Price Edict of Diocletian', at Academia.edu. www.academia.edu/23644199/New_English_translation_of_ the_Price_Edict_of_Diocletianus, accessed 9 June 2018.

Kyle, Donald (2007). *Spectacles of Death in Ancient Rome.* London: Routledge.

Langford, Julie (2013). *Maternal Megalomania: Julia Domna and the Imperial Politics of Motherhood.* Baltimore: Johns Hopkins University Press.

Larsen, Darl (2018). *A Book About the Film: Monty Python's Life of Brian.* Lanham, MD: Rowman.

Lee, A.D. (2015). *Pagans and Christians in Late Antiquity: A Sourcebook.* London: Routledge.

Lefkowitz, Mary R., and Maureen B. Fant (2016). *Women's Life in Greece and Rome: A Sourcebook in Translation*, fourth edition. London: Bloomsbury.

Lendon, J.E. (2002). *Empire of Honour: The Government in the Roman World.* Oxford: Oxford University Press.

Lepper, F.A. (1948). *Trajan's Parthian War.* Oxford: Oxford University Press.

Levick, Barbara (2007). *Julia Domna: Syrian Empress.* London: Routledge.

Levick, Barbara (2000). *The Government of the Roman Empire: A Sourcebook.* London: Routledge.

Lewis, Naphtali, and Meyer Reinhold (1990). *Roman Civilization: Selected Readings*, two vols, third edition. New York: Columbia University Press.

Ligures Baebiani, http://archive.org/stream/inscriptioneslat21dessuoft#page/ 612/mode/2up, accessed 13 October 2019.

Livius.org: Articles on Ancient History. www.livius.org, accessed 22 September 2019.

Lomas, Kathryn, and Timothy Cornell (2013). *'Bread and Circuses': Euergetism and Municipal Patronage in Roman Italy.* London: Routledge.

Lott, J. Bert (2012). *Death and Dynasty in Early Imperial Rome: Key Sources with Text, Translation, and Commentary.* Cambridge: Cambridge University Press.

Macaulay, David (1974). *City: A Story of Roman Planning and Construction.* Boston: Houghton Mifflin.

MacMullen, Ramsay, and Eugene N. Lane (1992). *Paganism and Christianity, 100–425 C.E.: A Sourcebook.* Minneapolis: Ausburg Fortress.

Mahoney, Anne (2001). *Roman Sports and Spectacles: A Sourcebook.* Newburyport, MA: Hackett.

Martindale, Charles, and Richard F. Thomas, eds (2006). *Classics and the Uses of Reception.* Oxford: Wiley-Blackwell.

Matyszak, Philip (2019). *24 Hours in Ancient Rome: A Day in the Life of the People who Lived There*. London: Michael O'Mara.

Matyszak, Philip (2007). *Ancient Rome on Five Denarii a Day: A Guide to Sightseeing, Shopping and Survival in the City of the Caesars*. London: Thames and Hudson.

McCormick, Michael (1990). *Eternal Victory: Triumphal Rulership in Late Antiquity, Byzantium, and the Early Middle Ages*. Cambridge: Cambridge University Press.

McDonald, Marianne (2008). 'A New Hope: Film as a Teaching Tool for the Classics', in Lorna Hardwick and Christopher Stray, eds, *A Companion to Classical Receptions*. Oxford: Wiley-Blackwell: 327–342.

McGinn, Thomas (2004). *The Economy of Prostitution in the Roman World: A Study of the Social History and the Brothel.* Ann Arbor: University of Michigan Press.

McGinn, Thomas (1998). *Prostitution, Sexuality, and the Law*, second edition. Oxford: Oxford University Press.

McLaughlin, Raoul (2010). *Rome and the Distant East: Trade Routes to the Ancient Lands of Arabia, India, and China*. London: Bloomsbury.

Milnor, Kristina (2005). *Gender, Domesticity, and the Age of Augustus: Inventing Private Life*. Oxford: Oxford University Press.

Momigliano, Arnaldo (1992). *The Classical Foundations of Modern Historiography (Sather Classical Lectures)*. Berkeley: University of California Press.

Names for Roman Dogs. www.unrv.com/culture/names-for-roman-dogs.php, accessed 30 May 2018.

Neel, Jaclyn, ed. (2017). *Early Rome: Myth and Society*. Oxford: Wiley-Blackwell.

Newmyer, Stephen (2010). *Animals in Greek and Roman Thought: A Sourcebook*. London: Routledge.

Nixey, Catherine (2018). *The Darkening Age: The Christian Destruction of the Classical World*. Boston: Houghton Mifflin Harcourt.

Nosch, Marie-Louise (2014). *Ancient Textiles: Production, Crafts and Society*. Oxford: Oxbow Books.

Olson, Kelly (2008). *Dress and the Roman Woman: Self-Presentation and Society*. London: Routledge.

Owen, S.G. (1924). *P. Ovidi Nasonis: Tristium liber secondus*. Oxford: Clarendon Press.

Parkin, T., and A. Pomeroy (2007). *Roman Social History: A Sourcebook*. London: Routledge.

Pesta, Abigail (2013). 'On pins and needles: stylist turns ancient hairdo debate on its head', *The Wall Street Journal*, 6 February. www.wsj.com/articles/SB10001424127887324900204578286272195339456, accessed 22 September 2019.

Pharr, Clyde (1964). *Aeneid: Books I–VI*. Wauconda, IL: Bolchazy-Carducci.

Platner, Samuel Ball (2015). *A Topographical Dictionary of Ancient Rome* (1938), ed. Thomas Ashby. Oxford: Oxford University Press.

Pomeroy, Sarah (2007). *The Murder of Regilla: A Case Study of Domestic Violence in Antiquity*. Cambridge, MA: Harvard University Press.

Pompeii Bibliography and Mapping Project. https://digitalhumanities.umass.edu/pbmp/?p=1290, accessed 22 September 2019.

Rawson, B., ed. (2010). *A Companion to Families in the Greek and Roman World*. Oxford: Blackwell.

Rawson, B., ed. (1986). *The Family in Ancient Rome*. London: Croom Helm.

Reiss, Werner, and Garrett G. Fagan (2016). *The Topography of Violence in the Greco-Roman World*. Ann Arbor: University of Michigan Press.

Reynolds, L.D. (1983). *Texts and Transmission: A Survey of the Latin Classics*. Oxford: Clarendon Press.

Robinson, O.F. (2000). *Criminal Law in Ancient Rome*. Baltimore: Johns Hopkins Press.

Roller, M. (2006). *Dining Posture in Ancient Rome: Bodies, Values, and Status*. Princeton: Princeton University Press.

'Roman Economy: Prices in Ancient Rome' *Ancient Coins.Biz*. http://web.archive.org/web/20070113183811/http://www.ancientcoins.biz/pages/economy/, accessed 7 June 2018.

Roman Name Generator. http://fantasynamegenerators.com/roman_names.php, accessed 30 May 2017.

Rowlandson, Jane (2009). *Women and Society in Greek and Roman Egypt: A Sourcebook*. Cambridge: Cambridge University Press.

Rushkin, I. 'Note on Water Measurements by Frontinus', *LacusCurtius*. http://penelope.uchicago.edu/Thayer/E/Journals/LacusCurtius/Note_on_Water_Measurements_by_Frontinus*.html.

Sage, Michael M. (2008). *The Republican Roman Army: A Sourcebook*. London: Routledge.

Saller, Richard P., and Brent D. Shaw (1984). 'Tombstones and Roman Family Relations in the Principate: Civilians, Soldiers and Slaves', *The Journal of Roman Studies* 74: 124–156.

Salway, Bernet(1994). 'What's in a Name? A Survey of Roman Onomastic Practice from c. 700 B.C. to A.D. 700', *Journal of Roman Studies* 84: 124–145.

Schadler, U. 'XII Scripta, Alea, Tabula: New Evidence for the Roman History of Backgammon', in A. de Vogt, ed., *New Approaches to Board Games Research: Asian Origins and Future Perspectives*, Working Per Series 3. Leiden: International Institute for Asian Studies, University of Leiden, 1995: 73–97.

Schaps, David (2010). *Handbook for Classical Research*. London: Routledge.

Scheid, John, ed. (2001). *The Craft of Zeus: Myths of Weaving and Fabric*. Cambridge, MA: Harvard University Press.

Sear, David R. (2000–14). *Roman Coins and Their Values*, 5 volumes. London: Spink.

Sebesta, Judith Lynn (2006). *The World of Roman Costume*. Madison: University of Wisconsin Press.

Segal, Erich (1987). *Roman Laughter: The Comedy of Plautus*. Oxford: Oxford University Press.

Severy, Beth (2003). *Augustus and the Family at the Birth of the Roman Empire*. London: Routledge.

Shelton, Jo-Ann (1997). *As the Romans Did: A Sourcebook in Roman Social History*. Oxford: Oxford University Press.

Shumway, Edgar S. (1901). 'Freedom and Slavery in Roman Law', *The American Law Register (1898–1907)* 49.11: 636–653.

Sidebotham, Steven (2011). *Berenike and the Ancient Maritime Spice Route*. Berkeley: University of California Press.

Smallwood, Mary E. (2011). *Documents Illustrating the Principates of Nerva, Trajan and Hadrian*. Cambridge: Cambridge University Press.

Smith, William (1875). *Colonia*. Transcribed at *Penelope* online. http://penelope. uchicago.edu/Thayer/E/Roman/Texts/secondary/SMIGRA*/Colonia.html, accessed 15 June 2018.

Stephens, Janet (2008). 'Ancient Roman Hairdressing: On (Hair)pins and Needles', *Journal of Roman Archaeology* 21: 110–132.

Stillwell, N.H.H. (1981). *Roman Roads of Europe*. New York: St Martin's Press.

Sumptuariae Leges. in Harry Thurston Peck, *Harpers Dictionary of Classical Antiquities*,1898. Quoted. at the *Perseus Project* online. www.perseus.tufts. edu/hopper/text?doc=Perseus:text:1999.04.0062:entry=sumptuariae-leges-harpers, accessed 13 June 2018.

Sussman, Varda (2012). *Roman Period Oil Lamps in the Holy Land*. British Archaeological Reports. Oxford: Archaeolopress Publishing.

Swanson, Donald C. (1968). *Names in Roman Verse*. Madison: University of Wisconsin Press.

Syme, Ronald (2002). *The Roman Revolution*, revised edition. Oxford: Oxford University Press.Taylor, Timothy (2012). *The Sounds of Capitalism: Advertising, Music, and the Conquest of Culture*. Chicago: University of Chicago Press.

Treggiari, Susan (1996). 'Women in Roman Society', in Diana Kleiner and Susan Matheson, eds, *I Claudia: Women in Ancient Rome*. New Haven: Yale University Art Gallery: 116–125.

Treggiari, Susan (1975). 'Family Life among the Staff of the Volusii', *Transactions of the American Philological Association (1974–)* 105: 393–401.

Treggiari, Susan (1973). 'Domestic Staff at Rome in the Julio-Claudian Period, 27 BC to AD 68', *Histoire Sociale / Social History* 6: 241–255.

Varner, Eric R. (2004). *Mutilation and Transformation: Damnatio Memoriae and Roman Imperial Portraiture*. Leiden: Brill.

Veleia Inscription, *CIL* XI 1.147, in Herman Dessau (1892), *Inscriptiones latinae selectae*. Berlin: Weidmannos: 640–642. http://archive.org/stream/inscriptio neslat21dessuoft#page/640/mode/2up, accessed 11 August 2018.

Vindolanda Tablets Online. http://vindolanda.csad.ox.ac.uk/index.shtml, accessed 9 June 2018.

Warrior, Valerie (2002). *Roman Religion: A Sourcebook.* Newburyport, MA: Focus.

Wiedemann, Thomas (1980). *Greek and Roman Slavery: A Sourcebook.* London: Routledge.

Wilken, Robert (2003). *The Christians as the Romans Saw Them,* revised edition. New Haven: Yale University Press.

Wilson R.J.A. (1983). *Piazza Armerina,* reprint edition. Austin: University of Texas Press.

Young, Simon (2008). *Farewell Britannia: A Family Saga of Roman Britain.* London: Weidenfeld & Nicolson.

Zanker, P. (1988). *The Power of Images in the Age of Augustus.* Ann Arbor: University of Michigan Press.

INDEX